TEACHING THE

CULTURALLY DISADVANTAGED

A RATIONAL APPROACH

KENNETH R. JOHNSON

COLLEGE OF EDUCATION
UNIVERSITY OF ILLINOIS
AT CHICAGO CIRCLE

Science Research Associates, Inc., College Division
165 University Avenue, Palo Alto, California 94301

A Subsidiary of IBM

A middle-class white man is as disadvantaged in the black ghetto

as a black man is in the dominant (white middle-class) culture . . .

Poverty is the unifying thread of cultural deprivation.

The disadvantaged family is caught up in a cycle of inherited poverty—

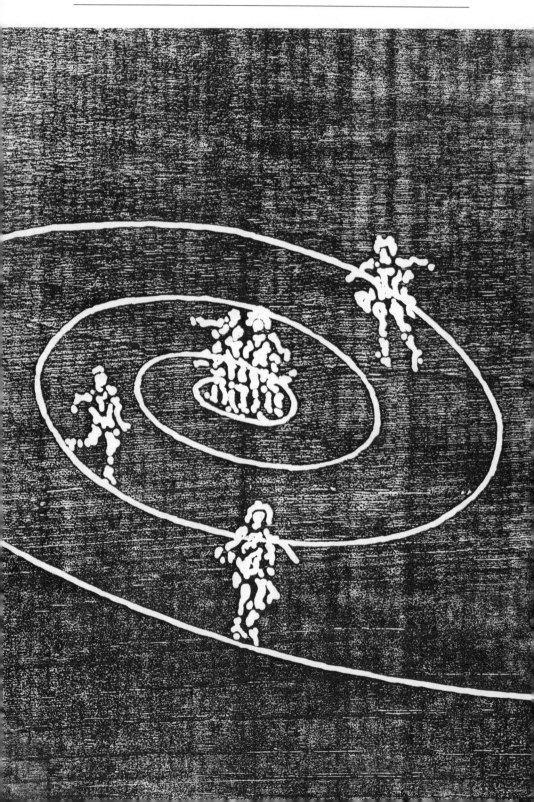

economic, educational, spiritual, moral, experiential, and aspirational.

Until it is broken, the children will continue to pass it on to their children . . .

Culturally disadvantaged children live in a negative environment—

bleak, oppressive, hostile, and debilitating.

The phenomenon of prophecy fulfillment tends to make children

live up to what is expected of them . . .

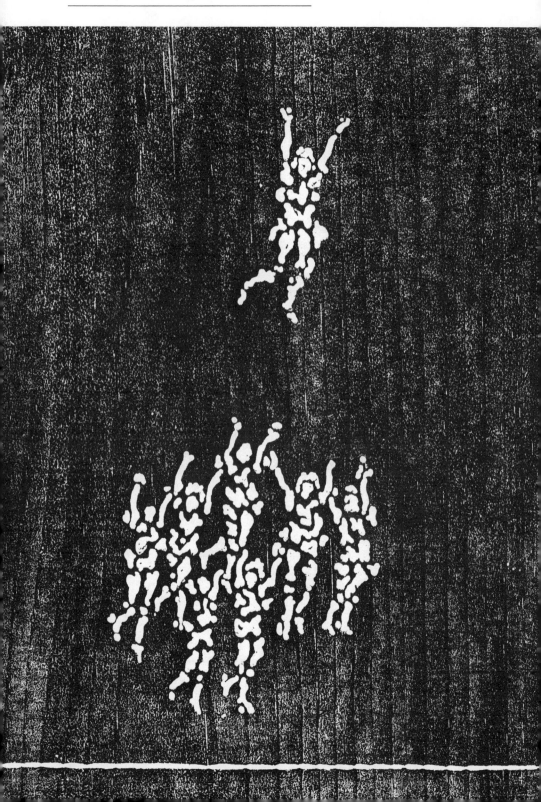

Design: Fetzer • Conover Graphics
San Francisco

Artist: Robert Bausch

Contents

Introduction

Teaching the culturally disadvantaged child is the major challenge in American education today. It is a challenge which must be accepted. First of all, our complex society needs the latent abilities of the disadvantaged that can be developed through education. Secondly, as Thomas Jefferson pointed out during the formation of our country, a democratic society cannot function properly unless all of its people are educated. Thirdly, our tradition of humanism tells us that the dignity of any human being must not be eroded by ignorance. Finally, education rather than ignorance should guide human behavior.

Recognizing and accepting the challenge of educating the culturally disadvantaged does not guarantee success. Many teachers do not have the training, the knowledge, or the tools to work with the culturally disadvantaged child. They need help. They need to know the available, workable tools that they can use to break the cycle of failure in which the culturally disadvantaged child is caught.

Time is running out. We have already wasted a great deal of it by refusing, until recently, to recognize the problem. To realize how negligent American education has been in facing the problems of teaching the culturally disadvantaged, one has only to examine the issues of the *Encyclopedia of Educational Research* over the past twenty years. Up to 1960 there is scarcely any mention of the culturally disadvantaged.

How times have changed! During the past few years the research, writing, proposals, conferences, and so forth on educating the culturally disadvantaged has increased so that one can hardly keep up with it. In fact, the volume is so great that one could lose the ability to discriminate between meaningful sounds and unimportant noise, "tuning out" these voices of concern much as the culturally disadvantaged child tunes out the ubiquitous noise in his environment or his teacher's voice during a reading lesson.

Even while all this attention is paid it, the problem continues to grow. It is difficult to estimate the number of children who cannot achieve in school because of their cultural background, since income is usually the only criterion used for identification. That is, families below a certain income level are classified as culturally disadvantaged. But the figure is often determined by legislation and it fluctuates according to the purpose and content of the legislation or the amount of money the legislatures are willing to spend. This method of classification is neither accurate nor consistent. In addition, there are also some culturally disadvantaged families that earn an income adequate for their material needs. Thus, there is no accurate count.

All authorities — sociologists, educators, government officials — agree, however, that the population of the culturally disadvantaged is increasing, especially in the cities. Some authorities have estimated that culturally disadvantaged pupils soon will comprise 50 percent of the public school population in many cities. In a few cities such as Washington, Detroit, Baltimore, and Chicago, this proportion is rapidly being approached. The significance of such figures is that a growing number of children in our schools cannot profit from the educational process.

The layman also is now beginning to see the social implications of this situation. In the past, the white, middle-class American (a member of the "in crowd") was rarely conscious of groups, even his own. Ask any white, middle-class American what it is like to be white and middle-class and live in America. He will be unable to give you a clear answer, and he may not even understand the question. It's like asking a fish what it's like living in water. However, ask any black, Mexican-American, Puerto Rican, American Indian, or Appalachian white a similar question — "What does it feel like to be (black) and live in America?" — and you will get a clear and lengthy answer. The white, middle-class American has finally heard these groups, especially the disadvantaged among them. He is aware of their problems — specifically, their educational problems — because the mass media has given them significant coverage. He even may have driven through the slums, unable to avoid their spreading blight; he may have fled to the suburbs just ahead of the advancing periphery of the ghetto. The times are ripe for action.

The culturally disadvantaged represent not only a tragic waste of human beings, but a threat to our security and our democratic society. They might be compared to blind Samson, who was led to the main supporting pillar of the temple of his oppressors and, with the last of his remaining strength, pulled the whole temple down upon himself and them. Unless the educational process can give them enlightment, the culturally disadvantaged may use their ignorance to strike at the supporting pillars of our society. There must be immediate, massive, and forceful action. Education must reach them soon.

A great deal of nonsense has been written by educators about teaching the culturally disadvantaged child. Educators who have never taught culturally disadvantaged children might be excused for the nonsense they have written, but those who have should know better. For example, literature on teaching the culturally disadvantaged is filled with "drum and tambourine" reports of how zealous teachers have achieved immediate, monumental, and miraculous results after some new approach has been used with loving application.

It's all right for teachers to love their pupils—especially disadvantaged pupils, who often receive too little love—but *concern* is a much more effective response to the pupils' needs. While concern is rational, love is emotional, and some problems cannot be solved by an emotional approach. This does not mean that teachers should not have affection for these children or feel empathy for them. They must do just this, if they are going to work effectively with them. But emotionalism has no place in the kind of uncluttered rational approach needed to solve the problem of educating the disadvantaged.

In addition, just because an approach is new does not ensure its effectiveness. Education seems to be affected with frequent periodic attacks of "faditis." Too many teachers have jumped on pedagogical bandwagons as they rolled across the educational scene, only to leave their pupils behind.

Some of the nonsense has been generated by school district research-and-evaluation sections. They have reported some shockingly fantastic results from special programs that were often based on poor experimental designs. Many of these reports are symptoms of faditis. However, it's a special kind of faditis with financial complications: money has a way of making all new programs successful. Research-and-evaluation sections are too often afraid to admit to a tightfisted superintendent and board of education that something new has failed. Educators sometimes do not recognize that analyzing a failure — seeing what doesn't work and learning what not to do — can be profitable.

The most prolific authors of nonsense about teaching the culturally disadvantaged child, however, are textbook publishers and producers of instructional materials. To take them at their word, culturally disadvantaged children will achieve remarkably (especially in reading) and experience a change in attitudes and behavioral patterns through the use of particular textbooks and materials. It would be wonderful if educating the culturally disadvantaged pupil were this easy. Unfortunately, there is no such magic available.

Too often, publishers present their regular materials for slow learners (nonachievers because of limited innate mental capacity) as materials designed specifically for the culturally disadvantaged child. There are some good materials available, however. The best way to find out if a certain instructional material is effective is to ask another teacher who has tried it.

Educating culturally disadvantaged children is terribly difficult and painfully slow. The teacher is severely handicapped by the lack of good research, by saccharine reports that give no help, and by the deluge of publishers' claims too incredible to warrant serious attention. However, when the teacher does have success with these pupils, it is immensely rewarding.

The purpose of this book is to provide teachers of culturally disadvantaged children with realistic and practical guidance, and to improve human relations and understanding among all who are engaged in the educational process from kindergarten through the twelfth grade. Specific objectives include:

1. To help teachers acquire some understanding of the groups of culturally disadvantaged children in American classrooms. Understanding these children is essential to teaching them.
2. To offer suggestions and techniques for teaching the culturally disadvantaged child.
3. To stimulate thought and promote discussion among teachers of culturally disadvantaged children.

CHAPTER 1

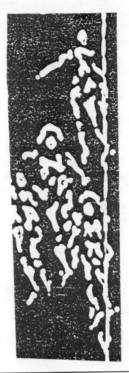

WHO ARE THE CULTURALLY DISADVANTAGED

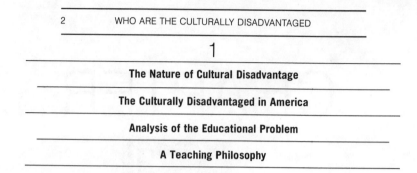

1

The Nature of Cultural Disadvantage

The Culturally Disadvantaged in America

Analysis of the Educational Problem

A Teaching Philosophy

There have been many attempts to formulate an accurate descriptive term for the groups of people that concern us here. While all terms are inadequate in one way or another, *culturally disadvantaged* is the term accepted and used by most educators. Other terms sometimes used are: *culturally deprived, culturally different, socially different, educationally deprived,* and *culturally handicapped.* While the term is not really important, it is important for teachers to understand the concept.

The Nature of Cultural Disadvantage

In 1891 Sir Edward Tylor defined culture as: ". . . that complex whole which includes knowledge, belief, art, morals, law, custom, and any other capabilities and habits acquired by man as a member of society."[1] Culture is all that man has learned as an individual in a society—it is a way of life, a way of acting, thinking, and feeling. No person who is a member of a society can be without a culture. One group's way of life may differ from another group's way of life, but every group has a culture.

Terms which imply a lack of culture are therefore inaccurate. Furthermore, it is not possible to place a value on any culture and label one better than another. Viewed as a group's way of coping with its physical and social environment, any culture is "good" in terms of its function. Presumably, behavior patterns that don't work would never develop or, if they did develop, would soon be discarded.

The term *culturally disadvantaged,* then, is a relative term. The teacher must always consider this question: When is the culturally disadvantaged child handicapped? The disadvan-

1. From *Primitive Culture* by Edward Tylor. Copyright 1891 by John Murray (Publishers) Ltd. Used by permission of publisher.

tage materializes when the child leaves his primary cultural group to function in the dominant culture. It is created by conflict between his subculture and the dominant culture. Only in a situation of conflict is the subculture of a minority child a handicap. But the situation occurs regularly in the classroom.

One instance of such conflict occurs when a member of a subculture attempts to communicate with the "outside world." Many culturally disadvantaged people speak a nonstandard dialect of English which limits their ability to communicate in the dominant culture, but upon which they must rely for communication in their own cultural environment. A person is also disadvantaged when his particular background of experience does not enable him to be sensitive to those cues of the dominant culture that call for a particular response.

For example, the disadvantaged child may learn few table manners at home. When food is served the primary objective is to eat it, not to practice accompanying acts of etiquette that are sometimes unreasonable and always indigestible. This child might appear crude to a middle-class observer; however, if he were to practice middle-class table manners in his home, he would probably go hungry.

The teacher can perhaps understand the disadvantaged pupil's position and the relative nature of the term *culturally disadvantaged* if he can put himself in the pupil's place. The average middle-class teacher would be culturally disadvantaged if he had to "make it" in Chicago's black ghetto, an Appalachian village, or the Mexican-American east side of Los Angeles. Imagine the handicap he would have if everyone around him spoke a language different from his, if everyone had a different code of behavior and a different system of values.

Theoretically, if a behavioral pattern is not effective in helping members of a group to adjust to their environment, then that pattern is discarded from the culture. In practice, however, the dominant culture sometimes does not permit the individuals of a subculture to drop an action, behavioral pattern, or attitude which on the surface seems ineffective.

For example, the lack of a positive self-concept in the black subculture is self-destructive. But our society, the dominant culture, makes it difficult for the black man to change his self-concept from negative to positive. It is difficult for him to believe in his own worth as an individual when he is held in low esteem by others.

One workable definition of the term *culturally disadvantaged* is "anyone who cannot participate in the dominant culture." Another is "one who is handicapped in growing up to live a competent and satisfying life in American society." A definition from the viewpoint of the teacher is "the child who has difficulty achieving in school because of his background."

An individual may be prevented from participating in the dominant culture by a lack of certain kinds of experiences, inability to speak standard English, skin color, ancestral origin, geographic location, and economic impoverishment. It should be noted that, despite the below-average IQ of this group, IQ is not one of these factors. All students who are culturally disadvantaged do not lack the mental capacity to become advantaged. The IQ scores are a symptom of the problem, not a cause.

Poverty seems to be the unifying thread in the concept of cultural disadvantage. While it is true that many of the culturally disadvantaged are also economically disadvantaged, culture is not equivalent to physical environment. Culture is not bad housing or dirty streets or dingy clothes or a hungry stomach. Since culture is tradition, mores, values, and institutions, it is possible to be poor but not culturally disadvantaged. Conversely, it is possible to be financially secure but culturally disadvantaged. Usually, however, the culturally disadvantaged are also economically disadvantaged.

There are degrees of cultural deprivation. That is, not all culturally disadvantaged pupils are disadvantaged to the same degree and kind. No two individuals can have the same background of experiences or the same lack of experiences in their backgrounds. Disadvantaged individuals vary in the degree to which they can participate in the dominant culture; and disadvantaged pupils vary in the degree to which they can achieve in the middle-class curriculum. Pupils may vary in their facility to use and understand standard English, in the amount and quality of the types of experiences they have had that facilitate and supplement learning in the middle-class school, in their acceptance or rejection of middle-class values, or in their conceptual development that grows out of environmental stimulation. Further, the degree that pupils can vary in one or all of the criteria of cultural deprivation covers a wide spectrum. In one way or another, and to a lesser or greater degree, their cultural background handicaps them in their efforts to achieve in school.

The difficulty with a label like "culturally disadvantaged" is that it does not allow for the above differences. It says nothing about variations in degree. It's a generalization and, like most generalizations, it is inaccurate. The only generalization that might safely be made about the culturally disadvantaged pupil is that each one is an individual. No two are alike. They share certain characteristics and all are handicapped in some way by their background, but each is an individual. Every classroom teacher must remember this.

The Culturally Disadvantaged in America

Minority group and *culturally disadvantaged* are not synonymous. However, there is a relationship: one's chances of being culturally disadvantaged are increased if one is a member of a minority group. While minorities, *as groups*, have not yet achieved their rights of full participation in American society, many of them are moving closer to this goal. We are concerned here, however, with those minority *individuals* who are standing still and even may be moving backward. (There is evidence that the gap between the dominant culture in America and the subcultures of disadvantaged minorities is rapidly widening.)

Perhaps as many as 50 percent of those not enjoying full participation in the dominant culture are Caucasian. But these culturally disadvantaged Caucasians are only a small percentage of the total white population, while the blacks, Mexican-Americans, Puerto Ricans, and American Indians not fully participating in the dominant culture constitute a large percentage of the total populations of these groups. In racial and ethnic terms, the main culturally disadvantaged groups are:

1. Black people in the rual South and in the black ghettos of our towns and cities. Their problems are particularly acute in Northern cities.
2. Mexican-Americans in the rural and urban Southwest and West. Many have recently migrated from Mexico.
3. Puerto Ricans in a few large Northern cities. Many have recently migrated from Puerto Rico.
4. Caucasians in the rural South and Appalachian Mountains. Some Caucasians from these areas have migrated to Northern industrial cities.
5. American Indians on reservations and in the cities of the Southwest and West.
6. Other ethnic groups including European immigrants, Cuban immigrants, and Eskimos.

Each group has special characteristics that make for a unique teaching situation. For example, the culturally disadvantaged blacks have a history of segregation and discrimination growing out of slavery; Mexican-Americans have a cultural background that is not native to the United States; the Southern and Appalachian whites have been geographically isolated from the dominant culture. Each of these ethnic groups has developed a subculture of its own. That is, each has developed its own way of coping with its particular environment. Furthermore, the repressive forces of the dominant culture (social and economic discrimination, segregation, inherited poverty, geographic isolation) combine with the subcultures these groups have developed to make it extremely difficult for individuals of these ethnic groups to attain full participation in the dominant culture.

In his book *Assimilation in American Life,* Milton M. Gordon has pointed out three functions of the subculture that seem to help perpetuate the disadvantaged way of life: the subculture gives its members identification; the subculture provides a patterned network of groups and institutions that allows an individual to confine his primary relations to his own ethnic group; and the subculture refracts the dominant cultural patterns of behavior and values through the prism of its own cultural heritage. The last function points out that subcultural groups must change the behavior patterns and the values of the dominant culture to fit their own particular ways of life. But in changing behavior patterns and values they become more unlike the dominant cultural groups, thus decreasing their chances of acceptance.

Teachers who work with culturally disadvantaged pupils are certain to increase the effectiveness of their instruction as they grow in understanding of the particular groups they teach. Toward this end, succeeding chapters of this book will deal with the background, characteristics, and special problems of disadvantaged groups. The main racial and ethnic groups will be discussed individually since each group has its own problems.

Analysis of the Educational Problem

The curriculum assumes that every child who enters school has a middle-class orientation and a middle-class background of experiences. Since the culturally disadvantaged child has neither, the standard curriculum operates against him from the first day he enters school. To make matters worse, many classroom teachers often demand that the culturally disadvantaged child adhere to the expectations of the curriculum. If the child doesn't, he is made to feel that something is wrong with him. The problem is: Change the child, or change the curriculum.

The reasons why the culturally disadvantaged child is unable to achieve in the curriculum must be examined. The disadvantaged child comes to school with a background of experiences that does not prepare him to achieve in a curriculum based on a background of experiences that can be obtained only in a middle-class cultural environment. As soon as he enters kindergarten or first grade, the effects of his different background begin to operate. His family life may have prepared him well for his particular subcultural environment—he may know a nonstandard dialect adequately, he may have learned to be aggressive, to ignore noise, to detect a threatening attitude in another, to shift for himself—but his family has not given him the experiences which the middle-class curriculum expects of all children. The curriculum begins instruction on the foundation of these expected experiences.

The experiential foundation includes adequate standard English; rudimentary time and quantity symbols; and general information about the where, what, and how of things valued by the dominant culture. The culturally disadvantaged child has gotten none of these from his family or cultural environment. Thus he starts school already behind. If he is to catch up, he must work at a faster-than-normal rate. But this is not usually possible: the impoverished background that causes him to be behind also prevents him from progressing at even a normal rate. The culturally disadvantaged child seldom catches up. In fact, some investigators have suggested that he falls farther and farther behind as he grows older. Too often, he just gives up completely and drops out of school.

Recently there have been many programs to begin schooling earlier for disadvantaged children. (The Headstart Program is the most notable of these.) These programs have been initiated on the assumption that the school can provide the experiences that are lacking. Perhaps these programs are a partial answer to the problem of adequately preparing the disadvantaged preschool child. However, there are additional, basic material needs that must be met before these children can match the achievement of middle-class children. Until they are satisfied, the difficulties in educating the culturally disadvantaged are compounded. Many of these basic needs are not satisfied because of economic impoverishment. It will be difficult for these children to profit from the middle-class curriculum or develop middle-class patterns of behavior until their economic base is substantially improved.

Educators tend to define basic needs in terms of what makes their job easier or what keeps the curriculum static. In other words, they tend to define basic needs in terms of curriculum expectations. Visit the slums of Harlem, the "black belt" of Chicago, the rural wastelands of the Southwest, the sharecropper country in the South, and then tell the disadvantaged child that his basic needs are more experience with books, more adult conversation, better manners, more trips to the zoo, or any of the other prizes of middle-class affluency! These are *educational* needs.

Basic Needs

Specifically, what are the basic needs of the culturally disadvantaged? The culturally disadvantaged child needs an income level that will permit him and his family to live at a comfortable level. He needs adequate housing, free of the exploitation of absentee landlords and merchants; he needs to be freed from all the invisible forces that keep him locked in poverty. He needs improved health facilities, better neighborhoods, better police protection, freedom from segregation—the list could go on and on. *Basic needs can be summarized as social and economic conditions that permit the individual to develop culturally without negative factors operating to retard or limit that development.*

The school never really comes to grips with these basic needs—it refuses to face the reality of deprivation. Certainly the school cannot satisfy these needs, and perhaps this is one of the reasons they are ignored when the curriculum and the child meet. Coming to grips with basic needs does not necessitate satisfying them; the school can give its disadvantaged pupils more help in dealing with their needs. The school can help its pupils face the realities of deprivation and some of the conditions that accompany deprivation.

For example, the greatest social problem of the girls in one Los Angeles high school social-studies class was getting home without being insulted by the winos who bunched on the corners. Their second social problem was avoiding the sexual advances of older men who accosted them from cruising cars. The boys' greatest problem was resisting the dope peddlers in the school neighborhood. Where in the curriculum were these students given help to deal with these kinds of problems?

That same social-studies class was studying a unit called "Problems of Our Society." Included were such topics as surplus food, inflation, citizen participation in service organizations, extreme political groups, and other topics equally far removed from the real concerns of the students.

In fairness it must be pointed out that the class also studied some topics that were relevant to the students' situation. However, the teacher did not tackle the problems of greatest concern. These students needed to know how to organize for power to make city hall improve neighborhood conditions; they needed to learn methods of making absentee landlords conform to minimum building safety codes; they needed to know how to read an installment-buying contract to protect themselves and their families from economic exploitation. Although this school was located in the center of a disadvantaged area, it gave no real help in solving the problems of the disadvantaged population.

The culturally disadvantaged pupil probably feels that the school is either naïve, apathetic, or dishonest in its refusal to come to grips with his obvious problems and handicaps. The school cannot forget that success in meeting educational needs and attaining educational objectives is affected by the extent these basic needs are either satisfied or ignored. Obviously, the school should do whatever it can to help its pupils indirectly satisfy basic needs by giving them more training in how to survive in a hostile environment.

Beginning school without the background of experience necessary for achievement, and getting little help in meeting basic needs throughout his school career, the disadvantaged pupil feels that the curriculum operates against him. He may not be able to verbalize his feelings; instead, they are reflected in his negative reactions to the curriculum. Implied in this whole discussion of basic needs is an important curriculum question: Can the schools make *any* progress in the face of such enormous undermining forces? The answer is *yes,* and the validity of this answer is measured by the many pupils who have succeeded in becoming full participants in the dominant culture.

Educational Implications

The word *impoverished* has been used to describe the experiential background of the disadvantaged child. This word is not entirely accurate. A better word is *different:* the disadvantaged child probably has had as many experiences as the middle-class child, but his experiences are different. Still, there is some truth in the implication that the experiences of disadvantaged children are different in *quality.* Many psychologists feel that disadvantaged children do not have the kinds of experiences that develop the particular conceptual foundation necessary for school success. The impoverished environment in which they are raised does not provide stimulation to develop the cognitive skills or experiences out of which concepts necessary for achievement in a middle-class-oriented curriculum are formed.

Since the school cannot change the background that causes the culturally disadvantaged pupil's nonachievement, the school has to *change the curriculum.* The curriculum must be based on the pupil's background of experiences.

The IQ Factor

One of the greatest educational needs of culturally disadvantaged pupils is a change in the achievement expectations their teachers hold for them. Teachers can begin making this change by accepting the fact that disadvantaged pupils can learn, that they learn in spite of all limitative factors. Differences in ability to achieve with a disadvantaged background come from several sources. Not all disadvantaged pupils are disadvantaged to the same degree. Thus the limitative effect of their backgrounds varies according to the degree of deprivation. Also, not all pupils coming from backgrounds of seemingly equal deprivation are affected in the same way and to the same degree. Finally, some disadvantaged pupils are innately bright; their intellectual capacities compensate for their disadvantaged backgrounds and permit them to achieve at a satisfactory level.

The myth that culturally disadvantaged children cannot learn is probably attributable to the IQ score. Too often, the IQ score is looked upon as an absolute measure of a child's intellectual capacity. At best, intelligence tests measure achieved functional capacity, not innate intellectual capacity. The IQ score really tells nothing about an individual's native intelligence.

The weakness of IQ tests is revealed when the assumptions behind IQ testing are examined. First, IQ tests assume that innate intelligence (rather than learning) can be measured by inference from the amount of success that an individual attains in performing certain tasks. Second, IQ tests assume that individuals can successfully perform increasingly difficult tasks as they grow older. Third, IQ tests assume that there are standard tasks that all individuals learn at about the same time in their development; thus an individual's intelligence can be judged by comparing his performance with the average performance of all individuals of his age. These assumptions are inaccurate, and they penalize the culturally disadvantaged child.

The IQ score does tell something about *how much* an individual has learned in comparison with others of his same age group. Not only does it tell how much an individual has learned, but it also tells *what* the individual has learned. That is, the tests are made up of items that test makers assume have been learned by the average individual at a particular age level. Since we live in a middle-class society, these items are the expected learnings of middle-class individuals. The tests are also standardized on this group. Thus IQ Tests are biased. When a culturally disadvantaged child takes an IQ test he is penalized by his background. His background has not provided him with the experiences needed to perform as well as the average middle-class child.

Most IQ tests given in schools are group tests that must be read by the individuals taking them. Many culturally disadvantaged pupils are not good readers, so they perform poorly. On individual tests and so-called performance tests, where reading skills are not as important, they generally do better, but not as well as middle-class pupils.

Closely related to reading ability in taking IQ tests is the kind of vocabulary the child has. Children who speak a nonstandard form of English or a foreign language do not perform as well as middle-class children on items requiring standard English skills.

Certain cultural factors adversely influence the IQ test scores of culturally disadvantaged children. These factors include attitudes toward the content of the test items and attitudes toward taking tests. Many of the situations, objects, and problems are not a part of the disadvantaged child's culture in the same way as they are a part of the middle-class child's. In one of the questions given to Terman's gifted sample, pupils were asked to pick the correct description of policemen from the following: "they have it in for kids;" "they are glad to help you out;" "it is fun to fool them;" "they are just big bluffs." Many culturally disadvantaged pupils would answer incorrectly were they not bright enough to know what the test maker was looking for. Their real feelings, derived from their culture, would be in conflict with the "correct" response. Obviously, middle-class pupils would not have this built-in handicap.

Furthermore, to many culturally disadvantaged pupils, taking a test is just another school task. They are not motivated to achieve when taking a test as middle-class pupils are. This has been given as one of the reasons culturally disadvantaged pupils do less well even on so-called culturally unbiased or culture-free tests.

If the IQ test is not a valid measure of an individual's innate intellectual capacity, then why give it? This question has bothered educators for years. The New York City schools no longer give schoolwide IQ tests, and many other systems are considering abandoning them. Other educators point out that the IQ test is a good predictor of school achievement. However, it has no validity for culturally disadvantaged pupils because they do poorly in school and on the IQ test for the same reason. Rather, their impoverished background serves as a good predictor for both IQ test score and school achievement.

Some educators feel that IQ tests do more harm than good, especially with culturally disadvantaged children. Certainly, teachers of culturally disadvantaged children should not take IQ scores seriously, and definitely not as a measure of innate capacity. Instead of allowing the IQ score to stigmatize the child as a nonlearner, look upon it as a measure of his handicap. Accept the child where he is and proceed from this point to help him realize his potential.

A Teaching Philosophy

Most psychologists define learning as a change in behavior caused by experience. How learning takes place and what conditions must be present is one of the great controversies in psychology and a source of confusion for the classroom teacher. Faced with competing theories and findings often more applicable to rats and monkeys than to children, teachers have very few practical applications of understandable learning theory to apply in the classroom. In teaching culturally disadvantaged children, the problem of using learning theory and findings for direction is especially acute because so little research has been conducted on their specific learning difficulties.

However, there are some general principles of learning that can provide direction:[1]

1. *An individual learns from his own experience.* This is the basis for the appeal to change the school curriculum so as to begin instruction at the child's level.
2. *An individual must interact with his environment to learn.* The teaching-learning act is a partnership—it's not what the teacher does that produces learning, but what the teacher *leads the pupil to do.* The teacher must plan learning activities that yield the kinds of experiences that will attain the objectives of the curriculum. When teaching culturally disadvantaged children, the teacher must also provide the kinds of activities that yield those experiences which are lacking in their cultural environment.
3. *Two kinds of experiences produce learning: direct and indirect.* Direct learning involves *actual* contact with reality. Indirect learning involves *vicarious* contact with reality, usually through lecture or reading. The lecture method is especially ineffective with culturally disadvantaged children. Also, the younger the child or the more inexperienced the learner, the more direct the experience must be.
4. *The quality of learning is determined by the quality of the experience.*
5. *The quality of the experience is dependent on many factors:* interest and motivation, concentration, breadth of stimulation, variety of stimulation, and level of the learner's intelligence.

Motivating the child is the crucial factor in providing quality experiences. Many of these children have learned to live with

1. Based on unpublished lecture of Earl V. Pullias, Professor of Higher Education, University of Southern California. Used by permission.

reduced needs and satisfactions, and motivating them to achieve is difficult. Teachers must convince these pupils that learning is important and constantly reward them to encourage their participation. Also, culturally disadvantaged children (especially those at the secondary-level) must be convinced that a better life is attainable through education.

Teacher Attitudes

Culturally disadvantaged children need their teacher to have a *positive* attitude toward them. Admittedly, teaching these children is a difficult and trying task, but when a teacher develops an attitude of expected failure, this attitude can be communicated to his pupils. When it is, the pupils are apt to live up to these expectations. That is, a teacher notes the disadvantaged background of his pupils, their low IQ scores, and their lack of motivation, and concludes that these pupils cannot be expected to learn very much. Teacher action is affected accordingly. The invalid conclusion is reinforced because children often conform to expectations. They live up to the prediction. This phenomenon is called "prophecy fulfillment" or the "self-fulfilling prophecy."

The stigmatization of culturally disadvantaged children by their generally low IQ scores is the first trap teachers must avoid to keep from developing negative attitudes. However, there are other traps. Many teachers attempt to teach the standard curriculum without adapting it to the pupils' particular background of experiences, needs, or interests. An instructional program that is not based on the experiences of the pupils or does not meet their needs and interests is doomed to failure from the start. In fact, such a program may incite a sort of intellectual rebellion in which pupils ignore the efforts of the teacher and refuse to learn. When this occurs, many teachers conclude that their pupils simply are incapable of learning. Instead, a re-examination of the curriculum may be in order.

A problem closely related to this that causes many teachers to give up on disadvantaged children is the inadequate textbooks that must be used. Much has been written lately about the strange world with alien people speaking a foreign language that many textbooks present to disadvantaged pupils. These middle-class textbooks are totally unsuited to disadvantaged pupils. (This problem seems to be more serious at the elementary level than at the secondary level.)

Thus presenting a curriculum that has little relation to the backgrounds or needs of the pupils and trying to work with inadequate and inappropriate textbooks contribute to the poor success of disadvantaged pupils. Their inability to succeed frustrates many of their teachers; and teacher frustration changes to apathy or a generally negative attitude toward the pupils.

Teachers need to develop attitudes of expected achievement toward their disadvantaged pupils. The phenomenon of prophecy fulfillment or the self-fulfilling prophecy works both ways: it can influence failure, or it can influence achievement. How can teachers develop a positive attitude—an attitude of expected achievement—toward disadvantaged children?

First, the teacher must realize that these children can learn. The disadvantaged children who are achieving in spite of their backgrounds help to reinforce this. Second, the teacher must disregard the IQ scores of disadvantaged children as a measure of their potential. Third, the teacher should form a close relationship with the children he teaches in order to know them as individuals rather than as personifications of all the factors that imply failure. Knowing the children better will reveal their strengths and help the teacher to base his instruction on these, rather than adapting it to fit their easily recognized weaknesses. Finally, the teacher must develop a better understanding of the concept of the culturally disadvantaged. Understanding disadvantaged children and the problems of educating them will help teachers avoid the kinds of negative attitudes that aid failure. Perhaps this understanding will help teachers develop the kind of professionalism that is needed to face the problems of educating culturally disadvantaged pupils positively and with confidence. This is the only attitude that will succeed.

The Role of the Classroom Teacher

The classroom teacher is the most important factor in the education of culturally disadvantaged children. Recently there has been an increase of interest in teaching machines, programed learning, and other teacher-substitute devices. Some educators have suggested that these devices provide a means of educating the culturally disadvantaged child. They can serve a valuable supplementary function; however, it is naïve to suggest that these devices could take over the primary role of the teacher, particularly as regards culturally disadvantaged pupils. There can be no substitute for the teacher's role in educating the culturally disadvantaged. Essentially, the teacher has three functions: he is a link with the dominant culture; he acts as a model for the disadvantaged learner; and he initiates, directs, and evaluates learning experiences.

The classroom teacher is usually the only meaningful and direct link with the dominant culture. Through the teacher, the culturally disadvantaged child may confront the dominant culture and increase his understanding of it without the distorting effects of culture clash. The classroom teacher can bring the disadvantaged child to understand the benefits of the dominant culture and provide activities that give the kinds of experiences middle-class children receive automatically. In this role the teacher functions as a kind of guide to conduct the disadvantaged child into the dominant culture.

The second function of the teacher is that of a model. This is particularly important in developing a child's skills—the teacher may be the only person he sees regularly who speaks standard English. The teacher also acts as a model for the general behavioral patterns and the values of the dominant culture.

The classroom teacher's third primary function is to initiate, direct, and evaluate learning experiences. Initiating learning experiences requires the teacher to be aware of the kinds of experiences the learner needs—in other words, the teacher must know where to start. Once the needs have been identified, the teacher must motivate the pupil to become involved in the kinds of activities that will provide the desired experiences. When the learner is involved, the teacher keeps him focused on the activity; offers information, explanation, and interpretation; provides materials; and gives frequent encouragement and reward to sustain the activity long enough to yield a quality experience. Finally, the classroom teacher must evaluate the learning experience.

The function of the classroom teacher in initiating, directing, and evaluating the learning experience is basically the same whether he is teaching culturally disadvantaged children or middle-class children, elementary or secondary. However, with the disadvantaged child, diagnosis and readiness are more critical at the point of initiation. Also, the importance of the classroom teacher as mediator between the disadvantaged pupil and the environment, materials, and other stimuli is greater.[2] That is, the teacher must provide more explanations, more interpretation, more encouragement and reward. In evaluating the learning experience of disadvantaged children, the teacher must not become discouraged with small gains.

Finally, we come to the question of whether disadvantaged children *want* to be educated. At times, their actions and attitudes seem to indicate that they do not. We must remember, however, that they are products of a background that has conditioned them one way—they have never really had a choice between actions and attitudes that support education and actions and attitudes that reject education. The schools must give them this choice.

2. Edwards, Thomas J. "Learning Problems in Cultural Deprivation," in J. Allen Figurel (Ed.), *Reading and Inquiry*, Proceedings of the International Reading Association, 10, 1965. Reprinted with permission of Thomas J. Edwards and the International Reading Association.

Summary of Main Points

1. The problems of educating the culturally disadvantaged are increasing as the number of disadvantaged pupils increases.

2. The school population is comprised of an ever larger proportion of culturally disadvantaged pupils.

3. There is no accurate definition of the term *culturally disadvantaged*.

4. *Culturally disadvantaged* is a relative term.

5. The culturally disadvantaged child is handicapped by his background; his background limits his chances for success in school.

6. Minority groups have a disproportionate number of culturally disadvantaged pupils.

7. Poverty seems to be the unifying thread in the concept of cultural deprivation.

8. The curriculum of the school assumes that all pupils have a middle-class background of experiences and a middle-class orientation.

9. Achievement in school is not possible for the disadvantaged child until some of his basic needs are met.

10. The school fails to come to grips with the reality of deprivation.

11. The school curriculum must be changed to fit the disadvantaged pupil's different background.

12. Cultural deprivation adversely affects IQ scores.

13. Culturally disadvantaged pupils can learn; the teacher must project positive expectations.

14. The classroom teacher serves three primary functions: as a link with the dominant culture; a model; and an initiator, director, and evaluator of learning experiences.

Questions for Discussion

1. Why is it necessary to educate the culturally disadvantaged?

2. What kinds of problems in educating the disadvantaged need to be researched? What are some of the questions that need answering?

3. Give a definition of the term *culturally disadvantaged.*

4. Formulate a more accurate term for this concept.

5. Why are minority group individuals more likely to be culturally disadvantaged?

6. Point out specific expectations of the curriculum that assume a middle-class background.

7. List additional basic needs of the culturally disadvantaged pupil.

8. What can the school do to give culturally disadvantaged pupils more help in solving some of the pressing problems in their subculture?

9. What changes need to be made in the curriculum to bring it in closer touch with the experiences of the culturally disadvantaged pupil?

10. How can IQ tests be used meaningfully in educating culturally disadvantaged pupils?

11. What additional functions could be added to the role of the teacher in educating culturally disadvantaged pupils?

12. How can an understanding of the disadvantaged pupil increase the teacher's effectiveness?

Bibliography

Bloom, Benjamin S., et al. *Compensatory Education for Cultural Deprivation.* New York: Holt, 1965.

Conant, James B. *Slums and Suburbs.* New York: McGraw, 1961.

Crosby, M. "Portrait of Blight," *Educational Leadership,* 20:300–304 (February 1963).

Davis, Allison. *Social Class Influences Upon Learning.* Cambridge, Mass.: Harvard Univ. Press, 1948.

Della-Dora, Delmo. "Culturally Disadvantaged: Further Observations," *Exceptional Children,* 29:226–36 (January 1963)

– – –. "The Culturally Disadvantaged: Educational Implications of Certain Social-Cultural Phenomena," *Exceptional Children,* 28:467–72 (May 1962)

Edwards, Thomas J. "Learning Problems in Cultural Deprivation," in J. Allen Figurel (Ed.), *Reading and Inquiry,* Proceedings of the International Reading Association, 10, 1965.

Eells, Kenneth. *Intelligence and Cultural Differences.* Chicago: Univ. of Chicago Press, 1951.

Elam, Stanley, ed. "Educating the Culturally Deprived in the Great Cities," *Phi Delta Kappan,* 45:70–100 (November 1963).

Gordon, Milton M. *Assimilation in American Life.* New York: Oxford Univ. Press, 1964.

Harrington, Michael. *The Other America.* Baltimore: Penguin, 1962.

Haubrich, V. F. "The Culturally Different: New Context for Teacher Education," *Journal of Teacher Education,* 14:163–67 (June 1963).

Havighurst, Robert J. "Conditions Favorable and Detrimental to the Development of Talent," *School Review,* 65:20–26 (March 1957).

– – –. *Human Development and Education.* New York: Longmans, 1953.

Hunt, J. McV. *Intelligence and Experience.* New York: Ronald, 1961.

Jackson, Toby. "Orientation to Education as a Factor in the School Maladjustment of Lower-Class Children," *Social Forces,* 35: 259–66 (March 1957).

Keller, S. "The Social World of the Urban Slum Child: Some Early Findings," *American Journal of Sociology,* 68:471–80 (1963).

Kerber, August. *Schools in the Urban Crisis.* New York: Holt, 1965.

McAllister, Jane Ellen. "Affective Climate and the Disadvantaged." *Educational Leadership,* 22:481–86 (April 1965).

Passow, A. H., ed. *Education for Depressed Areas.* New York: Teachers College, Bureau of Publications, Columbia Univ., 1963.

Riessman, Frank. *The Culturally Deprived Child.* New York: Harper, 1962.

Rivlin, Harry N. "Teaching and Teacher Education for Urban Disadvantaged Schools," *The Journal of Teacher Education,* 16:135–86 (June 1965).

Sexton, Patricia C. *Education and Income.* New York: Viking, 1961.

Taba, Hilda. "Cultural Deprivation as a Factor in School Learning," *Merrill Palmer Quarterly,* April 1964.

CHAPTER 2

CHARACTERISTICS OF THE DISADVANTAGED CHILD

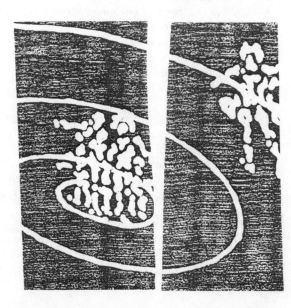

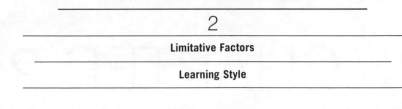

2

Limitative Factors

Learning Style

Limitative Factors

Although classifying the characteristics of the disadvantaged as social, psychological, or economic is convenient for cataloging, it is not necessarily accurate, because these characteristics are highly interrelated.

Briefly, the general characteristics shared in varying degrees by culturally disadvantaged children are:

- They have an experiential background that does not fit the expectations of a middle-class-oriented curriculum.
- They come from a rural background.
- They are economically impoverished.
- They are caught up in self-perpetuating spiritual, moral, aspirational, educational, and economic poverty cycles.
- They feel rejected by society.
- They have a poor self-concept.
- They are aggressive.
- They do not adhere to the values of the dominant culture —often, they are unaware of these values.
- They live in a negative environment that is ugly, crowded, filthy, noisy, and disorderly.
- They have a poor attention span.
- They have a conceptual development that does not fit the expectations of a middle-class-oriented curriculum.
- They are linguistically handicapped.

Not all culturally disadvantaged groups will exhibit a behavioral characteristic equally. For example, take the characteristic of aggressiveness. Culturally disadvantaged American Indian children are usually not aggressive; culturally disadvantaged Appalachian white children are moderately aggressive; and many culturally disadvantaged black children are extremely aggressive.

Further, just as individuals from a particular subculture will vary in the degree they are handicapped by their environment, disadvantaged individuals within a particular subculture will vary in the degree they exhibit these characteristics.

Rural Background

The majority of disadvantaged white and American Indian families and many of the disadvantaged blacks and Mexican-Americans live in rural areas. They scratch out an existence on meager farms as owners or sharecroppers, barely living better than the barnyard animals. Children born in the culturally barren rural regions of the United States (the South, Appalachia, and the Southwest) grow up in an environment that offers minimal educational experiences and stimuli and maximum hardship. Their geographic isolation prevents contact (conflict) with the dominant culture, so that they do not realize their handicap so long as they remain in the rural area.

However, most of these families leave the farms to improve their economic status. Then their handicap becomes manifest. Individuals who have spent their formative years in culturally barren rural areas do not easily adjust to an urban environment. The life style developed on the farm is inadequate for successful adjustment in the city. The educational and vocational experiences of rural immigrants do not qualify them to meet urban employment needs. Pupils coming to an urban school from a disadvantaged rural background are unable to compete. They lag behind even their disadvantaged cousins who have lived in the city all their lives. The higher the grade level at which they enter school, the greater the discrepancy between their achievement and the general achievement of the urban school population.

Even the child who is born in the city may have the experiences of a rural background. Many urban disadvantaged families are only one or two generations away from the farm. They live in areas of the city populated by those who share their ethnic identity and background. These segregated living patterns tend to perpetuate elements of the rural culture.

For example, the food stocked by stores and supermarkets located in disadvantaged areas reflects the rural diet of the local population. The small storefront churches in the black ghettos of Northern cities are a reflection of Southern rural areas where the church is the main black social institution. Usually the congregation is small, enabling every member to have a primary relationship with every other member, as in the rural social pattern.

Some of these retained patterns of rural living have little effect on the performance of the disadvantaged child in school. However, others operate negatively, and these the schools must work to change. Culturally disadvantaged children must learn that time concepts and time schedules are important in urban living. They must learn that attendance laws are more strictly enforced in urban school districts. They must learn to observe sanitation and health practices necessitated by more crowded living conditions. Finally, they must learn the "dialect of the city," even if they retain their rural dialects.

The language spoken by many disadvantaged children is probably the best reflection of the perpetuation of rural patterns in an urban environment. Disadvantaged blacks and Appalachian and Southern whites speak a language much closer to their rural dialects than to the language of the city in which they live.

In a sense, all rural children, culturally disadvantaged or not, are handicapped in school. Curriculum increasingly reflects the change of the United States from a predominantly rural society to an overwhelmingly urban society. Textbooks are prime examples of this shift. Research on the achievement differences between rural and urban pupils has significantly established that urban pupils generally do better on achievement tests, even if the groups are matched on all such variables as IQ, age, socioeconomic class, and race.

Although the core values of our society and much of what we consider the "good life" stem from our rural foundations, it is clear that vestiges of a rural society no longer applicable to a shifting, complex, industrial, urban society can constitute a severe handicap. A primary function of the school must be to provide the experiences missing from a rural environment that supplement and facilitate school learning.

Cycles of Poverty

Poverty is the unifying thread of cultural deprivation. Usually the word *poverty* means "economic poverty." When applying the word to culturally disadvantaged pupils, there are many more dimensions (although economic poverty is the prime contributing cause of all). There is educational poverty, moral and spiritual poverty, experiential poverty, and aspirational poverty. Culturally disadvantaged families often have a legacy of poverty extending over two, three, or more generations. The children of these families will grow up to inherit all the dimensions of poverty that have kept their parents in the empty basement of society. One educator, in referring to economic poverty, calls this process the "cycle of poverty."

Moral and Spiritual Poverty. There is more than one kind of poverty cycle, however. Another is the cycle of moral and spiritual poverty. Culturally disadvantaged children learn the morals and values of their families. Often these values are in conflict with those of the dominant culture, but they cannot be discarded easily — they are products of the environment. If the family remains in the impoverished environment, the same conflicting standards and values will be passed on to yet another generation. Many welfare workers in large cities have pointed out that one reason for the increasing number of unwed mothers who receive aid to dependent children is that girls raised on this system tend to duplicate the actions of their mothers. A new generation of "inherited illegitimacy" is thereby created.

Aspirational Poverty. Another cycle is that of aspirational poverty. Culturally disadvantaged children grow up in an environment that does not foster high aspirations. They are surrounded by social failure; they constantly hear the talk of poverty — unemployment, hardship, sickness, imprisonment. They do not set their aspirations very high. Consequently, few escape. When they become adults they pass on this heritage to their children, and the cycle continues. The schools can help break this cycle by helping culturally disadvantaged pupils to raise their aspirations.

Educational Poverty. The most significant implications for the school are found in the area of educational poverty. Culturally disadvantaged pupils often come from families that have known fewer than one or two generations of literacy. (Literacy may be defined here as the ability to barely read and write.) Such children do not learn the values of education from their families, and they do not see the results of education operating in their homes. Furthermore, their parents do not have a good understanding of the educational process.

Because of economic strain and lack of education, the parents of culturally disadvantaged children do not own books, subscribe to newspapers or magazines, or participate in activities that supplement education. Thus, many culturally disadvantaged children grow up in a home environment that is both economically and educationally deprived. They inherit poor attitudes toward education from such an environment.

Sometimes disadvantaged families are able to break the cycle of economic poverty. Times get better, the income increases, and basic material needs are adequately met. However, there is no assurance that the children of parents who have broken the cycle of economic poverty will be as fortunate when they grow up. The inherited educational attitudes still operate: After basic material needs are met, these families do not spend extra money on educational activities (books, trips, cultural activities, and so forth). They have not learned how to take advantage of a break in the cycle of economic poverty to eliminate other cycles of poverty. And if the other cycles are not broken, they will eventually lapse back into economic impoverishment.

Of all the cycles of poverty which operate against the culturally disadvantaged child, *educational poverty is the most crucial.* The cycle of inherited economic poverty is the generator of other cycles; however, breaking the economic cycle may have little effect on breaking the others. Education, on the other hand, gives the individual intellectual and spiritual enlightenment and the economic skills that he needs to break through poverty. (The federal government and many state and local governments have recognized this, and this is the reason so much money is being invested in educational programs for the culturally disadvantaged.)

Rejection

Culturally disadvantaged pupils learn very early that they are caught up in these cycles of poverty. From this realization, they develop feelings of rejection by society. Such feelings are not altogether unwarranted: society *has* rejected them. The dominant culture is now beginning to recognize the tragedy of human waste that accompanies rejection. However, the massive efforts which are being made to eradicate the accumulation of past tragedy and to prevent future tragedy must yet be seen by the culturally deprived population. The culturally disadvantaged must be made conscious of society's concern.

Poor Self-concept

Rejection breeds self-doubt and self-blame in the rejected individual. The individual grows to view himself as someone who is worthless. Self-assessment is made in relation to others — that is, the individual uses the collective image of society as a reference point to evaluate himself. He makes a qualitative judgment, consciously or unconsciously, as to *who* he is and *what* he is. The conclusion he reaches is his self-concept, the image he has of himself. Thus, self-concept is society's popularity contest in which all are entered and each is his own judge.

Since self-concept is an attitude, it must be learned. An individual develops his self-concept on the basis of various cues from his family, his neighborhood, his school, and the society. The disadvantaged family wears a label that none of its children can ignore. The child must wear it too. If his family is poverty-stricken in a society that measures success with a financial yardstick, if he has only one parent in a society where two are normal, if he is raised by parents who have given up and think little of themselves, and if his family is caught up in all the cycles of poverty, then the disadvantaged child can give little value to his family label. Since he also wears this label, he can give little value to himself. What his family is, he is.

Negative physical environment plays a strong role in the development of a negative self-concept. The accumulated rubble and filth of the slums or the empty wastes of rural areas suggest to the people living there that they can't be worth very much. All the other negative aspects of the physical environment—the exploitation, the crime, and the congestion; or the barrenness, the hostility, the apathy, the total neglect, and the isolation—all reinforce and perpetuate a negative self-concept.

The greatest influence on the development of a self-concept comes from the wider society. When disadvantaged children assess themselves in relation to the rest of society, they learn that there is no one below them, that every one else is above them. They are the bottom. From this, they conclude that they are not as good as others.

The rest of society is their reference point, and television has been one of the most effective means of clearly focusing this reference point. Television helps culturally disadvantaged children make the relative assessment necessary to form a poor self-concept. When they compare themselves and their situation to the America depicted on the TV screen, they do not measure up. (The wholesome, happy, affluent people that romp through the commercials contribute heavily to this evaluation.)

Government officials, law enforcement agents, merchants, and average citizens of the dominant culture all communicate lack of respect—even contempt—for disadvantaged individuals. The schools, too, perpetuate and reinforce the negative self-concept. Often, teachers unconsciously communicate attitudes of rejection, superiority, or contempt for their disadvantaged pupils.

Some teachers unwittingly *teach* disadvantaged pupils that they are inferior. For example, a teacher may make a child feel that he is bad when he fails to conform to the values or practices of middle-class culture regarding cleanliness, eating breakfast, aggressive behavior, respect for property and time schedules, and responsibility for homework assignments. This kind of action is damaging to self-concept. Teachers must realize that it is impossible for disadvantaged children to do many things that middle-class children do without conscious effort.

Textbooks, like television, provide a relative basis for self-assessment. Many reading textbooks help form negative self-concepts in disadvantaged pupils by presenting a romanticized middle-class culture and implying rejection of anyone who deviates from the description. Teachers, of course, give secondary reinforcement to the textbooks.

Growing up in a family that has inherited poverty, living in an environment that induces failure, being rejected by society, and being confronted with his own inadequacies in the school, the disadvantaged child learns to look upon himself with contempt. Furthermore, his negative attitude toward himself is continually reinforced. When he fails to change his negative self-concept to a positive one, he in turn produces children who develop a poor self-concept. Poor self-concept is still another cycle of poverty for the disadvantaged.

It is important that the teacher understand the significance of self-concept. If a child appraises himself in qualities that are mainly derogatory, this will color his view of the world. Furthermore, a child who views himself and the world in this way will demonstrate this viewpoint in his actions. If the child sees himself as someone who is liked, successful, and accepted by his teachers and society, then he will tend to conform to a role consistent with this view. If he sees himself as someone who is not liked, who is unsuccessful and rejected by his teachers and society, then his actions will be in accord, and his self-concept will be poor.

Sometimes his poor self-concept is acted out in aggression toward others or toward himself; sometimes it causes him to suppress *any* action—he just gives up. In either case, his self-concept *programs* him for expected failure. Since he expects to fail, he does fail—and this only reinforces his feelings of inadequacy.

Many culturally disadvantaged children never begin the cycle of achievement. That is, their expected failure diminishes their chances to experience achievement success that could generate the motivation to produce more achievement success, and so on. Instead, they are in a *reverse* cycle of achievement: their expected failure generates failure. Furthermore, many individuals don't believe that they can learn; one of the main tasks of the classroom teacher is to convince them that they can.

It was mentioned that teachers tend to hold up the middle-class culture as the standard that measures good and bad. To combat this influence, disadvantaged children should be made aware of the values that people have developed under different conditions. They should be taught that individuals of one way of life are not intrinsically better than individuals of another way of life. In other words, disadvantaged pupils should be made aware of the reality of deprivation. Disadvantaged children—especially those at the secondary level—should be given insight into their status and some of the factors that influence their status. This insight, perhaps, will help them relieve some of their frustrations, point out some escape for them, and help them to cope with their problems in a positive manner.

Also, the teacher can consciously help develop positive self-concepts in his disadvantaged pupils through constantly encouraging them to achieve, communicating an attitude of expected success instead of expected failure, and convincing them that they are as good as anyone else, in spite of all cues to the contrary. Other ways to build a positive self-concept are:

1. Treat the pupils as *human beings,* not as objects. Communicate a feeling of concern for them through classroom activities rather than through words.
2. With encouragement and praise, reinforce all kinds of behavior that reflect positive qualities of self-concept.
3. Reserve a minute or two each week to engage individual pupils in conversation. This will illustrate to each one that he is a somebody.
4. Point out to pupils examples of persons from situations similar to theirs who have made it.
5. Make the pupils aware of significant historical contributions made by persons from their ethnic groups.

Schools so far have done very little to improve their pupils' self-concept. An examination of the objectives of compensatory programs for disadvantaged children reveals that educators recognize the need to change self-concept—many compensatory programs list objectives to this effect. However, few programs outline a program of specific techniques and materials teachers can employ, or activities pupils can do, to attain the objectives. Changing self-concept cannot be accomplished through incidental learning; it should receive *planned* emphasis in programs for disadvantaged children. Self-concept is the key to human behavior: change an individual's self-concept, and his behavior is changed. A positive self-concept makes success possible; a negative self-concept produces failure.

Aggression

One of the products of a poor self-concept is aggression. Aggression is hostility resulting from underlying frustration. An individual who has a poor image of himself grows to hate himself. This individual is often hostile toward others, and his hatred breeds aggression. Built-up aggression seeks an outlet. Sometimes the individual strikes out at others; sometimes he turns his aggression inward and strikes at himself. In either case, he attempts to inflict punishment.

Aggression can explode in a series of individual acts of violence, or in the kind of collective catharsis that produced a Watts, California. Usually, collective explosions of aggression are expressed in teen-age gang warfare or other senseless acts of violence, destruction, and delinquency committed by groups of young people. When aggressive feelings are turned inward, the individual seems to punish himself, perhaps by dope addiction or by repeated acts that bring punishment from other people. Often, aggressive feelings are sublimated into positive activities, such as athletics, which permit the individual to release his aggression in a socially acceptable way. This may partially explain the outstanding athletic achievement of many culturally disadvantaged individuals. Culturally disadvantaged blacks, who have the poorest self-concept of any group and the greatest feelings of aggression, have achieved particularly outstanding records in athletics. Schools in the big-city ghettos consistently win more than their share of sports championships.

Poor self-concept is not the whole cause of aggression. Aggression is also a natural product of the disadvantaged social environment. Children who live in an environment populated by aggressive persons must be aggressive themselves in order to survive. If they do not learn this they soon become an object of aggression. (The term *jungle* is more than a figure of speech when it is used to describe the social environment of the culturally disadvantaged.) The disadvantaged child is taught very early to "hit back when somebody hits you." If he doesn't demonstrate the correct response for a hostile environment his parents' form of punishment will be physical, violent, and immediate—a pattern that reinforces aggression.

Culturally disadvantaged children are immersed in an aggressive environment. Aggression is the only pattern they have learned for dealing with frustration, disagreement, and hostility. When feelings of aggression are not expressed in physical acts, they often come out verbally, in threatening, insulting language.

Obviously learning cannot occur in an atmosphere where constant storms erupt; thus the school vigorously discourages overt physical and verbal aggression. Reason and discourse are promoted as a means of dealing with frustration, disagreement, and hostility. The school, operating out of a middle-class orientation, expects an individual to suppress aggression, especially during encounters with authority.

How does this affect pupils whose way of life teaches and reinforces aggressive behavior? The ways of handling aggression taught by the school often won't work in the pupils' social environment. There is a conflict between the demands of the school and the pupils' way of life. (Here is an example of the school attempting to solve a problem that originates outside the school and is caused by factors over which the school has little or no control.) Conflict between the school and disadvantaged pupils over aggression will continue until the social environment of the pupils changes, or until the school can find a means of controlling aggression within its walls.

Conflicting Values

Aggression is just one negative pattern of behavior resulting from acquired values—the attitudes and beliefs that determine an individual's preference for one behavioral pattern over another. The values of disadvantaged pupils are in frequent conflict with the values of the dominant culture. Because many of the values of the dominant culture are codified, those children whose values deviate greatly are potential or actual delinquents.

For example, one value many disadvantaged children do not share with the dominant culture is a reasonable and proper respect for legitimate authority. In any confrontation with an authority figure, such as a law enforcement officer, their reactions, or their behavioral patterns dictated by their attitude toward authority figures, cause them trouble. Other examples of conflicting values that cause trouble are lack of respect for the personal and property rights of others, inability to understand and observe the rules of common courtesy, and disregard for the laws of society (drinking, taking dope, gambling, stealing, and so on).

Of course, a differing value system is not the only reason these children get into trouble or break the law; there are many other factors, including self-punishment as a result of poor self-concept, dope addiction, satisfaction of primary drives like hunger or warmth, and ignorance of the laws. The different value system, however, is a main contributing cause of the high delinquency rate.

The tragedy in this conflict of values is that the disadvantaged child's values *inevitably* develop out of his impoverished and hostile environment. How can a child learn the value of deferred gratification if his chances of attaining gratification are slim? How can a child learn the value of saving if there is nothing to save? How can a child learn the values of ambition or achievement if his ambition is crushed? How can a child learn the value of hard work for future rewards if hard work is not rewarded in his environment?

Schools have had little success in accomplishing this reso-
lution of conflict—it is something educators constantly talk
about but rarely achieve. Changing attitudes and beliefs is involved, and the schools have concentrated on *cognitive,* or
intellectual, changes in pupils rather than *affective,* or value,
changes. If attitudes and values determine the behavioral patterns that are necessary for intellectual learning in school, then
it follows that the school must emphasize affective changes.

How can schools teach disadvantaged pupils the values
necessary for intellectual achievement and participation in
the dominant culture? First, in kindergarten, teachers should
begin to make the children *aware* of the values of the dominant culture, especially those values necessary for academic
achievement. Disadvantaged pupils often learn of these values
too late in their lives to make a change.

Second, teachers should make disadvantaged pupils aware
of the *benefits* of acquiring these values. Third, teachers should
reinforce the behavioral patterns from which these values can
be inferred. (This point cannot be overemphasized. Constant
reinforcement is necessary if a behavioral pattern is to be
learned.) Fourth, pupils should be shown the *conflict* between
their values (and the resulting behavioral patterns) and the
values of the dominant culture. This conflict should be explained as objectively as possible.

Finally, the approach that should be taken in teaching values
is to encourage disadvantaged pupils to employ, in appropriate
situations, those behavioral patterns derived from the values
of the dominant culture. In other words, since disadvantaged
pupils cannot use many of these patterns in their own environment, they should be taught the *alternate situations* where they
do apply. The school is certainly the main situation in which
disadvantaged pupils should employ these alternate patterns
of behavior derived from a value system different from their
own.

Negative Environment

Up to this point, characteristics resulting from psychological
and social factors have been emphasized. Other characteristics result from physical environmental factors. The physical
environment of the culturally disadvantaged child can best
be described by the word *negative.* Some investigators have
called the environment unstimulating. However, this is not
accurate; in many ways, the environment provides too many
stimuli (high noise level, congestion). Other investigators have
called the physical environment impoverished, and this is certainly an accurate though inconclusive label: impoverishment
alone does not necessarily produce the characteristics that

limit the achievement of disadvantaged pupils. Other terms used to label the physical environment of disadvantaged pupils are *bleak, ugly, depressing, hostile,* and *debilitating.*

The most striking impression of the physical environment of the disadvantaged population, whether it is urban or rural, is its incredible ugliness. There is a gloominess of city slums caused by the narrow range of colors they cast. The slums appear to reflect only the colors from the grayed end of the color spectrum—those buried colors at the ends of the rainbow. Shades of dull browns and dead grays predominate, and the layer of filth that covers everything tints all other colors brown or gray. Nothing stands out.

Slums look like the battleground for a fight for existence. The junk, the dilapidated buildings, and the disorganization intensify the impression of combat. Disadvantaged rural areas give the same impression: ruined buildings and broken objects seem to have been flung across the landscape by some destructive force. Even the people one sees in these big-city slums and bleak rural areas seem to be battle casualties.

It is amazing what little knowledge outsiders have of the physical environment of disadvantaged pupils. Even teachers who work in schools located in the heart of slums rarely see the totality of the ugliness. They travel to and from the slum schools by the most direct route, seeing as little of the slum as possible. Every teacher who works in slum schools should take a tour of the physical environment from which their pupils come. Instead of driving directly home, turn off the regular trail and drive through the canyons of deprivation. If you work in a rural area, turn off the highway and take the dusty roads that wind past the barren farms and shacks of the disadvantaged.

The insides of the homes in which disadvantaged families live are consistent with the ugliness outside. Often, the homes are both empty and crowded at the same time—they are empty of objects but full of people. There is an absence of furniture and other objects of comfort and necessity which middle-class people take for granted. The home and the neighborhood of the culturally disadvantaged child are generally ugly, disorganized, dirty, noisy, crowded, and void of the kinds of stimuli that are meaningful in the middle-class environment.

Here are some of the general effects of this negative environment:

- *Lack of awareness of order or organization.* An environment that offers little experience with order makes chaos the norm.
- *Lack of respect for property.* An environment that consists

largely of junk and run-down buildings produces a disre-
spect for property.

- *Poor attention span.* An environment that is disorderly and
noisy contributes to the development of a poor attention
span; individuals learn to tune out all sounds, and when
they come to school they are often unable to distinguish
between general noise and meaningful sounds.
- *Disregard for cleanliness.* An environment that is dirty provides little motivation toward cleanliness.

Finally, the most serious influence of a negative environment on young disadvantaged children is that it does not provide them with the kinds of experiences out of which the
concepts on which the curriculum is based can be developed.
That is, the social and physical environment of the disadvantaged child causes him to have a different conceptual development from that of the middle-class child. This does not mean
that his conceptual development is *inferior;* rather, because
it is different from the expectations of the curriculum, it con-
stitutes a handicap.

In general, the physical environment of the middle-class
child *automatically* provides the stimuli that generate the
concepts on which the curriculum is based. For example,
middle-class children have toys and many other objects to
manipulate, compare, and classify. This is not necessarily
true in the environment of the disadvantaged child.

On the other hand, there are stimuli in his environment out
of which concepts necessary for achievement can be generated.
The disadvantaged child needs help in extracting the meaning.
If a mediator were present (middle-class parents play this role)
to select, to point out, to present stimuli, and to give explanations, the child could gain the experiences and concepts necessary for achievement in the existing curriculum.[1] *The absence
of a mediator is the crucial factor in a negative physical environment.*

Language Handicap

Many culturally disadvantaged pupils speak a language that
is different from the language of the school. They may speak
a nonstandard variety of English; or their English may be influenced by their native foreign language. In either case, their
language handicaps them in school achievement. They are
"linguistically disadvantaged." Young children from disadvantaged homes are particularly disadvantaged in language. Their

© With acknowledgement to Thomas J. Edwards, Senior Language Arts Con-
sultant, Science Research Associates, Inc.

language development has not been as carefully guided as that of middle-class children, and it takes them longer to become proficient in their own language than for middle-class children to become proficient in theirs. Thus, they enter school not only speaking a different kind of English but a different, *incomplete* kind of English. Their disadvantage in language continues as they get older, so that language skills are the major academic need of disadvantaged pupils at every grade level.

Few disadvantaged pupils can be accurately described by the foregoing characteristics, which are only general tendencies. In discussing these general characteristics, the differences between disadvantaged pupils and middle-class pupils were emphasized. In truth, disadvantaged pupils are more like all other pupils than they are different. Unfortunately, the differences are educationally significant.

Finally, one very important and most accurate general characteristic must be stated: culturally disadvantaged pupils *are capable of learning.* Don't be misled by the bleak picture — many disadvantaged pupils have proved that in spite of tendencies toward these characteristics in greater or lesser degree they *can* acquire the learning that helps to overcome them.

Learning Style

The psycho-social characteristics of children from a disadvantaged culture cause them to develop a particular learning style. This learning style puts them at a disadvantage because it does not complement the orientation of the school curriculum. It has been suggested that the curriculum be adapted to the disadvantaged child's particular background of experience, his needs, and his interests. This kind of change in the curriculum involves a change in *content.* Another change is also required — this change involves *methods.*

The learning style of the culturally disadvantaged child is not efficient. At all grade levels it is slow, physical, nonverbal, problem-centered, and concrete-oriented — like the learning style of the young child. The disadvantaged child is unable to make the transition from this style of learning to the more efficient learning style of the older child. This is one reason why the achievement gap between the disadvantaged pupil and the middle-class pupil widens as they get older.

Teachers must work constantly to help their disadvantaged pupils acquire an efficient, mature learning style. A mature learning style is verbally oriented, problem- and content-centered, and present-, past-, and future-oriented. It entails the ability to deal with abstractions and to work for future reward and gratification. Until disadvantaged pupils acquire this mature learning style, methods of instruction *should be adapted to their present level of functioning.*

The learning style of the disadvantaged child operates within the framework of the general principles of learning:

1. An individual learns from his own experience.
2. An individual must interact with his environment to learn.
3. Two kinds of experiences produce learning: direct and indirect.
4. The quality of learning is determined by the quality of the experience.
5. The quality of the experience is dependent on interest and motivation, concentration, breadth of stimulation, variety of stimulation, and level of intelligence (innate capacity) of the learner.

Some of the factors that hinder the disadvantaged have been referred to in preceding pages. These factors are:

- *Different language development.* Culturally disadvantaged pupils are handicapped because of their inability to speak standard English. In addition, they are not verbally oriented in their learning style. (Note that much classroom instruction is carried on and transmitted verbally.)
- *Inability to distinguish between noise and meaningful sound.* This is closely related to poor language development, or inability to use language in the traditional ways of the school. Disadvantaged pupils do not attach the same significance to verbal stimuli as middle-class pupils do; consequently, they learn less from what they hear.
- *Inability to delay gratification.* Much of the learning in school does not provide immediate gratification; therefore disadvantaged pupils are apt to give up on a particular learning task long before they can receive any rewards from it. Instruction should be planned to yield immediate rewards whenever possible. At other times, constant encouragement and praise from the teacher must accompany the performance of the learning task.
- *Inability to sustain attention.* The short attention span of disadvantaged pupils demands that learning tasks be short and varied. These pupils generally will not devote attention to

any one task for sustained periods. This causes particular difficulty in primary grades. Young children have short attention spans anyway, but when they are both young and disadvantaged, their attention spans can best be described as compounded capriciousness.

One way a primary teacher can get around the doubly limited attention span is to make sure that all instruction is consistent with the learning style of the disadvantaged. Specifically, instruction should de-emphasize a verbal approach. There are other areas—visual-discrimination skills, manipulatory skills, and reacting physically with the environment—that must be developed *before* verbal skills and verbal reception are developed. If primary teachers emphasize the development of these skills, the attention span of disadvantaged pupils might be lengthened.

Throughout the middle and upper grades, the attention span must be constantly lengthened by gradually lengthening the time needed to complete particular tasks. This must be accompanied by instruction based on the interests and experience of disadvantaged pupils at increasing levels of difficulty.

Negative Attitude Toward Intellectual Tasks

There are still other factors that make up the learning style of disadvantaged pupils. Culturally disadvantaged children value physical prowess rather than intellectual prowess. Many school activities, to them, are sissy or square. Furthermore, they are not aware of the value of intellectual skills because they do not see the application of intellectual skills in their cultural environment.

Disadvantaged children are also present- and practical-oriented—they want to see an immediate use for something and an immediate benefit, whereas much of the learning in school has to be stashed away for future use. All these characteristics combine to produce a generally negative attitude toward intellectual tasks.

In order to change this negative attitude, culturally disadvantaged children must be given constant rewards for performing intellectual tasks. Whenever possible, they should be shown practical applications of learning. For example, they can be shown how a knowledge of percentages can uncover the exorbitant interest rates their parents are usually charged. (This will probably cause their parents to take a greater interest in education, too.) This technique of connecting learning to its relevant application—the solving of real problems in the pupils' environment—is a good tool for changing attitudes.

Inability to Recognize Adults as Information Sources

Culturally disadvantaged pupils, retarded as they may be in academic achievement, are often intellectual giants when compared to their parents. The ghetto child in the sixth grade, the Appalachian child who has three or four years of urban school experience, the Mexican-American or Puerto Rican child who speaks and reads English — all are often beyond their parents in intellectual achievement. Their parents cannot provide information relevant to the curriculum. Thus the children come to believe that adults are not sources of information.

This attitude begins to develop when the children are very young. Their parents are not likely to ask them, "What did you learn in school today?" Instead, they are more likely to want to know: "Did anyone pick on you today?" "Did the teacher treat you O.K.?" Disadvantaged parents are not likely to discuss academic matters with their children. If a child asks them a question requiring academic information, they usually will not be able to help much.

The older the child is, the less help the parent is able to give. By the time the child reaches fourth or fifth grade, his parents are no longer able to offer any assistance with school work.

The belief that adults are not sources of information then tends to be generalized — it may even include teachers. This is understandable when one realizes that little of the information disadvantaged children need is given by teachers. Instead, the information broadcast in the classroom is often impractical, incomprehensible, or earmarked for future use. Disadvantaged pupils cannot respond to information of this kind, and they do not regard the source of this kind of information as someone to go to for help in solving problems.

Kinesthetic vs. Verbal and Written Stimuli

In the face of the ineffectiveness of verbal stimuli, there are other means of transmitting meaning and stimulating learning. One of the most effective is extensive use of audiovisual materials. Audiovisual materials are dramatic and interesting. They enable the child to derive more meaning from the verbal part of the presentation through reinforcement by the visual part. In addition, pictures, filmstrips, movies, television, and displays are the most efficient and economical method of filling in the disadvantaged child's experiential void. Audiovisual aids should be used throughout all grade levels in the education of culturally disadvantaged children.

Psychologists suspect that disadvantaged children learn best when they are physically involved. Again, the outstanding athletic record of disadvantaged groups lends support to this: football requires many complex mental processes — quick evaluation, memory, strategy, interpretation—yet, disadvantaged boys learn these processes as well as or better than their middle-class peers. When learning football plays, however, participants *act out* the plays, rather than memorize them from a written or verbal description.

Perhaps classroom teachers should borrow the teaching methods of football coaches whenever they are appropriate and use them to teach cognitive learnings through physical involvement. (For example, in primary grades reading instruction may include tracing letters and words with fingertips or even with footsteps.)

Role playing is another activity that physically involves the pupil. This technique can be used at every grade level and in any subject. If primary-grade pupils are studying community helpers, they can act out various roles. The best way for secondary students to prepare for a job interview is to let them act out the roles of each of the interview participants.

Another way of physically involving children in a learning task is to let them take the place of symbolic representations. This method is particularly applicable when teaching arithmetic. For example, instead of writing an addition or subtraction problem on the chalkboard, groups of pupils can be used in place of numerical representation. Children can walk through the computations.

Orientation Toward the Present

Another conjecture of psychologists and other investigators in the area of educating the culturally disadvantaged is that these children are present-oriented, like the very young child of any culture or social class. This factor is increasingly significant as the grade level increases and the content in the curriculum becomes more past-oriented, especially in literature and social studies.

Disadvantaged children lack interest in the past. Their past has generally been unpleasant and filled with bad times and hardship. (By way of contrast, middle-class individuals look on the past as the foundation of their present fortunate condition. They tend to look at the past to determine how to preserve its legacy in the present and the future.) For disadvantaged individuals, the past contains the elements of their tragedy— thus they do not want to perpetuate it.

In addition, the conditions of deprivation force disadvantaged pupils to constantly deal with day-to-day problems to sustain their existence. Thus the attention of disadvantaged pupils is consistently focused on the present. Their preoccupation with the pressing problems of deprivation prevents them from shifting their orientation to the past.

The problem of time orientation of disadvantaged pupils is particularly acute in social studies. Social problems and historical events of the past have no apparent relevancy to the present. One of the purposes of teaching social studies, however, is to develop social concepts (in addition to telling the story of the development of our society, inculcating patriotism, examining the roots of contemporary social phenomena, and so on).

Concepts are not bound by time. For example, the emergence of groups to power or the extension of democratic processes can be developed from a study of the civil rights movement just as well as from a study of colonial America. Such an approach to social studies has the advantage of focusing students' attention on the problems that presently concern them, rather than on those that concerned their forefathers.

The past can be understood *in terms of the present.* That is, social studies can be taught more effectively backwards than by taking a starting point in the past and progressing chronologically to the present. Current problems can be traced backwards to determine their cause. An approach like this has the additional advantage of helping disadvantaged pupils to understand their present condition so they can better cope with it.

Slowness With Intellectual Tasks

Disadvantaged children perform intellectual tasks slowly. Slowness should not, however, be equated with dullness. Some researchers have suggested that these children are slow in performing school tasks because they are physical learners. Other reasons might be lack of interest in the task, lack of adequate preparation for the task, poor language development, poor physical and emotional conditions, or lack of regard for speed.

Some investigators have suggested that slowness is a positive rather than a negative factor in the learning style of the disadvantaged. Slowness can be an asset in solving many problems. However, the dominant culture is keyed to speed, and so is the curriculum. Until disadvantaged pupils learn to operate at a faster pace, what seems to be an asset will actually continue to be a handicap.

Teachers should not be too much concerned with developing general speed in their disadvantaged pupils. Speed comes with competence. The important thing is to help the pupils develop competence in subject areas; speed will be a by-product. In the meantime, plan to allot adequate time for the completion of assignments; disadvantaged children do not respond to exhortations to hurry.

Inductive vs. Deductive Approach

Material presented in parts that move to the whole, rather than from the whole to the parts, is a better approach to use with disadvantaged pupils. In teaching paragraph development to disadvantaged pupils, the topic sentence should not be introduced first. Instead, pupils should be taught to write three or four sentences about a topic. After they are able to do this, they can be taught to write one sentence that tells what the other three or four are about. This sequence—from the supporting sentences to the topic sentence—is an example of the inductive approach.

Inability to Deal With Multiple Problems

Finally, disadvantaged pupils usually perform better when they are confronted with only one task or assignment. Thus teachers should not give multiple assignments or even multiple tasks within an assignment.

Summary of Main Points

1. Certain general psycho-social characteristics are associated with culturally disadvantaged pupils. Individual disadvantaged pupils, however, differ in the degree they exhibit these characteristics.

2. The general characteristics of culturally disadvantaged pupils have educational implications; the instructional program must be based on these characteristics, and the instructional program must help pupils eliminate the deficiency implied by the characteristics.

3. Culturally disadvantaged children inherit poverty in many different forms.

4. Culturally disadvantaged children are caught up in cycles of poverty which perpetuate their impoverished condition.

5. Educational poverty is the most important cycle of poverty to break.

6. Culturally disadvantaged children have a poor self-concept. This makes them failure-oriented.

7. The values of culturally disadvantaged children are in conflict with the value system of the dominant culture.

8. The living environment of culturally disadvantaged pupils is negative.

9. Culturally disadvantaged pupils speak nonstandard English.

10. Culturally disadvantaged pupils have a learning style that limits their chances of success in the curriculum.

Questions for Discussion

1. At what point is a person considered disadvantaged?

2. How many characteristics are common to disadvantaged pupils, and to what degree is an individual described by these characteristics to be considered disadvantaged?

3. Discuss the following: Disadvantaged pupils are more heterogeneous than other pupils.

4. Select one of the general characteristics and discuss its educational implications. Discuss ways the school can help correct the deficiency of the characteristic.

5. Select one of the cycles of poverty (economic, educational, aspirational, moral and spiritual, experiential) and discuss ways the school can break the cycle.

6. Discuss the following: Breaking any one of the cycles of poverty makes it easier to break the other cycles.

7. How does the following statement relate to self-concept?
   Tell a man what he is, and that is what he most likely will become; tell a man what he ought to be and that is what he most likely will work toward.

8. The term *culture clash* refers to the conflict that results when persons with different value systems come into contact with each other. Discuss the implications of culture clash in the classroom. What are some steps that can be taken to alleviate this conflict?

9. Select one of the factors that makes up the learning style of disadvantaged pupils and show how pupils are handicapped in a particular subject because of the way it is commonly taught. Suggest ways the teaching of the subject can be changed to fit their learning style.

10. What are some of the ways teachers can help older children change their learning style?

Bibliography

Barber, Bernard. "Social Class Differences in Educational Life-Chances," *Teachers College Record*, 63:102–29 (November 1961).

Black, Millard H. "Characteristics of the Culturally Disadvantaged," *The Reading Teacher*, 18:465–70 (March 1965).

Bloom, Benjamin S., et al. *Stability and Change in Human Characteristics*. New York: Wiley, 1964.

Bruner, J. S. "The Cognitive Consequences of Early Sensory Deprivation," *Sensory Deprivation*, ed. P. Solomon. Cambridge, Mass.: Harvard Univ. Press, pp. 195–207.

— — —. "The Course of Cognitive Growth," *American Psychologist*, 19:1–15 (1964).

Davidson, Helen; Gerver, Joan; and Greenberg, Judith. *Characteristics of Successful School Achievers from a Severely Deprived Environment*. New York: City Univ., October 1962.

Deutsch, Martin. "The Disadvantaged Child and the Learning Process," *Education in Deprived Areas*, ed. A. H. Passow. New York: Teachers College, Bureau of Publications, Columbia Univ. 1963, pp. 163–80.

Dougherty, Louise G. "Working with Disadvantaged Parents," *NEA Journal*, 52:18–20 (December 1963).

Frink, M. B. "Self-Concept as It Relates to Academic Underachievement," *California Journal of Educational Research*, 13:57–62 (March 1962).

Larson, R., and Olson, J. L. "A Method of Identifying Culturally Disadvantaged Kindergarten Children," *Exceptional Children*, 30:130–34 (1963).

Rich, J. M. "How Social Class Values Affect Teacher-Pupil Relations," *Journal of Educational Sociology*, 33:355–59 (May 1960).

Riessman, Frank. "The Overlooked Positives of Disadvantaged Groups," *The Journal of Negro Education*, 33:225–31 (Summer 1964).

Trager, H. S., and Yarrow, M. R. *They Learn What They Live*. New York: Harper, 1952.

Wylie, Ruth C. *The Self-Concept*. Lincoln, Neb.: Univ. of Nebraska Press, 1961.

CHAPTER 3

THE CULTURALLY DISADVANTAGED BLACK CHILD

3

The Scope of the Problem

Contributing Factors

The Role of the Teacher

Educational Goals

All that has been written about culturally disadvantaged children in Chapters 1 and 2 applies to culturally disadvantaged black children. In addition, there are factors that pertain specifically to disadvantaged blacks and affect efforts to educate them. Right now, a big part of the black population is in desperate shape—socially, economically, educationally—even psychologically. In this chapter we will examine those areas of the problem that affect education.

The Scope of the Problem

Abraham Lincoln signed the Emancipation Proclamation more than one hundred years ago; yet many black people are still locked in a kind of slavery. Approximately two-thirds of the black population is held in bondage by the snares of cultural deprivation—too many blacks are enslaved by all the cycles of poverty that perpetuate social tragedy; and this is the American tragedy. For example, black people as a group have a pathetically low educational level. Literacy among blacks is a comparatively recent thing. Thus many black children do not acquire positive attitudes about education; they do not really see the benefits of education distributed throughout their subculture; and they do not develop a good understanding of the educational process. These black children grow up to pass this tragic inheritance on to their children, and the cycle is repeated.

Another cycle that enslaves blacks is economic poverty. As a group the blacks are at the bottom of the income scale. Economic poverty has been the rule rather than the exception; it is traditional with many blacks—and traditional economic poverty generates itself, ironically growing greater on less and less.

As a group, the blacks lead in almost every area of social pathology—broken homes, illegitimacy, delinquency, crime, school dropouts, and so on. Furthermore, efforts to save them from social drowning are handicapped by racism. Efforts to treat one sickness are impeded by another; thus both must be treated simultaneously. Racism helps to generate and accelerate the cycles of poverty in a peculiar way: racists point to the results of prejudice to justify their prejudiced attitudes.

As a civil war was needed to free black people from their former condition of slavery, an effort just as massive is needed to free them from their present condition. Unless the concern of America is focused on the problems of culturally disadvantaged blacks, their lives will continue to be controlled by the forces of deprivation. This is a kind of slavery because individuals caught up by these forces are unable to control their own lives and destinies.

Strengthening the economic base of black people is probably the first of many actions that must be taken to free them from the slavery of cultural deprivation. They will not be able to enjoy the benefits of our society until they are able to satisfy their basic needs. They need more money. It's that simple. Of course, this is true for all culturally disadvantaged groups.

In his book *The Other America*, Michael Harrington estimates that 40 million Americans are living in poverty. The seriousness of the economic problem of black people is revealed in contrasting the number of poverty-level blacks with the total number of Americans who live in poverty. There are about 22 million black people in the United States. Using the most commonly used criterion for poverty, a yearly income below $4000, the number of blacks living in poverty is somewhere between 60 and 70 percent of the total black population. Black people, who comprise roughly 10 percent of the total U.S. population, account for more than 25 percent of the total poverty population.

Racism and its products, social and cultural segregation, are historical causes of the plight of the blacks. They are the forces that have caused them, often legally, to be excluded from full participation in the dominant culture. In the South, emotions generated by racism have been translated into laws to exclude blacks from the dominant culture; in the North, emotions generated by racism have been sublimated into more subtle methods of exclusion. The results have been equally effective.

Many observers have pointed out that the blacks are not the only group that has been at the bottom of American society. Formerly disadvantaged groups were segregated at the time that they joined the blacks at the bottom of the social and economic ladder, but after a few generations they became assimilated into American society, leaving the blacks still at the bottom. There is an obvious reason why these groups were able to accomplish the process of assimilation. They were able to lose their identity; their identity could not easily be discerned. Black people have been prevented from assimilating precisely because they have *not* been able to lose their identity. Their blackness has made them visible targets for continued oppression, has stigmatized them, and has generated emotions that block assimilation.

Blackness has made exclusion easy. This blackness must be recognized and dealt with when any of the problems of black people are scrutinized. Testimony of their former servitude is cast in their blackness, and that is the root of all their problems. Their blackness, however, is not the only factor that has prevented them from being assimilated into the dominant culture as other groups have been.

Prejudice against black people has always been more intense than prejudice against other groups. Furthermore, prejudice against blacks is permeated with an emotionalism that makes their assimilation a threat against white supremacy and racial purity—both emotional, irrational, and racist crutches to buttress white self-concept. Finally, other groups were assimilated at a time when their bodies were needed for labor. Black people, for whom assimilation has been delayed because of high visibility and intense racial prejudice, are no longer needed in the work force. Technology, coupled with the lack of opportunity racism has created to prevent blacks from qualifying for skilled jobs, has made untrained blacks obsolete in our society.

In a way, *all* black people—all 22 million of them—are culturally disadvantaged. Blacks are still prevented from full participation in the dominant culture solely because of race. Therefore, all are culturally disadvantaged regardless of education, income, life-style, or value system. Not all are culturally disadvantaged to the degree that it handicaps their academic achievement, however.

The situation for middle-class blacks is rapidly improving. In fact, middle-class blacks already have had the door to the dominant culture opened for them, and they are passing through this door to full participation with increasing ease, while their less fortunate black brothers are slipping farther behind. Thus the gap separating culturally disadvantaged blacks from middle-class blacks and the dominant culture is widening.[1]

---

1. Daniel Patrick Moynihan, *The Negro Family* (Washington: Office of Policy Planning and Research, U.S. Department of Labor), 1965.

It is interesting that many jobs at the top of the job ladder have been opened to blacks, while jobs at the middle of the job ladder, particularly those middle-level jobs controlled by the craft unions, remain closed. The situation is ironic, because the vast majority of blacks (the lower-class blacks) who need better jobs are blocked by discrimination and fear from getting them, while the minority of blacks who are already economically secure (the middle-class blacks) have greater job opportunities.

Education is one massive program that must be conducted to help black people break out of their contemporary slavery. Education is one of the surest means of helping blacks — or any culturally disadvantaged people — participate in the dominant culture and derive the benefits that accrue from that participation. Education can be the passport. Increasingly, desperate desires of black people to be integrated have resulted in violent knocks on the doors of the dominant culture. Most of the participants in the riots that flare up have been young blacks of school age — from elementary to high school age. Education, rather than senselessness or hopelessness, must come to guide the actions of these young people.

In the South, the majority of culturally disadvantaged blacks live in rural areas; in the North, the majority live in the cities. The disadvantaged black population in Northern cities is being steadily increased by the migration of Southern rural blacks with the high black birthrate contributing heavily to the population shift. The numbers of blacks are increasing so rapidly in Northern cities that the problem of educating the culturally disadvantaged has become the problem of educating culturally disadvantaged black students.

Already, black students constitute *close to 50 percent* of the public school population in many cities; in some cities (Washington, Chicago, Baltimore, and Philadelphia), the majority of the public school population is black. Many of these blacks are culturally disadvantaged.

The movement of black people from rural areas to urban areas is shown clearly in figures from the United States Bureau of Census: in 1900, 90 percent of the black population lived in the South, and 80 percent lived in rural areas. In 1960, 73 percent of the black population lived in urban areas. The increase in urban blacks has been most notable in the big cities of the North, where the problem of educating culturally disadvantaged blacks is most acute. The larger the city, the greater the chances of a black student going to an all-black school. This further isolates black students from contact with the dominant culture.

Contributing Factors

Slavery

The present condition of the black people can be explained in great part by their background. The roots of deprivation, in almost any area in which blacks experience it, can be traced back to slavery.

The cruelty of the American system of slavery is unequaled. Of course, any system of slavery is cruel; but the American system was particularly destructive because it did not recognize or treat black people as human beings. Instead, it considered blacks as property—objects, things, tools for labor. The apologists for slavery often try to explain away some of the evils of the system by asserting that a warm relationship developed between slaves and their masters. Even though one may treat one's property with care, especially if it is of economic value, this kind of relationship was not the rule. Nor could any kind of relationship compensate for apparent lack of human identity.

The system of slavery was not a strong foundation on which to build the means for acculturation. On the contrary, slavery prevented blacks from developing a way of life that could be fused with the dominant culture when they were freed. The state of freedom that existed immediately after the Civil War, during the Reconstruction, probably increased the gap between the way of life developed during slavery and the dominant culture. Black people were never prepared for the sudden freedom that victory by the Union forces gave them. They were turned loose ill-prepared for assimilation, and the stigma of color marked them as persons unacceptable for assimilation.

Black people were first imported as slaves into this country in 1619. They were emancipated in 1863. Thus they spent almost ten generations as slaves. This is more than twice the length of time they have been free. *It took a very strong people to make the advances blacks have made in so short a time despite former servitude and continuing repression.*

Probably the two most important things for the classroom teacher to remember when dealing with the topic of slavery is to build self-concept by capitalizing on the gains black people have made since emancipation (always pointing out that these gains were made in spite of barriers), and to utilize the topic of slavery to shed understanding on the present conditions of black people in America. It is really important for black children to understand the roots of their deprivation, because out of self-understanding grows self-help. And this is something blacks desperately need.

Another guideline to follow when discussing slavery is that this subject should always be dealt with objectively and truthfully. If teachers or textbooks attempt to romanticize slavery and play down its cruel reality, black students tend to become cynical. Most of them know the truth about slavery. They check the teacher's honesty and integrity during any discussion of the subject. And the teacher who is not truthful or objective on this topic becomes suspect of dishonesty or lack of integrity in other areas. This means that teachers must often fill in the gaps in textbooks, as many textbooks do not handle slavery objectively. Be objective, but sympathetic; be truthful, but not overenthusiastic.

Discrimination

Discrimination was built into the system of slavery, and after the slaves were freed, new means to impose discrimination were developed. In the South it was a system of legal discrimination; in the North a system of subtle, "sublegal" discrimination, equally as effective. Both were a *conscious* effort to exclude black people from full participation in the dominant culture.

Discrimination through the years has particularly hurt black people in income, in housing, and in education. No one is more aware of the debilitating and destructive consequences of discrimination than its victims. For many black students, the most obvious examples of discrimination are the schools they attend. Legal discrimination or segregated housing patterns have created many black schools. Apart from any discussion of the merits of integrated schools, schools with all-black populations reflect the system of discrimination that operates against blacks, shutting them off from the dominant culture.

Discrimination is the most discussed topic in the black subculture. No other topic receives even half as much attention as this one. If teachers recognize that this is the most important concern of black people, the relevancy of the topic to the classroom is unquestioned. The teacher must realize that black children, even very young ones, look for both evidences and oversights of discrimination in the learning situation at all times.

For example, during the pledge of allegiance to the flag, they think about the phrase ". . . liberty and justice for all." In social studies, the words *equality* and *democracy*, or the omission of the black man's role in American history, have a special meaning for black students.

What should the classroom teacher do? Is it necessary to constantly discuss discrimination? Is it necessary to stop each time the problem is alluded to and point it out? Of course not. Classroom teachers who work with black children should, however, discuss the problem objectively whenever an apparent conflict between democratic principles and the reality of discrimination occurs.

Objectivity is always required. In addition, several positive aspects of the subject can be brought out. First, black children can be shown how other blacks have surmounted discrimination barriers. This has a raising effect on self-concept and aspiration level. Secondly, an understanding of the system of discrimination helps blacks to understand their society, and this leads to effective ways of removing discriminating barriers. Finally, pointing out to black students that these barriers can be surmounted strengthens their faith in democracy.

This last point is especially relevant today. The riots indicate that many blacks have rejected the democratic process as a means for achieving equality. The democratic processes were rejected because they often did not work for black people, or they worked at too slow a pace.

On the other hand, riots work. While politicians continue to assert that riots don't solve anything, in actuality, riots cause the dominant society to improve the lot of the ghetto population. After each riot, action is taken to eliminate grievances. (Think of all the programs that were instituted immediately after the riots in various cities.) This reinforces the riot pattern. It also implies that society must be attacked before it will move to meet the demands of ghetto residents, that the democratic processes don't work well for black people.

Many blacks feel so alienated from the dominant culture that they have given up ever being integrated. So-called black nationalist groups have developed that advocate, ironically, the same philosophy that produced their alienation. Some of these groups, especially in the big city ghettos, are dangerously active among black youths.

This presents another challenge to the schools. The actions of these groups must be counteracted. While the schools spend a great deal of time, especially at the secondary level, insulating young people from the appeals of communism, the threat of communism isn't nearly as immediate as the threat of extreme black nationalism. Black youths must be shown that their future lies in correcting the inequities of our democracy, not in rejecting our democracy. Rejection of democracy can result only in greater tragedy.

The Black Subculture

The historical twins of slavery and discrimination have caused blacks to give their own peculiar ethnic twist to some of the characteristics shared by other ethnic groups, to acquire other characteristics, and to be affected by other factors with educational implications.

Individuals are products of their culture. They learn the particular way of life of the group into which they are born. Sometimes this group is a relatively distinct but not a totally separate part of a larger whole—in other words, a subculture. This is the case of black people. The system of discrimination and segregation that has operated against them for so long has caused them to develop a way of life that differs from the dominant culture. Their subculture is their way of coping with life. Patterns of behavior, institutions, attitudes, and values passing from the dominant culture into the black subculture must first be passed through the prism of the historical experiences of black people. In this process they are refracted and bent to fit the particular needs.

Thus the black subculture is a result of the conditions of life set by the dominant culture, the freedom the dominant culture allows blacks, and their historical experiences. Within belong the majority of families classified as culturally disadvantaged.

The Black Family

Before children are products of their culture, they are products of their families. The family is the basic social unit of American life, the crucible in which socialization is forged. The basic tenets of the culture are transmitted by families to their children. The school gives depth and dimension to the transmission, but if the family has been ineffective in transmitting the basic tenets, or if they are different from the expectations of the curriculum, then the children have extreme difficulty achieving in school. Many culturally disadvantaged black children come from families that have not met the expectations of the curriculum. In addition, many black families are suffering from economic and social handicaps that also affect the children's school achievement.

Many black families are in bad shape. The deplorable condition of the family in the black subculture is shown in every index of family breakdown, such as divorce, desertion, separation, matriarchal families, indigent families, illegitimacy, and aid to dependent children. The situation is so bad that the black family has become a serious concern of the federal government; many programs in the war on poverty are indirectly designed to strengthen the black family.

Matriarchy. It is estimated that 25 percent of all black families are headed by women. (The figure is higher for urban families than for rural familes.) This kind of family structure is so far out of touch with the family structure of the dominant culture that it tends to severely retard the progress of the whole group. The matriarchal structure particularly crushes and erodes the self-concept of black men and boys, and it imposes a heavy burden on black women — frequently they have had to be both mothers and fathers, providers and caretakers.

The historical basis for this matriarchal structure is slavery. The Christian religious framework could not contain both slavery, as practiced by the South, and the concept of brotherly love. This conflict forced slave owners to consider blacks in nonhuman terms.

With this viewpoint, the system of slavery did not support the institution of the family as a unit. Black families were divided to the economic advantage of the slave owner. If the family was lucky, one buyer would purchase them all — but this was *not a primary concern of the buyer*. In instances in which children were too young to be separated from their mothers, the father went to one buyer and the mother and children to another. Thus the natural dependency of young children on their mothers helped to develop the matriarchal pattern.

Slaves could not develop strong marriage ties on the plantations; strong marriage ties were not supported by the attitudes of the slaveholder. Children born of these loose unions were looked upon as being the mother's responsibility. This was a natural result of the inability of the father to be a provider for the family in a normal sense, and of the fact that the children didn't belong to either the mother *or* the father — but were the property of the slaveholder. Fathers often lived on distant plantations, and the consequent difficulty of visiting also served to weaken family ties and prevent a normal family structure from developing. Not to be overlooked were the unions between master and slave. Many children were born of these unions, and they always remained with the mother.

The matriarchal structure of the black family developed in slavery because of the mother's fundamental role in relation to the child. The structure did not change after the slaves were freed, and subsequent social and economic factors perpetuated it. While it is important for the teacher to realize that a black family consisting of a mother, a grandmother, and children *can* be a wholesome, functioning family, male absenteeism nevertheless is a serious problem.

Economic Poverty. The other force that has had a debilitating effect on the structure of the black family is economic poverty. Between 60 and 70 percent of black families have incomes of less than $4000, which marks the poverty level. (Only 26 percent of white families have incomes below this figure.) It is difficult for families with such a meager income to adhere to the life-style of the average family of the dominant culture. Furthermore, economic poverty breaks down family structure, and since black people are disproportionately affected by economic poverty, the structure of many black families has been affected.

In 1964, 29 percent of the black male population was unemployed at one time or another.[2] As unemployment goes up, the breakdown of the family increases. When the male head of family becomes unemployed, the family passes through several stages toward breakdown. First the family becomes broke, then it exhausts its credit. At this point the women take over: first the social worker (usually a woman), then the wife, who administers the welfare funds for the upkeep of the home. The husband really isn't needed for the survival of the family at this point. This process destroys his self-concept. (In addition, intermittent unemployment makes the steady income of welfare attractive for the wife and children. Many black husbands are put out or they have to "cut out" for the economic survival of their families.)

Another economic factor that tends to break up the black family structure and perpetuate the matriarchy is the advantage the women have over the men in obtaining employment. Historically, the black women have held this advantage; they also are ahead as regards moving into higher paying jobs or jobs with higher status. Perhaps this explains the significantly greater academic achievement of black women over black men: the women can see a real use for education.

Presently, about 60 percent of all black women are in the work force. The relative ease of the women to find employment has tended to make them economically independent of the men, and this independence also contributes to family breakup. (While the self-concept of the black male naturally suffers because of this, the real sufferers are the children. The door keys hanging around the necks of the children of working mothers are, albatross-like, symbolic of all the destructive forces pressing down on the black subculture.)

The process of family breakdown holds specific implications for educating the children. In the first place, the kind of families generally described in textbooks may tend to confuse black children, particularly the younger ones. (Older children are familiar with the normal structure of the American family in the dominant culture, while they recognize the structure of many disadvantaged black families.) The classroom teacher

2. *Ibid.*

can't allow his pupils to remain confused about family structure. He is obligated to support the value of the family as a *stable unit,* with all its essential components: children, mother, *and* father.

The best approach to take with very young children seems to be to deal with each family presented in the text as an individual family. Do not generalize that most families fit the structure of a family presented in the text, and avoid contrasting the two types of family structures.

In the later primary grades and the middle grades, a generalization should be made without negatively rejecting other structures. Stories depicting families with a female head should be used to show that there is room for all. (In this case, the family structure should not be romanticized the way stories of this kind usually are in texts. Again, treat the family as an individual instance.) Admittedly, the whole problem of the conflict in structure between the pupils' families and the textbook families is a delicate one. Perhaps the best guideline is to use common sense that grows out of an understanding of the children.

The discrepancy between the valued family structure of the dominant culture and the family structure of the black subculture should be dealt with objectively when working with secondary students. The discrepancies should be pointed out and the reasons for their existence examined. Again, it is recommended that these students be given self-understanding to develop self-help. They must learn the values of the dominant culture if they are to enter it. While these older students are aware of family breakdown as an *effect* in the black subculture, they are not aware of the *cause.* The school should connect the relationship and clear up some of the confusion.

It is ironic that basic facts of family structure are presented and dealt with more in the primary grades, when the children are least able to understand the discrepancies, and less in high school, when students have both the capacity and the need to understand them.

When the American family is studied at the secondary level, the topics discussed are usually not the basic structure of the family and the forces of destruction attacking this structure. Instead, topics like family budgets and the importance of selecting a good mate are dealt with. While all students should study these topics, culturally disadvantaged black students also need a strong course in sociology including, among other things, a thorough study of basic family structure, the advantages of this structure in our society, and the causes of family breakdown.

Male Absenteeism. The absence of a male head in many black families has a particularly debilitating effect on boys. Too many black boys grow up without a male model, and they attend schools dominated by women (particularly in the elementary grades). They learn their male roles the best way they can; often they learn the male role in the streets from their immature peers or the adult models that are found there.

Immaturity causes the boys to select as models adults who occupy exciting, flashy, and money-making roles. In the urban ghetto, this means that the black boy often takes for his model the hustler, the "touch," the pimp, and other undesirable residue of human waste from the sores of urban neglect. These types are esteemed in the ghetto—they are the ones who have money, dress sharp, drive the Cadillacs—they have achieved a topsy-turvy success out of social neglect and breakdown. They are looked up to, romanticized in black songs and folktales ("Frankie and Johnny," "Stagger Lee"), and are often objects of women's affection.

The problem of the lack of a male family head is just as serious in small towns and rural areas. Lacking shady characters as models, many disadvantaged black boys in these areas learn their male roles at their mothers' knees. This is no place for a boy to learn how to be a man. There is an ethnic joke that the first thing a black mother teaches her daughter is that a black man "ain't no good."

One place disadvantaged black boys should be able to find male models is at school. Unfortunately, women dominate elementary schools and make up almost half of the personnel in secondary schools. The problem is most acute at the elementary level because of the formative age of the children. Not enough men are entering elementary teaching.

Almost every elementary school, however, has at least *one* male teacher. With a little flexible scheduling, this one male can be used effectively as a model: he can exchange places with women teachers—especially in the primary grades—for part of the day. Perhaps in ghetto schools a "floating" male teacher can be assigned a regular schedule to teach part of each day in rooms taught by female teachers.

The Ghetto

Ghetto life has a greater influence on black children than merely providing poor models for the boys. The black ghettos of American cities wield against their young people all the inhibiting power of a negative environment. In fact, America's black ghettos are the worst kind of negative environment. In every city the black ghetto leads in crime, disease, family breakdown, substandard housing, and most other social disruptions. Being raised in such an environment *in itself* handicaps a student; no one living in the ghetto can escape being scarred by it.

Originally the word *ghetto* was the name of the Jewish section in sixteenth century Venice. Now the word has come to stand for the areas in cities where black people live, locked behind invisible walls. Few blacks in America's cities are able to live outside the ghetto. Economic level is not the qualification for living there—black skin is the only qualification. Thus the ghetto can present an interesting contrast: good and bad, religion and immorality, middle class and lower class, wealth and poverty, joy and sorrow—all the opposites one can think of are nowhere else found in such incongruous juxtaposition. This is one reason why black children are usually more worldly wise than children of other groups.

The limiting effect of the ghetto's invisible walls is in preventing blacks from coming into direct contact with the "outside world." Many young blacks have never been outside those walls; they meet the outside, populated with strangers and unfamiliar in its physical appearance, only through their textbooks. Since the walls of the ghetto keep its inhabitants locked in and untouched by the dominant culture, the ghetto subculture perpetuates itself. Unlike most ghettos of other ethnic groups in the past, today's black ghettos are expanding both in size and density of population.

Self-concept

Self-concept has been defined as "an individual's assessment of himself." The assessment is made by comparing himself with others, or having himself compared to others. Some of the causes of negative self-concept of culturally disadvantaged students were discussed in Chapter 2. All of these causes apply to culturally disadvantaged black students. In addition, some contributing causes stem from the peculiar status of blacks in America: the inability of some black men to fill the role of head of family, the historical fact of being former slaves and continuing victims of discrimination, the stereotype that the dominant culture has held up as a model of black people, and the stigma of black skin (which encompasses the other stigmata of kinky hair, thick lips, broad nose, or any other physical feature identifiable as black).

The Stereotype. Some black writers, including James Baldwin, Richard Wright, and Ralph Ellison, have stated or implied that the Negro was invented by the white man. What these writers are referring to is the stereotyped image of black people that has developed. This stereotype projects blacks as good-for-nothing, shiftless, immoral, inferior, simple children of nature who are inclined to steal, rape, and kill. Yet somehow they are also loyal and obedient; they know their "place" and keep it (except when some "outsider" stirs them up). This image is inconsistent and contradictory; yet this is the stereotype that the dominant culture historically has held of black people.

Fortunately, as our society matures, this stereotype is fading. Its influence, however, is still active on the black self-concept, like a dark shadow extending out of our historical immaturity. This stereotype has a negative influence because it taught blacks *who* they were and *what* they were—and, if they did not accept this, it taught them what they were *expected to be*.

There is always some truth in a stereotype. For example, the stereotype of happy-go-lucky blacks seems to hold a great deal of truth. Culturally disadvantaged black children *are* surprisingly happy and cheerful, in spite of the adversity surrounding them. Most black children learn from their culture not to take troubles too seriously because they have little control over them.

The peculiar thing about stereotyping is that it tends to prove itself. In the case of blacks, society forced them into conditions in which the qualities fitting the stereotype could develop. When those qualities did develop, they reinforced the stereotype.

In addition, the process of prophecy fulfillment tends to cause some individuals to conform to the stereotype. That is, an individual ". . . belonging to an oppressed and exploited minority, which is aware of the dominant cultural ideals but prevented from emulating them, is apt to fuse the negative images held up to him by the dominant majority with their own negative identity."[3]

Adherence to the stereotype, then, also reinforces the victim's negative self-concept formed through relative assessment. Thus the label given to black people has helped to influence the development of a negative self-concept in two ways: first, many blacks tended to conform to the label (the stereotype) by the process of "prophecy fulfillment" and this provided a frame of reference for relative assessment; secondly, even if blacks *did not* conform to the label in actions, their self-concept was damaged as they were told over and over again what was expected of them.

---

3. Erik H. Erickson, "The Concept of Identity in Race Relations: Notes and Queries." Reprinted by permission from DAEDALUS, Journal of the American Academy of Arts and Sciences, Boston, Massachusetts, Volume XCV, Number 1, p. 155.

Instructional Materials. The curriculum has contributed its share in upholding a negative image of black people. Literature and music provide many examples in which black characters are portrayed negatively or are referred to in negative terms ("The Gold Bug," "Black Sambo," *Huckleberry Finn, Robinson Crusoe,* "Old Black Joe," "Swanee River"). In addition, the omission or slight attention given to the role of blacks in the development of our country's history is a kind of negative "silent comment." Such examples as these in the curriculum have helped to damage black students' self-concept. It is imperative that teachers reject curriculum materials that may have a destructive influence.

Some good materials will have to be rejected—materials so rich in intellectual value that their worth seems to overshadow any negative influences they may have. The rejection of such material is unfortunate but must continue until black children are able to look at one black without suspecting that his negative qualities are assigned to every black by the dominant culture, and until the dominant culture can look at one black without generalizing his negative qualities to all blacks.

Because of the peculiar status of black people in America—and the treatment accorded to black people because of their status—just being black makes a child vulnerable to a negative self-concept. Black children learn very early—perhaps as early as three years of age—that they are black, that they are at a disadvantage in our society simply because of their skin color.

The Stigma of Being Black. Visible body signs that make an individual different in physical appearance from the "normal" population cause the marked individual to take on personal qualities unrelated to the mark. The normal population tends to impute a wide range of imperfections on the basis of the mark. The normals react negatively because of irrational conclusions reached on the basis of the irrelevant fact of physical difference.

The stigma of black skin has made black people easy targets for persecution and discrimination. It has become a symbol for all the troubles of black people. The blacks themselves have tended to believe that black skin, in itself, is bad.

Many ethnic "in" jokes ridicule or refer negatively to black skin. Often black mothers of newborn babies are more concerned about "What color is the baby?" than the lack of physical deformity. Also, it is interesting and revealing that black people divide hair into "bad" and "good" categories: bad hair is "Negro" hair and good hair is hair with Caucasian qualities. Thus the two most visible physical marks that identify black people have been looked upon as bad both by blacks and whites. This kind of attitude about one's physical appearance can only be damaging to self-concept.

Individuals who are stigmatized attempt to hide, or "correct," what society sees as their failing. In the past, black people have attempted to correct their black skin by lightening it, and their kinky hair by straightening it. The great amount of advertising space in black publications given over to "stigma-correcting" products reflects the intense desire of blacks to remove the stigma. Significantly more advertising space is given to products that attempt to correct the stigma of black skin or kinky hair than to any other group of products. These ads continue to reinforce negative attitudes regarding skin and hair by implying that they are indeed inferior.

Also revealing are the many slang words and phrases blacks have to refer to the stigma of black skin and kinky hair. (The popularity of hats among blacks probably has been due to their desire to hide their "bad" hair.)

The color black in our culture has always been associated with things that are "bad." The color black carries a negative value judgment. Black is the color of mourning; a "black night" is a forbidding night; a "black moment" is a time of trouble; a "black heart" is an evil heart; the villain is the fellow in the dark clothes.

Thus black people have been taught by a kind of stimulus generalization that their skin color is bad, and the way they are often treated reinforces this. It has been difficult for them to develop a positive self-concept when they have been constantly reminded that their color is, *in itself,* bad.

Black History. The most frequent suggestion for helping black students improve their self-concept is for schools to teach black history. The advocates of black history have not clearly defined what it is, or explained how it would be included in the curriculum. They have vaguely defined black history as "the part black people have played in the development of our country."

Black people have made many great contributions, and these contributions should be presented in the curriculum fully and accurately, without sentimentality or condescension. But the contributions of blacks were not made in a vacuum: they are an integral part of the whole development. Therefore, it is inconceivable that the contribution of blacks should be treated as something distinct and separate from the total effort to build a great nation.

Furthermore, even if black history can be thought of and treated as a separate subject, it is questionable whether it should be. Admittedly, the role of black people in our country's history has often been underplayed or ignored. The reality of segregation in life has resulted, regrettably, in the omission of the role of black people. Black children are keenly aware of this omission. However, to define the role of the blacks separately and distinctly, and to establish separate courses in black history is really curriculum jim crow. The role of black people must be taught within the *whole framework* of our country's development, as an integral part of courses in United States history.

One of the topics that should be studied in history classes is the civil rights movement. This movement is a source of great pride for black people, especially since the 1963 march on Washington. The civil rights movement has given a boost to the self-concept of every black individual. It has given blacks identity, and many of them are becoming increasingly nationalistic. Thus many black people now accentuate their black characteristics: they wear their hair "natural" instead of straightening it, and they describe themselves as "blacks" instead of "Negroes" or "colored people." (A few years ago, the term *black* was taken as an insult.)

Black people are taking increasing pride in their African roots, their dialect, their food, and the humor that has grown out of their adversity. (A whole new crop of comedians are probably the most articulate spokesmen and interpreters of the black subculture to the dominant culture.) They are not ashamed of being black any more, and this loss of shame is due to a new identity and boosted self-concept gained from the civil rights movement.

A movement that started with the goal of social integration, the civil rights movement has actually created pride in those things that have prevented black people from being integrated. In similar fashion, teaching black students about black history or the civil rights movement may improve their self-concept but at the same time make them more nationalistic — and this will make integration more difficult.

Black Literature. Many schools now include black authors in the literature program. This should continue at an increased rate. Black authors help black people to understand themselves and to define themselves, and so contribute to the formation of a positive self-concept.

A tendency exists to exclude the best and most relevant black authors. Too often, the only ones included are "safe Negroes," that is, blacks who have said the things or lived the kinds of lives that conform to white expectations, such as George Washington Carver, Marian Anderson, Booker T. Washington, Jackie Robinson, Ralph Bunche, and Charles Drew.

The black writers who speak directly to the needs and interests of black people are often excluded from the literature program, for one reason or another (too militant, too mature, too radical, too liberal, too communist). Writers like W. E. B. Dubois, James Baldwin, Ralph Ellison, Eldridge Cleaver, Richard Wright, and LeRoi Jones are examples of significant, relevant, and effective black writers often excluded from the literature program for such purported reasons. The real reason they are excluded is that they do not conform to the expectations that whites impose on blacks.

The Role of the Teacher

The role of the teacher is essentially the same for all disadvantaged groups. The teacher is a link with the dominant culture, a model, and the initiator and evaluator of learning experiences. The isolation of the black people, however, makes the first role the most important in instructing black children.

To the black child, a teacher is more than a link with the dominant culture—teachers are a link with the entire white world. Because of increased segregated living patterns, black people living in the ghettos today have less contact with white people than in any previous generation. Contact with the white world is often indirect, and regrettably much of the contact is a result of the civil rights conflict as reported in the mass media. (These reports usually emphasize the negative aspects of the conflict.) Also, for many black children, contact with the white world takes place in unpleasant ways, such as through the police or exploitative merchants. Thus black students often make the generalization that the entire white population is against them.

The teacher of black children must serve as a *positive* link with the white world. He must communicate the concern that the vast majority of white people have for the culturally disadvantaged blacks. Specifically, the job of the white teacher is to convince black children that the sensational acts of bigotry reported in the press and their own unfortunate encounters with bigoted people do not justly represent the feelings and actions of all white people. This will be a difficult task. The teacher can counter the work of bigots most effectively by doing a sincere job and pointing out examples of cooperation between blacks and whites.

Another special objective for teachers who work with black children is to raise their aspiration level. Blacks have long been correct in thinking that opportunities didn't exist for them. Recently, however, increasingly more opportunities have become available. Thurgood Marshall, a black man and a Supreme Court judge, stated in a recent speech that it is impossible for a qualified black to be without a job. This message must be communicated to black children by their classroom teachers. They must be shown that opportunities are open that may not have existed just a few years ago.

Ebony magazine runs profiles of blacks in worthwhile positions. This material might be profitably introduced in the classroom. Industrial field trips serve as another way to make black children aware of greater opportunities. Many school systems have used new federal funds to initiate programs incorporating field trips and other kinds of cooperation with industry. *Seeing another black person performing a job is the most convincing evidence that the opportunity exists.*

Finally, another role special to working with disadvantaged black children has to do with achieving the goals of equality. Currently, black people in America are involved in a struggle to achieve equality, a struggle which has been called "the black revolution." The struggle is not new; black people have waged the battle for equality for many years. The intensity of the struggle, however, has increased in recent years, and this has caused observers of it to give it a new label.

The essence of the revolution is simply this: *black people in America will no longer accept racist treatment from the dominant society.* All barriers of racism are being attacked with increased intensity. In addition, the black revolution has caused black people to redefine themselves. No longer will they be defined by others; self-definition is a product of the revolution.

Teachers working in ghetto schools must realize that all blacks—particularly secondary students—are caught up in this revolution. It's the most important thing in their lives. White teachers who agree with the primary goal of the black revolution—full equality—have a very important role to play in black schools. *If a white teacher doesn't agree with this goal, then he should get out of the black school.* Those teachers who are in agreement with the goal of the black revolution can demonstrate their support through committed teaching and in their teaching relationships with black students.

Educational Goals

The goals of education for black children must be the same as the goals of education for everyone else. Deprivation *does not* determine different goals; deprivation *does* determine different methods, approaches, materials, and increased efforts and concern for reaching educational goals.

Vocational education, traditionally given as a solution to this problem, will not solve the long-range needs of American society. First, vocational education would continue to make the white man's floor the black man's ceiling. Second, our democratic principles do not allow us to educate one group of people to fill particular occupational roles in our society.

The first strong advocate of vocational education was the black leader Booker T. Washington. His views on vocational education, expressed over half a century ago, are *still* the arguments given by contemporary advocates of vocational education for black students. The Job Corps program and the vocational program for black students recommended by James B. Conant in his book *Slums and Suburbs* are examples of the "Washington solution" to the race problem. Booker T. Washington wanted to train blacks to be blacksmiths, bricklayers, carpenters, and tailors; today, the advocates of vocational education want to train blacks to be welders, drill-press operators, repairmen, and janitors. A comparison of these aims reveals years of inaction.

Classroom teachers must encourage their black students to stretch beyond the limited goals of vocational education or our society risks the stagnation of 22 million people. If vocational education is overemphasized, the aspiration level of black students will remain low. Also, the absence of black models who have successfully attained the full range of educational goals will discourage intellectual effort on the part of black students.

Black students won't do much stretching unless they see others like themselves who have successfully completed the stretch beyond mere vocational educational goals. The reality of our society, which places so much importance on *group* identity instead of individual identity, causes minority individuals to recognize their potential in others who match them in color and ethnic background. Finally, every individual — regardless of color or deprivation — has the right to develop to his full potential. Vocational education alone does not afford this opportunity.

Summary of Main Points

1. The social and economic status of blacks is a major domestic problem.

2. The problem of educating culturally disadvantaged black children is most acute in the cities.

3. Slavery is the root of the black problem; the problem has been perpetuated by discrimination.

4. Segregation has caused black people to develop a subculture.

5. The structural and economic problems of many black families are grave.

6. Culturally disadvantaged black youths often lack good models.

7. Ghetto life serves to seal off blacks from the dominant culture.

8. The black self-concept is damaged by the relative status of blacks in our society and the value judgment our society places on the color black.

9. The special functions of teachers who work with culturally disadvantaged black pupils are to act as a link with the white world and to make their pupils aware of increasing opportunities.

10. Vocational education should not be emphasized for black pupils.

Questions for Discussion

1. Is education the best hope of improving black economic and social status?

2. Discuss some of the dangers to our society if the black population continues to be disproportionately disadvantaged.

3. Discuss the importance of changing the prejudiced attitudes of the dominant culture. What part can the schools play in this kind of education?

4. What efforts are needed to improve the status of blacks in addition to the efforts now being made by the federal government?

5. Is slavery really the root of the black problem? Are there any equally important roots that have not been discussed?

6. Discuss the need for dealing objectively and openly with the topics of slavery and discrimination.

7. Should education prepare black students to face life *as blacks* in our society, or *as American citizens?* To what extent should the reality of discrimination and prejudice be taken into account?

8. Suggest ways that culturally disadvantaged blacks can be taught the value of the American family structure.

9. Should black history be taught in schools as a separate class?

10. Should black students receive a "special" education that emphasizes vocational skills?

Bibliography

Baldwin, James. "A Talk to Teachers," *Saturday Review,* 46:42–44 (December 21, 1966).

— — —. *The Fire Next Time.* New York: Dial Press, 1963.

Billingsley, Andrew. *Black Families in White America,* Englewood Cliffs, N.J.: Prentice Hall, 1968.

Brody, Eugene B. "Color and Identity Conflict in Young Boys: Observations of Negro Mothers and Sons in Urban Baltimore," *Psychiatry,* Vol. XXVI (May 1963).

Butts, Hugh F. "Skin Color Perception and Self-Esteem," *Journal of Negro Education,* 32: 122–28 (1963).

Clark, Kenneth B. *Dark Ghetto.* New York: Harper, 1965.

Daedalus: The Negro American — 1. Vol. XCIV (Fall 1965).

— — —: *The Negro American — 2.* Vol. XCV (Winter 1966).

Frazier, E. Franklin. "Problems and Needs of Negro Children and Youth Resulting from Family Disorganization," *Journal of Negro Education,* 19:269–77 (Summer 1950).

— — —. *The Negro Family in the United States.* Chicago: Univ. of Chicago Press, 1966.

Handlin, Oscar. *Race and Nationality in American Life.* Garden City, N.Y.: Doubleday, 1957.

Harlem Youth Opportunities Unlimited, Inc. *Youth in the Ghetto.* New York: Harlem Youth Opportunities Unlimited, 1964.

Harrington, Michael. *The Other America: Poverty in the United States.* Baltimore: Penguin, 1963.

Herson, Phyllis. "Some Personal and Sociological Variables Associated with the Occupational Choices of Negro Youth," *Journal of Negro Education,* 64:337–51 (January 1959).

Kardiner, Abram, and Ovesey, Lionel. *The Mark of Oppression: Explorations in the Personality of the American Negro.* Cleveland: World Publishing, 1962.

Kvaraceus, William C., et al. *Negro Self-Concept: Implications for School and Citizenship.* New York: McGraw, 1965.

Myrdal, Gunar. *An American Dilemma.* New York: Harper, 1944.

Office of Policy Planning and Research, U.S. Department of Labor. *The Negro Family: The Case for National Action.* Washington: U.S. Department of Labor, 1965.

Pettigrew, Thomas. *A Profile of the Negro American.* Princeton, N.J.: D. Van Nostrand, 1964.

Redding, J. Saunders. *On Being Negro in America.* Indianapolis: Bobbs, 1962.

Silberman, Charles E. *Crises in Black and White.* New York: Random House, 1964.

Warren, Robert Penn. *Who Speaks for the Negro?* New York: Random House, 1966.

CHAPTER 4

OTHER MAIN DISADVANTAGED GROUPS

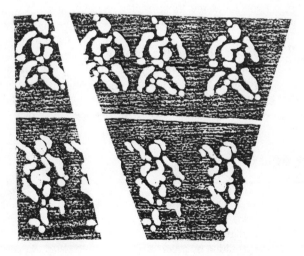

4

Mexican-Americans

Puerto Ricans

Appalachians and Southern Whites

American Indians

Four major ethnic groups combine with the black race to comprise virtually the total disadvantaged population: Mexican-Americans, Puerto Ricans, Appalachian and Southern rural white immigrants, and American Indians. Most of the individuals in each of these groups are culturally disadvantaged. Like the disadvantaged blacks, each of these groups has unique factors that make its deprivation different. This chapter will focus on the handicaps that children of these groups bring to school and the educational implications of these differences.

The Appalachian and Southern rural whites who have migrated to the cities are, like the blacks, products of a subculture that does not adequately prepare them to participate in the dominant culture: they are products of a relatively distinct but not totally separate culture. Their way of life is a dulled and distorted reflection of the dominant culture.

The term *subculture,* when applied to the Mexican-Americans, Puerto Ricans, and American Indians does not mean quite the same thing as it does when applied to the other groups. The subcultures developed by these ethnic groups are not derivatives of the dominant American culture. They are products of altogether different cultures—ways of life that work in another time or place, but not in this time and place. Individuals from these cultures are really, then, *culturally different*; and the difference between their culture and the dominant culture makes them disadvantaged.

Mexican-Americans

Few teachers really understand the cultural background of Mexican-American pupils; consequently, few teachers work effectively with these children. Instead, they allow themselves to be guided by a stereotyped image in which Mexican-Americans are by nature undependable, irresponsible, indolent, dirty, and unhealthy; they have questionable moral standards; they refuse to learn English and stubbornly cling to their native Spanish; they refuse to help themselves and ignore educational opportunities; they are taciturn and laconic.

The acceptance of this deplorable stereotype is understandable — most teachers have only limited and narrow access to information about Mexican-Americans *in terms of their own culture*. An understanding of the Mexican-American child in these terms will help teachers get rid of this stereotype and see the child as a product of his cultural background.

Many Mexican-Americans are the descendants of an agrarian culture and, as such, they have grown up in tradition-bound homes in which families lack a real sense of social responsibility and have limited experiences in civic affairs. There is a strong tendency in such families to preserve the agrarian Mexican culture.

The more recent a child's introduction to American urban society, the more marked will be the differences between his values and attitudes and the values and attitudes of the dominant culture. Some of the urban values are in direct conflict with the values that made survival possible in an agrarian society in Mexico. The very meaning of life is involved in these opposing value systems.

Mexican-American pupils find themselves trying to straddle two different cultures. This situation is more complex than that of either the disadvantaged blacks or the disadvantaged white groups: the black children and the Caucasian children are products of a subculture (a way of life that deviates in *degree* from our dominant culture), whereas Mexican-American children are products of an entirely different culture (a way of life that differs in *kind* from our dominant culture).

As Mexican-Americans try to adjust to the dominant culture, they sometimes create problems in both their homes and their schools. Many of these people are unable to reconcile the differences between their agrarian culture and the urban-oriented dominant culture of America. They are unable to make an adjustment. As a result of this conflict, the children grow to feel that they belong to neither culture — that they have no real identity. To complicate matters, many Mexican-Americans are victims of social and economic discrimination, and they share the label of second-class citizenship with the black population.

Mexican-American children are well aware of the stigma of second-class citizenship. Very early in their lives, they learn (as many black pupils do) the subordinate role which the dominant culture has assigned to them. The lack of emphasis placed on competition in the Mexican-American culture may contribute to this feeling. However, it largely results from a kind of self-hate or from low personal expectations reinforced by reality: disproportionate numbers of these people do remain permanently at the bottom of the social scale.

Origins

Mexican-American pupils can come from any one of seven major groups, each having a great deal in common with the others, along with its own unified characteristics. These seven major groups are:

1. Descendants of early California or Texas families.
2. Second- or third-generation offspring of families who came to this country as political refugees during the revolution of 1910-1920.
3. Second- or third-generation offspring of families who came to this country as agricultural contract laborers during World War I.
4. Children of *braceros,* or farm workers, who have come to this country recently.
5. *Tejanos* — migrants from Texas (found in California).
6. Recent immigrants from Mexico.
7. *Hispanos,* who consider themselves more Spanish than Mexican.

Pupils in the first three categories (descendants of early California and Texas families, early political refugees, or early agricultural workers) are generally found to be Americanized. They often have little knowledge of their Mexican heritage, and they probably speak little Spanish. Pupils in the next three categories (recent arrivals) generally speak Spanish and tend to hold tightly to Mexican traditions and customs. Pupils in the last category (the *Hispanos*) are generally well assimilated, probably because their economic status is usually higher. (There is question whether their economic advantage causes them to classify themselves as *Hispanos,* or whether their economic advantage results from their being *Hispanos.*)

The Mexican-American Family

Structure. Most Mexican-American families have a rigid patriarchal structure. Although the mother is the center of the family, the father has all the authority. When the father dies, the eldest son inherits the father's authority over the immediate family. There is also an extended family structure. That is, the family unit includes not only members of the immediate family — parents and their children — but also grandparents, aunts, uncles, and *compadres* (friends and relatives or godparents, who can assume parental responsibility for the children). *The Mexican-American child owes his primary loyalty to this family organization.*

Knowledge of this family structure gives teachers insight into some of the problems of educating Mexican-American children. For example, the lack of interest often shown by parents and pupils may be due to conflict between school demands and family demands. Many teachers have complained that Mexican-American children exhibit a lack of initiative — they depend on being told explicitly what to do and how to do it. Perhaps this lack of initiative is due to the subordinate role the individual must assume within the Mexican-American family structure.

Another problem is the excessive school absence rate of Mexican-American children. Primary loyalty to the family often requires that students miss school to fulfill family obligations. Sometimes the reason for absence may seem trite to the teacher. However, if he can realize that the demands of the family *always* come first (regardless of how unimportant these demands might appear to an outsider), he will appreciate why the absence rate is so high.

Male-Female Roles. The Mexican-American family structure very clearly defines the male and female roles. Thus a Mexican-American child rarely has any doubt about his role. A boy is nurtured on the idea that he is developing into a man, and this means he is *macho* and must behave a *lo macho* ("like a male") or *ser muy hombre* ("be very much a man"). In other words, boys are encouraged from birth to develop clearly masculine qualities. This accounts for the bravado in so many young Mexican-American males, the need to defend honor, and the urge to establish a masculine image before women. Mexican-Americans have a word for this: *machismo.*

This clear understanding of identity and male role may also explain why some woman teachers have trouble disciplining Mexican-American boys. It may be one reason why so many Mexican-American boys drop out of school early: a boy is *macho* if he is working, earning money, and standing on his own two feet.

Mexican-American girls also learn their role early in life. Essentially, the role of the woman in the Mexican-American family is to perform all the duties that maintain the family, including caring for the children, cooking, and cleaning. The woman is always subservient to the male head of the family.

The conditions of modern life — particularly modern urban life — may seriously disrupt or upset the ideal family structure described here. Increasingly, the father is unable to provide an income that will support such a structure, and the mother must go to work. When this happens, the father's *machismo* suffers and his head position in the family is eroded. The mother, with the new independence she receives as a contributor to the family income, demands a more dominant role in family decisions. Thus the traditional roles of the parents are altered and conflict occurs.

The children are greatly affected by this: when the traditional family structure breaks down they lose their sense of security and also a great deal of parental control. The disintegration of the family unit may contribute to some of the negative school behavior of Mexican-American children.

Values

Most Mexican-American children are affected by two basic philosophies in their culture. These philosophies are expressed in the expressions *Dios dirá* ("God will tell"; or, "It is in the hands of God"); and *Hay mas tiempo que vida* ("There is more time than there is life"). The first places responsibility in the will of God. Health, sickness, life, death, success, failure, wealth, misfortune—everything that affects the life of an indivivual—is in God's hands. God determines what is to be. This concept of life places limitations on planning for the future, developing ambitions, or carrying through the expectations which are placed on individuals in our society. It also provides Mexican-Americans with a rationalization for failure.

The second philosophy ("There is more time than life") complements the first. It encourages procrastination and relieves the pressures of deadlines and promptness; it allows for improvidence—why worry about tomorrow, when tomorrow may not come? Philosophically then, the curriculum and the teachers are in conflict with their pupils: the American middle-class viewpoint does not accept such a concept of life.

The teacher should understand that as an attendant part of this value system, his Mexican-American pupils will respond better to a reward given as soon as a job is completed. In addition, they probably do better with work that can be finished in a short time than with a lengthy assignment. Short assignments followed by immediate rewards are very important in any instructional program for Mexican-American children.

The Barrio

Mexican-American children grow up in what they call *barrios,* and what generally are called ghettos. *Barrio* means "neighborhood" or "community." Many *barrios* exist within the ghetto. Mexican-Americans who are born in the ghetto or come to live there at an early age grow up understanding that this is their section, their part of town. Many reach adolescence without ever having left their section of town. These youngsters mature within a circumscribed area of overcrowded housing, poverty, disease, and crime. They see and share their parents' loss of dignity when seeking necessary aid from charitable agencies.

When families can afford to move they leave, and behind them remain those people least able to function effectively in the complex urban framework. This group, helpless in its immobility, gives the ghetto situation a perpetuating strength. Reinforcement is supplied by the continual arrival of immigrants from Mexico and from other ghettos.

Individuals are trapped because their families are trapped. Ironically, besides confirming a feeling of inferiority, *the ghetto inculcates in its inhabitants a security that makes them fearful of leaving.* In the ghetto, *their* language is the dominant language, *their* customs are the accepted customs, *their* food is the most available food in the stores. The ghetto is home.

Fear of unfamiliar surroundings is transmitted to the young people who, in many cases, refuse to leave the ghetto for any reason. While some young people can find work within its boundaries, the ghetto offers very limited employment situations, so there is little need to develop skills that would provide greater vocational opportunity. Other young people will venture out of the ghetto to seek employment. Feelings of inadequacy and insecurity outside the ghetto may be interpreted by a prospective employer as lack of interest, lack of confidence, or poor qualifications. The employer may be free from prejudice, yet he will discriminate, for he wishes to protect his business from seemingly harmful or debilitating influences.

Thus outside his element the young Mexican-American encounters what he has feared—discrimination and suspicion, both nonexistent in his *barrio.* He will not place the blame for his rejection on himself or his limitations. Instead, he will react with hatred. His hatred will breed aggression, and his aggression may bring him into conflict with the law. The entire encounter will firmly establish in his mind the certainty of his inability to function adequately in this world beyond the confines of the ghetto.

Self-concept in Transition

Teachers often observe that their Mexican-American pupils are taciturn and laconic. A weak self-image is one basis for this kind of behavior. Mexican-American children have developed a poor self-concept because of causes common to all culturally disadvantaged children. In addition, there are particular contributing factors.

First, Mexican-American pupils are labeled second-class citizens because of their cultural background (especially their *language* background). Second, their difficulty in adjusting to the cultural and intellectual demands of the curriculum causes them to be regarded as intellectual inferiors. Third, they receive little understanding from either home or society. Fourth, like culturally disadvantaged blacks, Mexican-American pupils often live in dilapidated areas that seem to reflect on the quality of the inhabitants. Finally, Mexican-Americans are victims of prejudice and discrimination because of their heritage, socioeconomic level, and physical appearance. (This last point is the most important factor that is *not* being dealt with in all of the mass efforts to improve the lot of disadvantaged groups.)

Negative self-concept in Mexican-American youth may be, in part, a question of identity—that all-encompassing preoccupation that marks the stage of adolescence. All young people go through a search for identity. The Mexican-American youth is no different: he is bombarded by the same advertisements and general commercialism as the youth of the dominant culture. (This is the chief way our society helps individuals discover their identity.)

Mexican-Americans are not "Anglos," and they cannot affect the "Anglo" fashions, fads, grooming, and behavioral patterns without producing incongruous results. Still, they use the dominant culture as a model. Like all young people, they put emphasis on physical appearance. They choose many of the "identity labels" from the dominant culture, and unconsciously alter them to be consistent with those of the Mexican-American culture. This increases their alienation from all sides. The parents cry, "*¡No somos asi!*" ("We are not like that!") Then teachers say, "No, you don't look right; you have it all wrong!" The disapproving teachers are representatives of the alien culture that has spawned these unacceptably dressed and groomed, generally mixed-up youngsters.

Attitudes Toward Education

Mexican-American parents often regard school as a requirement imposed on them by the government rather than as a means to an end. They do not generally discuss school in positive and constructive terms with their children. They see their responsibility for educating their children as stopping at the door of the school; the children must deal with the school experience by themselves. They must overcome their language handicap, understand the new values thrust at them, and find worth in what they are being taught—all without parental support and reinforcement. Furthermore, these children must weigh and choose sides in the conflict between the values of their culture and the values of the dominant culture, also with little parental guidance.

Brighter, more mature pupils can often compete with their middle-class peers while they shoulder these burdens. But these are the exceptions. The majority usually succumb to the frustrations inherent in their solitary struggle. The outcome is that many Mexican-American pupils decide that they are incapable of achievement and classify themselves as inferior. This kind of self-concept either precipitates antisocial behavior in the school and the community, or causes Mexican-American pupils to become withdrawn. They may become either delinquents or dropouts.

Putting Understanding to Work

We have reviewed a number of characteristics that are applicable to Mexican-American children in varying degrees. There are great numbers to whom such characterization is a gross exaggeration, and great numbers to whom these characterizations are not at all applicable. The latter are probably not culturally disadvantaged. Our concern is with those for whom the description is accurate. These are the young people who need to be reached. These are the ones whose talents and abilities are wasted. They need teachers who have developed insight into their problems.

How is this insight applied in the classroom? Let us observe a typical classroom where the majority of pupils are Mexican-American. On the opening day, the teacher is met by the usual anticipatory syndrome. The salutation of some children is a bobbing of heads, while others boldly ask, "Who are you? What is your name?" Some will not look in the teacher's direction but quietly and submissively find seats. This behavior should indicate to the teacher that his class is already divided into three basic groups:

1. The bold children, who may well be more Anglo than Mexican.
2. The children who merely nod their heads, who are probably 50 percent Anglo and 50 percent Mexican (half assimilated).
3. The submissive, quiet children, who are more Mexican than Anglo.

Measuring Abilities. Between these groups are varying degrees of assimilation. A less obvious division than behavioral response is academic ability. The teacher will have to develop methods that will give real evidence of each individual's ability. IQ and subject-achievement scores available in the counselor's office are generally not an accurate appraisal.

Few mental-measurement and achievement tests account for cultural factors, experience differences, intellectual opportunities, and all the other relevant factors that comprise the difference between the culturally disadvantaged child and the average Anglo child.

The teacher, himself, must determine the reading, spelling, and reasoning level of his pupils. This is an extremely difficult thing to do, because Mexican-American children do not respond well to formal testing. A test such as this might be used: the teacher reads a short story and asks the students to select from a choice of words on the chalkboard those that best tell what the story is about.

During the testing period the teacher should be aware of the children who cannot write down their words without first consulting a classmate, either verbally or visually. (An important word of caution: Do not consider the last behavior a form of cheating; accept it as an indication that the student is not really able to respond independently. It is interesting to note that the Spanish language has no word equivalent to the English word *cheating*.)

More indicative of student ability is a test given after the teacher has become familiar with each pupil's special pattern. A completely individual evaluation, it consists of engaging a child in conversation and inconspicuously assessing his understanding of subject matter, directional commands, general vocabulary, and American idiomatic expressions.

The group limited in these understandings will be quite small, because most Mexican-American children have developed defensive techniques that allow them to function rather adequately in most classroom situations. However, the teacher must not be deluded into thinking that this group is able to apply classroom learning outside the classroom. His pupils will return at the end of the school day to Spanish-speaking homes, to Mexican culture, to a system in which there is *little reinforcement of the learning that takes place at school*. It is essential that the teacher develop a program which is meaningful to these children in terms of the world *in which they already live,* as well as the world in which they will eventually live.

Such a program will stimulate the children to participate orally in explanations of what they have learned, to discuss it through key words and dramatizations. The hope is that such determined and varied reinforcement will enable them to internalize what they have learned.

Paradoxically, the more able group will be generally slow in their response. Theirs is a dilemma of mental calesthenics.

Confronted with their hodgepodge attempts to function in two cultures, they have developed a language that is often adequate in either culture but nonstandard in both. This group will probably be more Anglo in its philosophy and behavior than the other two. But the child of this group basically remains part of the Mexican culture, even though he comes from that part which has replaced or compromised many of the traditional Mexican customs and ways of life with Anglo ones. And the child's cultural values, the most difficult part of the child in which to effect changes, will determine much of his classroom attitude and achievement.

In working with individuals of this group, the teacher is compelled to understand that the youngster does not want assimilation at the sacrifice of identity. Therefore, in a program outlined especially for him, the teacher must point out that the child can succeed and achieve the highest goal possible. The teacher must demand of him the limits of his potential. Most important, *the teacher must identify the individuality of each student in terms of Mexican culture.*

Discipline. Considering the variety of pupils, it is almost inevitable that the teacher will come up against the issue of control. Knowledge of the Mexican culture will indicate to the teacher that these children respond best to a disciplined situation, with overtones of formality. A Mexican-American child sees a teacher as a person similar to his father in the family situation. The teacher is, in psychological terms, an authority figure. But the teacher's responsibility is to see that the authority reflects understanding, fairness, and acceptance. A great disservice is done to a child when the teacher displays a leniency toward habits that fail to conform to classroom or school routines, such as tardiness, neglect of deadlines, or failure to come to class.

A matter that could lead to complete breakdown of communication between the teacher and his students is the embarrassment of the child by the teacher. The Spanish language has no equivalent for the word *embarrass*. There are expressions for turning red as a result of receiving a compliment (*ruborizarse*), and for placing oneself in a compromising situation (*comprometerse*); otherwise, to embarrass is literally to dishonor (*deshonrar, insultar, infamar*).

Speakers of the Spanish language do not treat loss of stature lightly. When a teacher finds it necessary to discipline by heaping guilt on a youngster, he should never do it in front of the youngster's peers. Such disciplinary action must always remain an individual confrontation, handled without witnesses.

Puerto Ricans

Spanish Cultural Roots

Mexican-Americans and Puerto Ricans have similar cultural backgrounds, and many of the same considerations apply to pupils of both groups. For example, Mexican-Americans and Puerto Ricans are similar in value system, outlook on life, language, and family structure. The reason is obvious: the cultures of both groups stem from Spanish cultural roots. Both groups are culturally different from the Anglo society, whether or not they are disadvantaged. When individuals of these groups are also culturally disadvantaged, their problems of becoming assimilated and gaining full participation in our society are greatly increased.

One significant difference between the cultural backgrounds of the two groups is that the Spanish cultural roots have never been as deep for Puerto Ricans as they have for Mexican-Americans. Puerto Ricans tend not to hold as tenaciously to the cultural patterns they bring with them from Puerto Rico as Mexican-Americans hold to theirs. This means that Puerto Ricans are more susceptible to assimilation and acquisition of American cultural patterns.

For example, Puerto Ricans are more anxious to learn English than are Mexican-Americans, and they do not seem to be as eager to have their children learn or retain Spanish. Puerto Ricans seem much more ready than Mexican-Americans to become like the dominant culture in all areas. Their willingness to become acculturated helps them to avoid the contradiction of wanting full assimilation while totally retaining their own cultural identity.

In addition to Spanish cultural roots, there is a more potent factor operating to facilitate the acculturation of Puerto Ricans: they are already American citizens, and this gives them an automatic loyalty to the United States and its institutions. Also, the Puerto Rican population in America is overwhelmingly urban, and the closeness of urban living makes these people much more vulnerable to change than the partially rural Mexican-American population. By the second generation, Puerto Ricans are more American than Puerto Rican. In contrast, second-generation and even third-generation Mexican-Americans are bothered by the problems of cultural ambivalence.

Of course, the extent of acculturation for individuals of both groups is conditioned by their socioeconomic status. If an individual is culturally and economically disadvantaged, he cannot become fully acculturated. He is a member of the general subculture of poverty, having as much in common with other disadvantaged individuals, regardless of cultural or ethnic identity, as with more fortunate individuals belonging to his parent culture. This is the case for too many Puerto Ricans: the subculture they have developed in response to conditions here in the United States has made them neither culturally Puerto Rican, nor American middle-class.

The Great Migration

The island of Puerto Rico has a long history of poverty. The Spanish neglected its economic development, and until recently the United States did little to improve economic conditions. To the north she sat, a fat, rich land in which opportunity seemed to be waiting. Many of the same conditions that drew Europeans to America's shores stimulated Puerto Ricans to migrate. In addition, there were other factors: first, Puerto Ricans, as American citizens, gained easy entrance to this country; second, the distance between the United States and Puerto Rico was short. The distance seemed even shorter by plane. Thus began the first airborne migration in the history of the United States.

The slight distance has made it easy for many Puerto Ricans in the United States to "commute" to the island. The trip is only a few hours by plane from major Puerto Rican centers in America. The proximity of the two countries has also facilitated a cultural pipeline to Puerto Ricans in America which reinforces their old life patterns and retards assimilation.

Although the Puerto Rican migration is similar in many ways to the earlier European migration, there are distinctive factors that tend to prevent Puerto Ricans from becoming assimilated and from rising out of their disadvantaged position. Puerto Ricans have migrated at a time when there is no manpower shortage, so they have difficulty finding employment. They often are forced to take low-paying, unskilled jobs. Puerto Ricans have migrated after the technological revolution, when many of the kinds of jobs that were available to European immigrants no longer exist. Finally, *many Puerto Ricans are classified as black in this country,* and these people acquire the traditional employment difficulties of the blacks. These are the main factors that keep Puerto Ricans chronically culturally disadvantaged and at the bottom of the economic scale.

Puerto Rican migration has increased rapidly since World War II. In 1930, there were about 45,000 Puerto Ricans in the United States. By 1940 this number had increased to about 70,000; by 1950 the figure was 250,000. The 1960 census listed more than 600,000 Puerto Ricans in New York City.[1]

1. Reprinted from *Beyond the Melting Pot* by Nathan Glazer and Daniel Patrick Moynihan by permission of The M.I.T. Press, Cambridge, Massachusetts. Copyright 1963 by the Massachusetts Institute of Technology. Pp. 91-94.

Current estimates place well over a million Puerto Ricans in the United States. The high birthrate of this group will rapidly increase this figure. Most of the Puerto Ricans who came to this country settled in a few large Northern cities, and the greatest number settled in New York City. Arriving in the cities, Puerto Ricans squeezed into the crowded slums with other disadvantaged groups, usually taking over part of the slum for their own community — *el barrio Latino*.

In the typical migration pattern, the father goes to the United States and stays with friends or relatives until he finds a job and a place to live. Then the mother and children join him. Sometimes the children come one by one, or in small groups. This spaced migration results in varying degrees of adjustment to American life within the same family.

Puerto Ricans can be roughly divided into three groups: the old residents, who migrated to this country prior to World War II; those who were born in this country or who came here when they were very young; and the recent emigrants. The three groups demonstrate varying degrees of acculturation. The old residents and the recent emigrants tend to adhere closely to the Puerto Rican culture of the island. The Puerto Ricans who were born here or raised here tend to lose many of the cultural patterns of the island. They acquire cultural patterns similar to those of other disadvantaged groups, yet influenced by their Puerto Rican background.

Problems of Acculturation

Like Mexican-Americans, Puerto Ricans are products of a *different* culture that deviates further from the dominant culture than do the subcultures of the disadvantaged blacks, the Appalachians, and the Southern white migrants. This different cultural background is the cause of their most obvious handicaps in participating in American life. Their cultural background has a different value system, a different outlook on life, a different language, a different family structure — and these differences may place them at a greater disadvantage than even blacks, for example, who have altered their cultural patterns.

One aspect of this is language. The difficulties of full participation and advancement in the dominant culture for individuals who speak a foreign language are obvious. Puerto Ricans are acutely aware of these difficulties, and they are anxious to learn English. In spite of their preference for English, many Puerto Rican children come to school not really fluent in either Spanish or English. They speak a kind of English heavily influenced by Spanish ("Spanglish") that causes them difficulties in school, especially in reading.

It has been pointed out that some Puerto Ricans suffer the same kind of racial discrimination that black people suffer. Racially, Puerto Ricans are a mixture of Caucasian, Indian, and black stocks. The scale of physical appearance of these three races is a continuous blend: at one end of the scale are Puerto Ricans who are typically Caucasian, and at the other end are Puerto Ricans who are typically black. In the middle is a blend of the two extremes. Those individuals whose physical appearance is black are often doubly victimized, first by being Puerto Rican and then by being black. This situation, unfortunately, has caused some conflict between blacks and Puerto Ricans. The blacks resent Puerto Ricans who refuse to be identified as blacks even though they look like them, and the Puerto Ricans resent being classified with blacks, because they realize the stigma this classification carries.

The Puerto Rican Family

The structure of the Puerto Rican family closely resembles the structure of the Mexican-American family. Ideally, the Puerto Rican family consists of the father (who holds all authority and responsibility for supporting the family), the mother (who upholds the father's authority and the respect his position demands), and the unmarried children. Ideally, the father is the strongest figure in the family. Early marriage is common among Puerto Ricans, especially on the island. One investigator found that seven out of ten Puerto Ricans were married before they were twenty-one, many before they were eighteen.[2] This pattern of early marriage probably contributes to the high dropout rate of Puerto Rican students.

Like Mexican-Americans, the Puerto Rican family is extended to include grandparents, uncles, aunts, cousins, and *compadre* and *comadre* (co-parents), all bound up in a tightly organized unit. All demands of this unit have priority. Children are expected to be completely subservient to their parents. They are expected to love, honor, and respect their parents; they are expected to be "good," to be "seen but not heard," and to do what they are told. *Independence and self-reliance are not encouraged in children.* Boys are expected to develop *machismo;* girls are protected.

The demands of American society—particularly of urban living—tend to break down this ideal family structure. This kind of family structure, oriented to the demands of a Puerto Rican society, doesn't work in American society. For example, independence and self-reliance are positive attributes in Amer-

2. *Ibid.,* p. 89.

ican society, and children who are discouraged from developing these attributes will be at a disadvantage.

In addition, this kind of attitude toward the child's role conflicts with school, where these children are encouraged to participate in planning sessions with the teachers and to develop initiative and self-reliance. Many Puerto Rican parents don't understand the school's attitude on these matters.

Another concept of the Puerto Rican family that doesn't work to advantage here in this country is the concept of *machismo,* the encouragement of manliness in boys. Like Mexican-Americans, Puerto Rican boys are expected to exhibit those qualities identified with the male role. In the city, however, boys often show their *machismo* in ways that get them into trouble.

Other factors that contribute to the breakdown of the traditional Puerto Rican family structure are the length of time in this country and the proximity to other groups. The crowded conditions of slum living help break down traditional family structure by presenting alternate and more Americanized patterns. Also significant is the mild resistance that many Puerto Ricans have to change, especially when change is synonymous with "more American."

The Puerto Rican in School

Puerto Ricans generally have a high regard for education. Like most Americans, Puerto Ricans see education as a means for raising one's status. (On this point, they differ from Mexican-Americans.) Unfortunately, many culturally disadvantaged Puerto Ricans do not know how to express their positive attitude toward education through actions that support the educational process. Too often, their disadvantaged position works against them.

The positive attitude of many Puerto Rican parents is often reflected in the high aspirations they have for their children. For example, Puerto Rican parents often boast that their child will be a doctor, a lawyer, a "great man" rather than a workman. Most of the time these high aspirations are pitiful in contrast with the circumstances of the family's deprivation. One of the most important functions the school can have is to help these children realize the expectations of their parents.

Notwithstanding their positive attitudes toward education, the ideas that most Puerto Rican parents have regarding educational methods often conflict with school practices. This is particularly true of parents whose basic orientation is toward a Puerto Rican society rather than an American society. For example, some Puerto Rican parents who are not Americanized look upon the school as a surrogate parent—that is, they see the school as taking the complete place of the parent once the child enters its doors.

Another area of conflict between parents and school is the informal and democratic atmosphere of the classroom. For some Puerto Rican parents, the American classroom is too informal; these parents want the schools to be conducted in a formal, authoritarian way. A third area of conflict is cultural patterns. The parents and the school follow widely differing practices on such matters as children drinking coffee, calling teachers by their names, and participating in a discussion with a teacher. This kind of culture clash is most common between the school and recently arrived, un-Americanized Puerto Ricans.

Appalachians and Southern Whites

The culturally disadvantaged Caucasian is probably the most neglected of disadvantaged groups. The federal government, in recent years, has become increasingly active in helping culturally disadvantaged Caucasians, particularly those living in that vast poverty region called Appalachia. But the help has been mostly in one dimension — economic aid. There does not seem to be the same concern for cultural enrichment and educational advancement for culturally disadvantaged Caucasians as exists for other disadvantaged groups.

It has been pointed out that income is the most common criterion of cultural deprivation. Though income is not an entirely accurate criterion, it is the best single measure available for determining cultural deprivation. Depending on the minimum income used as a cutoff point, the number of culturally disadvantaged individuals is between 40 and 50 million. Caucasians are roughly half of this population. Thus Caucasians *are the largest ethnic group* among the disadvantaged.

A number of factors acting in concert may account for the lack of recognition of this group. For one thing, the disadvantaged Caucasian is not highly visible. Unlike the black, Mexican-American, Puerto Rican, and Indian, who have more or less distinguishable physical features that set them off from the dominant Caucasian population, the disadvantaged Caucasian blends imperceptibly with the dominant population.

Disadvantaged Caucasians have more freedom than other disadvantaged groups. They are not racially segregated; thus they have easier access into the dominant culture simply because they are not handicapped by other people's prejudices. Most disadvantaged Caucasians are Anglo-Saxon and Protestant; this gives them a definite advantage over the other disadvantaged groups. They are also less vocal. Many of them have a tradition of stubborn independence, and they do not protest their deprivation in as dramatic ways as do, for example, the blacks. Instead, many suffer deprivation in "quiet desperation."

Finally, many disadvantaged Caucasians live in Appalachia, an area of the country that is somewhat isolated and hidden from the sight of the rest of the population. Other disadvantaged Caucasians live in Southern rural areas that have traditionally been associated with deprivation, perhaps so long now that deprivation in this area has become natural and unnoticeable. It is the vast migration of these two groups from their homes to the cities which has brought the problem of culturally disadvantaged Appalachians and Southern whites increasingly into focus.

Appalachia

The area called Appalachia stretches roughly from the Eastern seaboard to the Midwest, and it includes parts of West Virginia, Virginia, Pennsylvania, Maryland, Ohio, Kentucky, Tennessee, Arkansas, Alabama, and Georgia. The heart of this area is the Appalachian mountains, and this is the section with the most extensive poverty. Actually, these mountains run through only a few states, but the entire poverty area surrounding these mountains has been termed *Appalachia,* a word which has become synonymous with *poverty.*

Before the word took on this new meaning, most people probably thought of it only as an area of great beauty, with gently rolling mountains covered with deep green growth and blue streams plunging into lush valleys, inhabited by happy, carefree people. The area is beautiful, and its physical beauty is ironic in contrast with the desperation of its population. The features that make the area beautiful are exactly the kinds of land features that make farming difficult and unproductive. In addition, the coal-mining industry that once provided employment for many people in this area has slowed to a virtual stop, and there are not enough other industries in the area to take up the slack and provide additional employment.

Almost every dimension of poverty and cultural deprivation touches the people of Appalachia. These are not the happy hillbillys romanticized in cartoon strips — they are people desperately trying to scratch out a living on unproductive farms or in barren, dirty little towns sitting like tombstones on top of dead mines. The whole Appalachian area just barely manages to stay alive on a welfare economy.

The other area of the country having large numbers of disadvantaged Caucasians is the rural South. Some of this area is included in the Appalachian poverty area, but much of it is in the cotton and tobacco belts of the South. The people living in this area suffer the characteristics of other disadvantaged groups: low income, poor health, substandard housing, and low educational level. They also share another characteristic with disadvantaged rural groups: many leave the farms and go to the cities. The reasons they migrate are obvious and classic: they go to the cities to improve their economic status.

During the 1950s more than 1,500,000 people left Appalachia to seek another life in the large industrial cities of the North. These were the young and adventurous, and they drained off the lifeblood of the area, leaving it more dead than ever. Most of the migrants found that they had left one kind of poverty for another: from the hills and pastures of Appalachian poverty, they plunged into the canyons of poverty of the big-city slums.

The migrants usually settled in areas of the cities where there were others like themselves. Thus they created and continued their own little pockets of poverty—a new kind of ghetto—in the big city. Many are unable to qualify for the sophisticated jobs offered by modern urban industry, and they find that the nonskilled jobs are occupied by blacks or other disadvantaged groups who arrived earlier. Some migrants return to Appalachia or the South, but many stay in the cities and struggle to make a living. The only thing that really changes for those who stay is the geography of their poverty.

Characteristics of Disadvantaged Whites

The cultural characteristics of Appalachian and Southern white migrants can be summarized in the following way.

1. They have strong family ties and connections with people of their own kind. They are clannish, preferring "home folks" (people with similar background) to others.
2. They are suspicious of outsiders, and they often shun the help of outside agencies.
3. They practice fierce individualism, even in the face of poverty and deprivation.
4. Their clannishness cuts them off from meaningful contacts with the dominant culture and perpetuates primary-group relationships; this restricts their chances for assimilation. Even though they are not handicapped by a negative racial identity, *their chances for assimilation are almost as limited as other disadvantaged people who are restricted by race.*

5. They are stoics, and they do not openly express suffering or hardship. This characteristic is probably due to their fierce individualism, and relates to why they do not seek help.
6. The father is usually the authoritarian figure in the family, while the mother is the center of love. Children are usually assigned definite roles and duties in the family, probably as a carry-over from the chore responsibilities of rural children. In the city, chores are often limited, and the children go about on their own, often unsupervised.

The cultural background of these people has developed in a rather isolated environment which presents few of the kinds of experiences that supplement education. They usually do not see the value of education; instead, they feel that a minimum amount of education is all one needs—just a little reading and writing. They are much more indifferent to education, as a group, than either disadvantaged blacks or Puerto Ricans. This indifference makes them much more uncooperative with the school. Children from this background often cause teachers more problems in discipline than do other disadvantaged children. Their fiercely independent attitude makes them resist authority. Their resistance usually does not take the form of overt aggression; they are more likely to resist authority with a stubborn sullenness.

Because of their racial identity, the Appalachians and the Southern white migrants have the best chance of all disadvantaged groups of being assimilated into the dominant culture. Education could be the means for them to accomplish this comparatively easy assimilation, but their negative attitudes toward education act as a severe handicap. Perhaps the most effective instructional programs for this group would begin with efforts to change their attitudes toward the educational process.

American Indians

The American Indians are probably the country's first disadvantaged group. Since the establishment of the first white settlement at Jamestown in 1610, American Indians have improved their status very little in relation to the dominant culture. Their way of life did not prepare them to resist the debilitating effect of contact with another culture. Historical and social factors have prevented a people indigenous to this land from being assimilated.

There are more than 500,000 Indians in the United States. Approximately three fourths of them live in rural areas, and most of these rural areas are parts of reservations located in the South and Southwest sections of the country. Although their numbers are not large, their deprivation is great: for example, the almost totally absent Indian middle class, the amount of government welfare funds spent on Indians in relation to their per capita income, their educational level, their average life span, and the rate of tuberculosis within the group are all indexes of the American Indians' deprivation.

Because their numbers are small, it may appear that a discussion of the Indians' educational needs is not important here—few teachers in public schools work with Indian children. However, such a discussion will further illustrate how a different and unexpected cultural background handicaps learning—especially if teachers ignore the difference. The great gap between Indian culture and the dominant culture clearly illustrates this concept.

American Indians, like Mexican-Americans and Puerto Ricans, are products of a different culture. Furthermore, their cultural background is so completely different from that of the dominant culture that of all disadvantaged groups they are probably the least prepared to participate. To complicate matters, there are numerous Indian tribes, all culturally different in varying degrees from one another. Treating the Indian tribes as if they were alike was the cause of many mistakes made in past dealings with Indians.

The enduring difference between the Indian culture and the dominant culture has made assimilation impossible for the bulk of the American Indian population. Of course, there are other factors that have helped to prevent assimilation. Racial prejudice and geographic isolation are two of these. Geographic isolation in the form of the reservation system has prevented the assimilation process from beginning. The reservation system has tended to decrease contact between Indians and the dominant culture. Thus the reservation system arrests assimilation, perpetuates cultural isolation, and sustains the Indians' disadvantaged position.

One solution to the problem that is sometimes suggested is that Indians be taken off the reservations and made to sink or swim in the dominant cultural mainstream. Those who suggest this kind of plunge for the Indian point to black people as an example of how successful this method of assimilation can be. Black people without a doubt are not as disadvantaged as the Indian, and those who recommend that the Indian be thrust into the dominant culture fail to realize that the blacks, even under slavery, were *more acculturated than the Indians are now.* Slavery afforded a better apprenticeship for acculturation than did the reservation system.

The advocates of immediate assimilation fail to recognize the inhibiting factors for assimilation that the Indian carries from his cultural background. The most significant of these factors is an entirely different value system: *the value system of American Indian culture is opposed to the highly competitive, specialized American value system.* In short, Indians simply can't survive with their value system in direct competition with the dominant culture. Yet, many Indians are going to encounter the challenge of "making it" in the dominant culture—population growth is forcing many Indians off the reservation.

Education plays an obvious and necessary role in helping American Indians improve their status. Of course, education alone can't accomplish this. The attitude the dominant culture holds toward Indians—and the overt discriminatory acts that stem from this attitude—will have to change before education can be wholly effective. Also, the basic needs of the Indian population must be satisfied before the educational catalyst can really accelerate the assimilation process.

The federal government has primary responsibility for educating Indians. In the past, part of the problem has been that the schools sometimes educated Indian children to live on reservations. This, in effect, did not prepare them to compete within the dominant culture when they left the reservation. On the other hand, Indian children who are educated to live in the dominant culture also often are not able to compete. At the same time, their education makes it difficult for them to return to their own culture. Indian children educated in this manner are doubly disadvantaged.

Fortunately, the federal government has recognized the nature of this problem, and better educational programs for Indians have been devised. These new programs recognize the importance for Indian children to retain their cultural identity; they also take into account the necessity of using the background of Indian culture as a starting point for developing the skills needed for participation in the dominant culture. These skills give Indian children a passport into the dominant culture, and continued contact with the dominant culture can help them acquire the kind of practical understanding necessary for assimilation.

When efforts to educate Indians have failed, the reasons usually can be traced to the most common cause for failure in educating disadvantaged children—that is, *not enough consideration has been given to the child's cultural background.* This has been especially true of Indian children. Teachers have often placed Indian children in situations that are inconsistent with Indian culture.

For example, the system of grading is inconsistent with the noncompetitive culture of many Indians: grades embarrass both the achievers and nonachievers. In fact, any classroom activity that reveals a difference in achievement (discussions, recitations, teacher comments, games, and so forth) embarrasses many Indian children. Division of labor is often strictly defined by sex in Indian culture and assigning boys and girls to identical activities causes culture clash. So does having Indian students participate in activities that violate tribal or cultural taboos (such as coed dancing), and failing to clearly define the difference between work and play.

However, the most serious problem of educating Indian students is that *contact with the dominant culture is necessary to develop patterns for participation in the dominant culture.* Contact with the dominant culture is required for using and testing these patterns. As long as many Indian children are restricted to reservation living, this contact is severely limited. They are likely to remain disadvantaged because they cannot learn the dominant culture in the kind of isolation created by reservation living.

While education and greater contact with the dominant culture seem to be the means for eliminating the disadvantages of Indians, this presents the Indians with a terrible and awesome choice: they must step out of a culture in which they are secure into a drastically different culture for which their background has not prepared them.

Summary of Main Points

1. The chances of being disadvantaged are increased if an individual is a member of a minority group.

2. Culturally disadvantaged black and Caucasian children are products of subcultures; culturally disadvantaged Mexican-American, Puerto Rican, and American Indian children are products of different cultures.

3. Mexican-American and Puerto Rican pupils show varying degrees of Americanization.

4. Mexican-American, Puerto Rican, and American Indian pupils are put in the difficult position of trying to straddle two cultures; sometimes this does not permit them to plant a firm footing in either.

5. Each of these minority ethnic groups has had a particularly difficult time becoming assimilated and acculturated.

6. Although the cultural backgrounds of both Mexican-Americans and Puerto Ricans have Spanish roots, Puerto Ricans tend not to cling as strongly to their Spanish heritage.

7. Puerto Ricans are overwhelmingly urban; the majority of the Puerto Rican population lives in New York City.

8. The foreign language background of many Mexican-American, Puerto Rican, and American Indian students severely handicaps their achievement in school.

9. Social and economic deprivation tends to break down traditional cultural values while preventing the development of many of the values of the dominant culture.

10. The problems of culturally disadvantaged Caucasians have received little attention in proportion to their number.

Questions for Discussion

1. Discuss the difficulty of adjusting or getting along in the dominant culture (including the school curriculum) for: (a) students who are products of a subculture; and (b) students who are products of a different culture. Which students would have the most difficulty? Why?

2. What are some of the difficulties in discipline, role identification, self-concept, and value orientation for students who come from strong patriarchal families and attend femininely dominated schools?

3. Some students who come from different cultures may not be able or willing to abandon many of their native cultural patterns, even when these patterns place them at a disadvantage. How far should the schools go in Americanizing students from other cultures? How much of the native culture should the schools reinforce and teach?

4. What are some of the main factors that prevent the ethnic groups discussed here from assimilating as fast as have some other ethnic groups in the past? What can the schools do to help?

5. Of the ethnic groups discussed here, which one will have the most difficulty becoming assimilated or acculturated?

6. If a hierarchy of educational needs could be listed for each of the groups discussed in this unit, what needs would be at the top of the list? Are the schools now equipped and organized to meet these needs?

7. Has the reservation system worked to the advantage or disadvantage of the American Indian pupil? Why?

Bibliography

Board of Education of the City of New York. *The Puerto Rican Study 1953–57*. New York: Board of Education, 1958.

Collins, Henry Hill. *America's Own Refugees*. Princeton, N.J.: Princeton Univ. Press, 1957.

Craw, Lester D.; Murray, Walter I.; and Smythe, Hugh M. *Educating the Culturally Disadvantaged Child*. New York: David McKay, 1966.

Dworkis, Martin B. *The Impact of Puerto Rican Migration on Governmental Services in New York City*. New York: New York Univ. Press, 1957.

Glazer, Nathan, and Moynihan, Daniel Patrick. *Beyond the Melting Pot*. Cambridge, Mass.: The Massachusetts Institute of Technology Press, 1963, pp. 86–136.

Handlin, Oscar. *The Newcomers: Negroes and Puerto Ricans in a Changing Metropolis*. Cambridge, Mass.: Harvard Univ. Press, 1959.

Harrington, Michael. *The Other America*. Baltimore: Penguin, 1963.

Hodgkinson, Harold L. *Education in Social and Cultural Perspectives*. Englewood Cliffs, N.J.: Prentice-Hall, 1962.

Kluckhohn, Clyde, and Leighton, Dorothea. *The Navaho*. Garden City, N.Y.: Doubleday, 1962.

Lenior, Clarence. *The Puerto Ricans: Strangers —Then Neighbors*. Chicago: Quadrangle Books, Anti-Defamation League B'nai B'rith, 1965.

Lewis, Oscar. *Children of Sanchez*. New York: Random House, 1961.

Madsen, William. *Mexican-Americans of South Texas*. New York: Holt, Rinehart & Winston, 1964.

McWilliams, Carey. *North From Mexico*. Philadelphia: J. B. Lippincott, 1948.

Manuel, Herschel T. *Spanish-Speaking Children of the Southwest: Their Education and the Public Welfare*. Austin, Tex.: Univ. of Texas Press, 1965.

Marden, Charles F., and Meyer, Gladys. *Minorities in American Society*, 2d ed. New York: American Book, 1962.

May, Edgar. *The Wasted Americans*. New York: Harper & Row, 1964.

Mills, C. W.; Senior, Clarence; and Golden, Rose K. *The Puerto Rican Journey*. New York: Harper & Row, 1950.

Padilla, Elena. *Up From Puerto Rico*. New York: Columbia Univ. Press, 1958.

Rose, Peter I. *They and We*. New York: Random House, 1964.

Rubel, Arthur. *Across the Tracks*. Austin, Tex.: Univ. of Texas Press, 1966.

Sexton, Patricia C. *Spanish Harlem: The Anatomy of Poverty*. New York: Harper & Row, 1965.

Simpson, George E., and Yinger, J. Milton. *Racial and Cultural Minorities*. New York: Harper & Row, 1958.

Wakefield, Dan. *Island in the City: The World of Spanish Harlem*. Boston, Mass.: Houghton Mifflin, 1959.

Woods, Sister Frances Jerome C.D.P. *Cultural Values of American Ethnic Groups*. New York: Harper & Row, 1956.

Zea, Leopoldo. *The Latin American Mind*. Norman, Okla.: The Univ. of Oklahoma Press, 1963.

CHAPTER 5

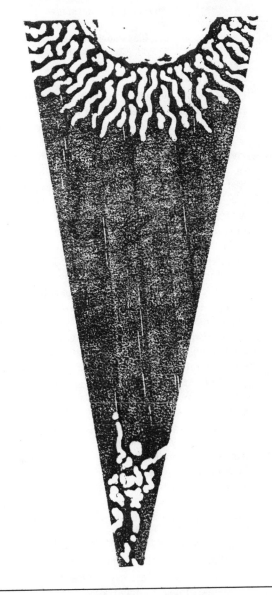

THE TEACHING RELATIONSHIP

5

The Need for Research

Getting to Know the Child

Working With Disadvantaged Parents

Programs for Disadvantaged Children

Classroom Management

The discussion of the main ethnic groups that make up the culturally disadvantaged population suggests that each group must be uniquely dealt with in any area of the instructional program. The children of each group have different problems with language, respond differently to various disciplinary procedures, base their learning on different backgrounds of experiences, and have their own unique attitudes and problems that may inhibit learning. To be effective a teacher must be aware of all the variables caused by ethnic background. To be aware of the pupils' deprivation is to understand only partly the problem of educating them.

Educators have just recently achieved a greater understanding of deprivation and the special considerations implied in teaching disadvantaged children. In the past, children who did not achieve in school because of cultural limitations were treated as slow learners. They were dealt with as if their learning difficulties were the result of limited innate mental capacity. This viewpoint has been reflected in the kinds of textbooks and materials produced for culturally disadvantaged children in the past—their learning materials have been identical to those produced for slow learners. Educators who are interested in the culturally disadvantaged recognize that the child who does not achieve *may not be a slow learner* according to the traditional definition of the term.

The terms *culture shock* or *culture clash* have been used to describe the conflict that occurs when teachers and pupils fail to work together because of cultural or social-class differences. Sometimes culture clash results from the teacher's realization that his pupils don't share his value system, goals, or attitudes toward education. Sometimes the shock is the result of teacher-pupil conflicts that can occur in any classroom situation, except that these conflicts are intensified because of cultural or social-class differences. Other times the shock is created out of the frustrations teachers experience in trying to solve massive problems within the limited context of the educational process. Culture shock is the result of teachers and pupils marching to different drummers.

The failure of the school curriculum to help disadvantaged children make substantial progress is based on two main factors: the inability of the school to meet the basic needs of its pupils, and the pupils' lack of experiences that facilitate learning. These two factors are inseparable.

Disadvantaged pupils are more like all other pupils than they are different because they have *the same basic needs* — they have the same basic physical needs, the same basic emotional needs, and the same basic psychological needs. The satisfaction of their basic needs is frustrated by cultural deprivation. The school is the primary agency of society to compensate for the deprivation that these children suffer. To be successful in helping disadvantaged pupils, the school has to learn what it can and what it cannot do — what is *possible* — along with appropriate and effective methods.

The Need for Research

The rapidly expanding research in the area of education for the culturally disadvantaged is, potentially, the teacher's most valuable source of understanding. Although many other avenues to understanding are open to the teacher — for example, observation, experience, information and insights provided by other teachers — ultimately, research must provide the kinds of information and insight that can't be acquired through usual classroom operations.

The final answer to the question "How can culturally disadvantaged pupils be educated?" will have to come from research findings. The complexity of the many vital questions involved requires the intensive focus of the research process. Classroom teachers usually don't have the resources — training, facilities, school organization, and time — to conduct research; and the primary function of the school must be education, not research.

This does not mean, however, that the classroom teacher and the school are not involved in the research process — they have to be. It is up to teachers to raise many of the questions that must be answered; teachers have to hypothesize and suggest means to test their hypotheses. The school must cooperate closely with researchers in uncovering the answers to vital questions. This has not always happened in the past because schools have been so exclusively involved in the educational process.

Perhaps administrators feared that research results would reveal deficiencies in many areas. This urgent educational project must now take precedence over the perpetuation of hiding shortcomings. As schools become involved, increasing numbers of teachers must also become actively involved in *conducting* research. In this respect, also, the cooperation of the school district is needed: the district must be more willing than it has been in the past to permit—even to encourage—its classroom teachers to take part in the research process.

In the meantime, it is important that teachers keep abreast of significant research in spite of the limited time they have and the inevitable fatigue that results from teaching culturally disadvantaged pupils. The teacher cannot dodge the responsibility of reading research reports and translating the findings into effective classroom applications.

In addition to increasing teacher understanding and answering general questions about culturally disadvantaged children, research can serve more specific functions. For example, research can point out effective approaches and methods to use in teaching culturally disadvantaged children; it can indicate means of motivating these children; it can tell what kinds of programs should be started (or stopped); it can establish the framework for the kinds of materials needed to help culturally disadvantaged children learn. In short, research can be one of the teacher's most valuable tools in working with culturally disadvantaged pupils.

Research is now providing needed answers to many vital questions. Since 1960 the acceleration of research on educating culturally disadvantaged children has been phenomenal. Much of this research has been descriptive (identifying and listing characteristics of these pupils) and a great deal of it has been assessment (contrasting these pupils with other pupils). Now there is a need for the emphasis to shift from describing and assessing to answering more fundamental questions.

There are indications that such a shift has begun. Some schools, in spite of their limitations and resources for conducting research, have instituted innovative programs, action programs, or experimental programs based on teachers' hunches and "classroom pragmatism" rather than basic research. These efforts have yielded some of the most valuable information on educating culturally disadvantaged pupils.

Yet to be answered are many questions. The most significant can be grouped under three broad headings: those that refer to pupils; those that refer to the teacher-pupil relationship; and those that refer to the instructional program (including methods, materials, content, and organization).

Pupil-Research

Do culturally disadvantaged children really have a particular learning style? Chapter 2 describes the learning style of culturally disadvantaged pupils and summarizes the methods and conditions that seem to facilitate learning. More research is needed to firmly establish the validity of these assumptions about learning style and to determine how culturally disadvantaged pupils can develop a more mature and efficient way of learning. More research is needed to determine whether or not the learning style of culturally disadvantaged pupils is irreversible.

Why is it that some culturally disadvantaged children do well in school, while others do poorly? More research is needed to determine why pupils with similar backgrounds and the same innate mental capacity show such a wide range of achievement. One of the most puzzling questions about educating culturally disadvantaged children is why some overcome their handicap, achieve in school, and make it into the dominant culture. If the specific factors that help them accomplish this can be identified, perhaps other disadvantaged pupils can be taught to do it. Maybe disadvantaged children can be guided through a program that leads them out of cultural deprivation and into the dominant culture. Or, if the salient factors of nonachievement caused by an impoverished cultural background can be identified, perhaps the school can better combat them.

How do cognitive skills develop in culturally disadvantaged children? Research is needed to determine exactly how such cognitive skills as summarizing, generalizing, hypothesizing, classifying, defining, symbolizing, relating, and modifying are impaired in culturally disadvantaged pupils and whether this impairment is irreversible. Research in this area will involve finding out just how cognitive skills develop; perhaps a more extensive Headstart Program based on this research can be designed to help culturally disadvantaged children develop the cognitive skills necessary for academic success.

Additional research is needed to establish the relationship between nonstandard language skills and cognition. That is, *does nonstandard language handicap cognition significantly enough to negatively affect achievement?* Or, do children who speak a nonstandard variety of English have a *different* cognitive development as opposed to an *inferior* cognitive development? Because of the interrelation between cognition and language, research in these areas must be coordinated.

What effect does slum living have on children? It is obvious that a slum environment is detrimental to the development of children and that it has a limiting influence on their school achievement. Many studies have pointed out the debilitating influences of a slum environment. More studies are needed, however, to pinpoint the effects of slum living on cognitive development: the specific experiential lacks resulting from slum living; the effects of crowded living conditions on social adjustment, learning, and school achievement; and the effects of a noisy home environment on the listening ability of children.

Until such time as slum conditions can be eliminated, educators must use the slum environment as an experiential foundation on which to begin learning. Research on the effects of slum living can give direction on how to plan activities and devise methods and materials to do this. In other words, this kind of research can, perhaps, indicate how even a slum environment can provide positive aspects to reinforce learning. It can reveal ways in which schools can change the curriculum so as to use a *negative* environment to produce *positive* changes in pupils.

How can self-concept be raised? Some assumed ways for building a positive self-concept are listed in Chapter 2, but research is needed to establish their effectiveness. Does identification with successful models significantly raise self-concept? Does a study of the blacks' role in American history, for example, raise the self-concept of culturally disadvantaged black pupils? Can the teacher improve a pupil's self-image through friendly, personal conversation?

The fact is, although these suggestions seem to be effective, educators really don't know. From kindergarten through high school, the curriculum must include a sequential program on improving self-concept. Perhaps this kind of sequential program is just as important for disadvantaged pupils as one in language arts, mathematics, social studies, or any other subject area.

What is the relation between the parents' attitude and the child's achievement? It is axiomatic among educators that a positive attitude toward education increases the chances for the pupils' success. Although many disadvantaged parents have a positive attitude toward education, too many do not. This indicates that ways must be found to influence parents. Ways must be found to involve them in school activities. (The traditional approach has been through PTA activities, but this has not been successful; the PTA is typically composed solely of those parents who are upward-mobile. The approaches used to involve disadvantaged parents must appeal to them — they must be based on *their* cultural background, rather than on a middle-class background.)

On the other hand, some disadvantaged pupils do achieve in school even though their parents have a negative attitude or, at best, a neutral attitude toward education. This indicates that perhaps research in this area might concentrate on how to help disadvantaged pupils achieve in school *regardless* of their parents' attitude. (The task of educating disadvantaged pupils is difficult enough; the additional task of educating their parents might be too much for the schools to handle.)

Specifically, the following question must be answered: Does parental attitude, by itself, really affect the achievement of disadvantaged pupils, or is a positive attitude toward education just one manifestation of a particular kind of family environment which produces the conditions and experiences that facilitate learning?

Research on the Teaching Relationship

What kind of teacher is effective with culturally disadvantaged pupils? Some teachers work better with younger children than with older children; some teachers work better with slow-learning children than with bright children; and some teachers work better with culturally disadvantaged children than with advantaged children. While many of these teachers have acquired their ability with culturally disadvantaged children through training and experience, others seem to come by it naturally. This hints at the old question of whether good teachers are born or made. Both are probably true to some degree.

However, all teachers have to acquire an understanding of the learning process, knowledge of the content to be taught, and skill in organizing and presenting the content to the learner. These are the tools of teaching. Understanding these tools is the science of teaching, and the unique ways that teachers apply these tools is the art of teaching. Some teachers do seem to have been born with a talent for this art.

Perhaps the art of teaching can't be taught, as some have argued; but the science of teaching—specifically, the science of teaching disadvantaged pupils—can be. Research projects are required to identify the acquired characteristics that make teachers of culturally disadvantaged children function effectively. The results of this kind of research could lead to better teacher-training programs.

Interest in disadvantaged pupils and dedication to helping them achieve is also necessary to produce success. Many of the tools of teaching can be learned from effective teachers of disadvantaged children. This kind of informal training occurs every day in schools; valuable methods, techniques, and approaches for teaching are acquired through casual observation and friendly discussion. It would be useful for schools to set up in-service training led by faculty members who are especially successful in teaching their disadvantaged pupils. This would make it possible for teachers to find time in the busy school week to sit down with those teachers and discuss ways to upgrade the efforts of *all* the teachers in the school.

Do teachers from a disadvantaged background work especially well with culturally disadvantaged children? And do teachers who share the same ethnic background as their pupils have a kind of built-in potential for effectiveness? On the surface, it would seem that teachers of the same cultural or ethnic background may understand the problems and needs of the pupils better than others. Also, these teachers are not likely to draw the suspicions that disadvantaged families often have toward teachers. For example, a black teacher cannot be accused of being racially prejudiced toward black pupils. (This accusation is often made by black parents when any difficulty occurs between their children and a Caucasian teacher, and the accusation too often becomes a bigger problem than the original one.) Mexican-American or Puerto Rican teachers who speak Spanish have an obvious advantage in dealing with children and parents from these groups. One study showed that the attitudes of black teachers toward black pupils was decidedly more positive than the attitudes of Caucasian teachers toward black pupils.[1] This relationship might prove out for all of the disadvantaged groups.

Various interpretations might be given to the results of this study: maybe the Caucasian teachers were able to be more objective than the black teachers; maybe the black teachers inflated their responses to raise their own self-images because of their strong identification with their pupils. In any case, the more positive attitude of the black teachers undoubtedly was communicated to the pupils. A positive attitude has a positive influence on a child's performance. If it can be firmly established through research that teachers from similar cultural or ethnic backgrounds have a greater potential or automatic effectiveness when working with disadvantaged children, more disadvantaged pupils must be encouraged to enter the teaching profession. (In fact, more disadvantaged pupils must be encouraged to enter the teaching profession by whatever reason.)

Questions on *what* makes a good teacher for disadvantaged pupils and *how* good teachers are made are complex. Certainly, the education of culturally disadvantaged pupils will not improve on a vast scale until more answers are provided.

---

1. From "Teaching and Students: The Views of Negro and White Teachers" in *Sociology of Education.* © Fall 1963 by the American Sociological Association. By permission of author and publisher.

In the meantime, colleges and universities must continue to train teachers for culturally disadvantaged pupils. Up to the present time, our institutions of higher learning have not done a very good job in this area, chiefly because so little is known. Most of their training programs are oriented toward training teachers for middle-class children. Teacher trainees are taught how to translate a middle-class curriculum to middle-class pupils with methods and techniques that appeal to middle-class people. Often, practice teaching is done in a school that has a middle-class population. Teachers who have gone through this kind of program are not prepared for the task they face when they go into the "inner-city" schools, the "difficult" schools, the "target area" schools, or whatever else the schools with disadvantaged pupils are euphemistically called.

Another reason teacher-training programs give inadequate preparation for teaching disadvantaged children is that, too often, the instructors themselves have had little or no experience with culturally disadvantaged children. Some ways must be found to involve more of the successful teachers of disadvantaged pupils in teacher-training programs; usually, these teachers are involved in teacher-training only when they have practice teachers.

Most teachers come from a middle-class background that has not brought them into contact with the culture of deprivation. This, coupled with a teacher-training program that perpetuates a lack of contact with disadvantaged pupils, ensures inadequate preparation for the situation most new teachers face in schools with disadvantaged pupils. Yet, the greatest number of vacancies in the large cities exists in these schools.

Fortunately, many colleges and universities — particularly those located in large cities — have recently begun programs that train teachers specifically for disadvantaged pupils. Some of these special training programs are very good. They incorporate into their curricula a great deal of what is known about teaching disadvantaged pupils and they give their trainees valuable experience in working with disadvantaged pupils during the practice-teaching semester. More of these kinds of programs need to be started.

Program-Research

Which factors merit the greatest consideration in planning instructional programs? Instructional programs for disadvantaged pupils are often planned on the basis of *what* is to be taught instead of *who* is to be taught. Because of disadvantaged pupils' nonachievement in subject areas, there is a preoccupation with subject and content rather than with children. This is true in spite of the frequent use of such clichés as "the whole child" and "the child-centered curriculum." That educators usually operate in contradiction with what they say is proven by the actual inappropriateness of the curriculum and the phenomenal lack of success that culturally disadvantaged pupils experience with the curriculum. For example, the process of reading is analyzed to determine the most logical way to present this subject. This analysis is important, but more important is *the nature of the child to be taught.*

Research findings have generally established the nature, or characteristics, of culturally disadvantaged pupils. Yet this knowledge does not provide primary guidance in planning instructional programs. Instead, subject matter tends to be cut into smaller and smaller pieces to be fed at a slower and slower pace. This kind of approach implies that the characteristics of disadvantaged children indicate that these children can digest the standard curriculum menu in smaller-than-usual morsels. Perhaps, instead, the menu needs to be changed.

What changes are needed in the school and the curriculum? The majority of educators agree that the school and the curriculum must be changed. Along with this, most educators would accept the statement that since the school can't change the background of the disadvantaged pupil, it has to *accept the child and change the curriculum.* So that learning is facilitated, the required changes must be appropriate to the background of the disadvantaged child. But the changes should not be so extensive that he becomes satisfied with the culture of deprivation and adjusts to it.

These questions concerning pupils, teachers, and programs are overlapping and interrelated. Thus many of these questions should be investigated simultaneously. For example, research to find out what makes a good teacher and research to improve teacher-training programs are inseparable; research on the characteristics and learning style of culturally disadvantaged children and research to plan better instructional programs for these children must be conducted concurrently and cooperatively. Hopefully, more teachers will accept the responsibility for finding and contributing their own answers in these areas.

Getting to Know the Pupil

Identifying the Culturally Disadvantaged Child

Identifying the culturally disadvantaged child in a school where he is in the majority is not a great problem. Identification is made easy by the high density of pupils and the many manifestations of deprivation which result. When schools are located in a neighborhood overwhelmingly populated by culturally disadvantaged families, the problem may be identifying the child who is *not* disadvantaged. On the other hand, in schools that are not located in disadvantaged neighborhoods where there are few such children, identifying the culturally disadvantaged child sometimes can be a problem.

Identifying the culturally disadvantaged pupil is easier in elementary schools than in junior and senior high schools. One reason for this is that elementary school populations are more homogeneous culturally and socially. Secondary schools have large attendance boundaries, encompassing neighborhoods of varying cultural and social classes. In secondary schools the teacher-pupil relationship is usually not as intimate as it is in the elementary school. Thus identifying the disadvantaged is more difficult. In addition, students at the secondary level may have learned to hide their deprivation by a quiet withdrawal from the mainstream of activity. This is particularly true if the disadvantaged pupils are a minority in the school population.

Finally, ease in identifying culturally disadvantaged pupils is related to the degree of their deprivation. Obviously, the greater the degree of deprivation, the easier is the identification. Specific characteristics that will help teachers to identify culturally disadvantaged pupils are:

1. *Limited experiential background.* There is a lack of *quality* experiences that facilitate learning.

2. *Transiency.* Disadvantaged pupils have a high frequency of residential changes and school transfers. (It is not uncommon for some elementary schools in disadvantaged areas to turn over almost the whole school population in one year or less.)

3. *Poor attendance.* Attendance patterns are often irregular, with many short-term or one-day absences.

4. *Poor health.* Poor health contributes to poor attendance. Disadvantaged children are generally not as healthy as middle-class children; they particularly need dental care. Part of their poor health is due to inadequate diet—not enough food and poor selection of foods. (Disadvantaged children often walk to school in the morning drinking soda pop and eating potato chips or candy.) Among the contributors to poor health are unsanitary living conditions, congenital defects, and lack of rest.

5. *Lack of supervision.* Disadvantaged children often wear door keys around their necks because their mothers work. (Too often, the mothers are the sole support of the family.)

In addition, the school nurse, the attendance officer, school administrators, and classroom teachers are valuable sources who can give information to help identify particular disadvantaged pupils.

Avenues to Understanding

The gap between middle-class teachers and their culturally disadvantaged pupils has been pointed out many times. This gap is more than a social-class difference. The social-class dichotomy is descriptive; but after the social classes of teachers and pupils have been described, what does the description really tell about the need for teachers to understand culturally disadvantaged pupils or ways to acquire this understanding? Social-class differences tell nothing about the dynamics of the teaching-learning process. When this process is considered, however, the gap that separates middle-class teachers and culturally disadvantaged pupils becomes significant.

Teachers repeatedly report the inadequacy of their preparation for teaching culturally disadvantaged pupils. The most common complaint, especially of new teachers, is that they don't understand these pupils. Research is the most promising means of providing teachers with answers that will increase their understanding of culturally disadvantaged children and, subsequently, their teaching effectiveness. There are other avenues to understanding, however, that teachers themselves can take, including workshops and college courses in teaching the disadvantaged, observing and interviewing culturally disadvantaged pupils, and drawing on the community of disadvantaged children for information. The most obvious of these is reading.

Reading. The bibliographies at the end of each of the chapters in this book list many references, including works on the problems of teaching disadvantaged children, that can help teachers understand their disadvantaged pupils. There is another kind of literature, however, that is not often referred to in bibliographies on teaching disadvantaged pupils, and this is the literature produced by artists—novelists, playwrights, and poets. The works of the social scientists, the psychologists, and the educators primarily stimulate the intellect to attain understanding. The literature produced by artists is an emotional stimulation.

Often, understanding is increased with an emotional response. Thus, to really understand culturally disadvantaged pupils (and ethnic groups), a teacher must *feel* some of the problems, some of the pains, some of the frustrations and the alienation of disadvantaged people. This kind of experience comes vicariously from reading works of art.

Artists bring disadvantaged people to life. Through the dramatization of their problems and situations, others gain a deeper and different kind of understanding than can be achieved from studies, reports, statistical graphs and charts, and textbooks. It is not suggested that works of art provide a better understanding of disadvantaged people; rather, works of art lend depth and balance to the understanding.

For example, Lorraine Hansberry's play *A Raisin in the Sun* presents an authentic picture of a black family. This play particularly depicts the matriarchal dominance in some black families and their hope of a better life. Even the language of the play captures the flavor of the urban Negro dialect. Claude Brown's novel *Manchild in the Promised Land* is another example of literature that can help teachers understand disadvantaged children. This novel particularly describes the negative environmental forces that threaten to destroy or succeed in destroying disadvantaged youngsters. The writings of James Baldwin articulate the alienation of black people; Langston Huges particularly captures the humor and dreams of blacks in his poetry and Jesse B. Simple stories.

Other examples of literary works that give depth to understanding disadvantaged and ethnic groups are: *Children of Sanches* (this work is really an anthopological study of a Mexican family—however, the story is told in the words of the Sanchez family and it is included here because of its strong emotional appeal and the beauty of its narratives); the stories of Jesse Stuart; *Tobacco Road,* by Erskine Caldwell; *Up from Puerto Rico* by Helen Padilla (this is another descriptive study that fits into the classification of works of art); *West Side Story*; and John Steinbeck's classic novel *Grapes of Wrath*, which takes the reader into the life of a poverty-stricken family. Steinbeck has also written shorter works that portray the lives of disadvantaged Mexican-Americans in California. These works, and others of this sort, offer a different approach to understanding disadvantaged groups.

Workshops, In-service Training, and College Courses. An informal exchange of information among teachers, a kind of unstructured in-service training program (and a valuable one) is continually carried on in schools. Increasingly, school districts are conducting formalized, structured workshops and in-service programs to help teachers understand disadvantaged pupils and improve instruction for these pupils. Many of these programs are particularly valuable for dealing with the problems that are most pressing and common to a specific group of teachers. Another point in favor of these programs is that they are conducted by experienced teachers who have an understanding of disadvantaged pupils and can transmit this understanding to others.

Another kind of in-service program consists of college and university courses in understanding and teaching disadvantaged children. Some of these courses are very helpful, particularly those offered by colleges and universities in large urban areas. Usually, college and university courses are not as specific as in-service programs conducted by school districts. This may, or may not, be a weakness. One sure weakness of many of these course, however, is that they stress general understanding of the culturally disadvantaged, and the instructors too often lack direct, personal, or recent classroom experience with disadvantaged children.

Probably the most valuable kind of in-service program can be conducted by individual schools through regularly scheduled faculty meetings where experienced teachers can share their understanding of disadvantaged pupils with other teachers. Individuals from the community such as ministers, merchants, community leaders, and parents can be invited to contribute. This function can bring the school and the community closer together.

The Classroom. Observing disadvantaged pupils in the classroom is another obvious way to achieve greater understanding and to pick up effective ways of working with them. For example, the teacher should notice how his disadvantaged pupils participate in class discussions and react to differences of opinion. Disadvantaged children often are unable to conduct constructive discussions, particularly those that examine opposing points of view, because they become increasingly aggressive as a discussion progresses. Classroom discussions turn into verbal combat. The discussion may be structured to avoid arguments by channeling it through the teacher and eliminating student-to-student exchanges.

Class discussions, however, reveal much more than aggressive tendencies. Frequently, the pupils reveal a great deal of information about themselves and their situation that can help teachers to understand them. Too often, a teacher misses this opportunity for understanding his pupils because he requires them to respond according to middle-class norms or his own expectations.

When pupils respond according to their viewpoint and

experiences, the teacher may cut them off by telling them their responses are incorrect. Or he may coax his pupils to respond in the expected way. Children soon learn to anticipate this, and many of them refuse to volunteer their remarks; others learn to play the game of telling the teacher what he wants to hear. Instead of cutting the pupils off during discussions or attempting to force them into the expected middle-class response, the teacher must permit the pupils to respond according to their individual experience and orientation.

When teachers listen, they learn a lot. For example, the relationship between the police and the disadvantaged community is crucial and serious. In a discussion of policemen as community helpers (in elementary schools) or as protectors of society (in secondary schools), the children's opinions reveal causes of friction between the disadvantaged community and the police.

Another frequently discussed topic in classrooms is family structure and intrafamily relationships (particularly, the role of individuals in the family). This topic not only helps teachers to understand the disadvantaged family, but can often point out the wide gap between the role-expectations of disadvantaged family members and the role-expectations of middle-class family members.

For instance, disadvantaged secondary pupils often reveal a relationship between males and females that is detrimental to family stability. (Fighting is expected and accepted between husbands and wives; husbands should keep most of the money for themselves, since they work for it; infidelity is the rule, rather than the exception.) Disadvantaged elementary pupils reveal surprising concepts of family structure and family relations (particularly, a lack of basic understanding of the family as a unit).

A classroom discussion of values is still another way to understand many of the differences between middle-class and disadvantaged pupils. These are only a few examples of ways in which the teacher can use discussion periods not only to teach his pupils, but also to learn something about them.

Another area worth observing is that of positive response. Positive responses, of course, help teachers to understand the kinds of activities and subject matter that facilitate learning. They also may give insight into pupil needs. For example, black pupils are often extremely attentive whenever classroom discussions or materials deal with the historical problems of blacks. This kind of positive response suggests that this topic satisfies a greater need for a positive self-concept. (Mexican-American students often exhibit the same kind of intensive attention whenever their cultural heritage is discussed.)

The kinds of books and reading material pupils select themselves help teachers make similar inferences regarding pupil needs. Disadvantaged pupils (like all other pupils) sometimes select reading materials to meet specific needs, and their selections can give the teacher an opportunity for meeting these needs in other activities.

Other ways that the teacher acquires understanding during classroom activities are: noting what the children talk about among themselves; having the children fill out questionnaires pertaining to their interests or aspirations; keeping anecdotal accounts of individual children (these accounts often reveal recurrent incidents that establish definite patterns); examining school records for such information as average IQ scores, number of illegitimate children, and birthplaces of pupils and their parents.

Finally, one of the easiest ways for a teacher to increase his understanding of disadvantaged children is to ask his pupils questions. If a teacher wants specific information, why shouldn't he discreetly ask his pupils for it? Within the classroom, there is no better source of information.

The Community. The community surrounding the school is another source of understanding. Observing the people and their activities, seeing the buildings as compartments of poverty rather than as the dismal façades of some abandoned movie set that they resemble, visiting the people who live behind the façades, attending meetings of community organizations, reading community newspapers, and inviting individuals to contribute information—all make for more effective teaching.

Teachers usually take the most direct route to school, and they rarely see the ugliness of the disadvantaged community or the drama of life that is acted out daily on its streets. It is surprising how much one can learn from just a casual tour through a disadvantaged community—the kind of tour that one can take on the way home from school. All it takes is a few extra minutes—just ten extra minutes a day for five days should provide a complete tour of most neighborhoods.

There are some specific things a teacher should notice when he drives through a disadvantaged neighborhood. For example, the unusual number of taverns and liquor stores shows that many parents spend too much money on liquor. The children's welfare is sacrificed for a temporary escape from their intolerable situation.

Also, notice the many small crowds of men huddled on street corners, engaged in activities that do nothing about filling family pocketbooks. These men are on the corner because there is no place to go. (In many areas of the country, the unemployment rate of disadvantaged communities is as high as one-third of the male population.) These idle men certainly dull the aspirations of children and the role-identification they represent to boys is contrary to the role expectations of the dominant culture. When these men are parents, the effect of their idleness on the well-being of their children is tragic.

Teachers should also note the incredible amount of activity that occurs on the streets of many disadvantaged neighborhoods. In warm weather, people seem to burst out of the crowded walls of slum tenements or shoddy shanties to flood the streets with activity. This extension of the living area from inside to outside suggests why disadvantaged pupils find the classroom so confining. There are many other inferences that can be made from observing street activity. For instance, note the young age at which children are permitted to play without adult supervision, the type of play the younger children engage in and the activities of the older boys and girls, the expressions of the people in the streets, and the preponderance of activities that merely sustain life rather than enrich living.

While driving through these communities, the teacher should also listen to the voices of the people, particularly the kind of language the people use. Specifically, note the noise level and the nonstandard language or foreign language of disadvantaged communities. The noise level of the voices is necessitated by the noisy environment and the density of the population. Disadvantaged pupils may learn not to listen; or they may learn not to distinguish meaningful sounds. The different language systems (nonstandard dialects of English or foreign language) used in disadvantaged communities also have implications for the school program. For example, the universality of a particular language system in a disadvantaged community indicates that the school has an impossible task in trying to force pupils to give up that language.

A teacher can infer understanding from the physical aspects of the community as well as from observations of the people. The ugliness of the disadvantaged community points to the need for providing a pleasant school environment; the physical chaos of the community helps the teacher understand the pupils' need for order in the school; crowded slum conditions help the teacher realize that disadvantaged pupils need at least a desk at school as their own private property. The physical condition of some disadvantaged communities is so bad that the environment seems unreal. Its hard to believe that people really do call such places home.

If the school is allowed to reflect the negative environment of the surrounding community, then some of those behavioral patterns operative in the surrounding community are brought inside the school — and many of these patterns are detrimental to learning.

A walking tour is another way to see the disadvantaged community. This kind of tour should be taken, of course, during daylight and, preferably, with others. Much of the literature on the culturally disadvantaged recommends this kind of community visit; seldom, however, are teachers warned of the dangers involved. The fact is, many disadvantaged communities are not safe for strangers — they aren't even safe for the people who live in them. Disadvantaged communities invariably have the highest crime rates, and teachers should use common sense about walking around these communities. One safeguard is to be accompanied by a pupil. Pupils are also good tour guides: they can point out things that might otherwise be missed and they can interpret and answer questions.

Making visits to community organizations, especially the churches, is another way to increase understanding. Some community organizations in disadvantaged communities will welcome teachers. In many instances, however, the church is the only real community organization. These churches never turn away visitors. In fact, a teacher is likely to be treated as an honored guest and may even be asked to say a few words to the congregation. (The services of many of the churches attended by disadvantaged blacks and Appalachians are unstructured and flexible enough to permit this.)

In the event that an invitation is preferred, the teacher has only to tell his pupils that he would like to attend a church service or a special church program. This will not be considered an imposition or forward action, and the pupils will be glad to extend an invitation. The teacher who asks for an invitation probably will receive several.

Visiting the churches in a disadvantaged community is good public relations for the school. The teacher can meet and talk with parents on the parents' home ground. Often, disadvantaged parents are much more communicative away from the school, and they will be pleased at the interest in their children that a church visit implies.

Many disadvantaged communities publish newspapers, and teachers can learn a great deal about the community from reading them. In addition, in many cities there are newspapers published for the black, Mexican-American, and Puerto Rican populations. These papers are valuable in learning about these ethnic groups. Of course, a newspaper printed in Spanish is not very helpful if one does not read Spanish; but black newspapers are printed in English and contain information that can help teachers understand the black population, especially the integration goals of blacks and the attitude of blacks toward the dominant culture.

When reading a black newspaper, however, there is something the "outsider" should be aware of: the reports of scandals, the wild headlines, the exciting leads, and the disproportionate space allotted to crime are the come-on to get people to buy the newspaper. They also tell a great deal about the unfortunate condition of many black communities in the city they serve. But the real key to understanding black people is found on the editorial page and feature pages. These pages can give an outsider an inside view of the grievances, the aspirations, the goals, and the needs of the population. Quite frequently the writing is good and the views expressed are a consensus. Reading the black newspaper is probably the easiest way to learn something about a city's black population.

Working With Disadvantaged Parents

Understanding the Parents

The general characteristics of culturally disadvantaged children that limit their achievement are acquired from their culture through learning. In other words, disadvantaged pupils are products of their culture. Specifically, these pupils are products of a particular kind of family, because the family is the primary means of transmitting culture. Thus culturally disadvantaged pupils are reflections of their parents. For example, culturally disadvantaged pupils speak nonstandard English or a foreign language and they have a value system different from that of the dominant culture, a poor self-concept, low aspirations, and a poor understanding of success. Their parents necessarily share these characteristics.

Teachers often fail to realize that parents of culturally disadvantaged children are also culturally disadvantaged. Some teachers seem to believe that cultural deprivation is a kind of immaturity of the pupils. They do not recognize that the parents also operate on a different level and speak a different language than the school and the teachers.

Cultural deprivation is not exclusive to a particular age level—it is a handicap of a whole group of people who share a particular way of life. Thus teachers and parents have different frames of reference when dealing with the same problem — they look at problems from different cultural perspectives. This often causes confusion, even conflict, when the teachers and the parents of disadvantaged pupils meet. For example, the teacher who complains to a parent about a pupil fighting may be shocked when the parent indicates that there is nothing wrong with fighting, that the pupil was *taught* to fight when someone got out of line. This is an example of culture shock at the parent-teacher level.

The school can't possibly change the parents. The characteristics that keep them disadvantaged and affect the achievement of their children are many, and the task of changing the pupils is about all that the school can handle. Yet many school districts are attempting the impossible task of changing disadvantaged parents through parent-involvement programs. Some districts are even trying to make disadvantaged parents into middle-class parents!

A few of these programs are accomplishing limited objectives with disadvantaged parents in adult- and parent-education programs. But the problem of completely changing disadvantaged parents — making them able to participate in the dominant culture — is so great that these programs cannot hope to succeed. This does not mean that all programs should be abandoned, and certainly not those programs that help parents get better jobs to increase their incomes. A better income can be one of the keys to unlock the entrance to the dominant culture.

The limitations of these programs, however, must be recognized. These programs can't eliminate some of the causes or effects of cultural deprivation: an absent father can't be provided or returned to the home; the color of one's skin or one's ethnic background can't be changed; an entire value system can't be restructured appreciably by attending class one night a week; disadvantaged parents can't fill their experiential void and work at the same time; the welfare agency won't increase monthly payments; the landlord won't fix the hole in the roof.

The question that must be asked at this point is: If the pupils are products of their culture — specifically, products of their families — and if the school can't change the parents (eliminate their cultural deprivation), how then can the pupils be changed? The answer is: The school *can* influence the parents in those areas that *directly* pertain to the pupils' success in school. For example, the school can convince parents that education is important; the school can convince parents that regular attendance is necessary; the school can change their attitude toward learning from apathy to excitement; the schools can make them realize the cooperative role they share with the school in helping pupils achieve academic success.

The school *can* effect changes in these areas, and these are the areas the school should emphasize in parent-education programs and school programs to involve parents. In other words, *emphasize the changes that directly pertain to pupil success, and suggest changes in terms of how they will affect the pupils, not the parents.* The many Headstart Programs around the country and the remarkable Banneker School Program didn't try to make disadvantaged parents into middle-class parents. What these programs did was to change the parents' attitudes about the things that directly affected their children's achievement.

The important points emphasized here are that parents of culturally disadvantaged pupils share the same characteristics that have been listed to describe the pupils, and that the school and teachers must work with these parents within the framework of limitations these characteristics impose. The school should concentrate on changing those characteristics of the parents that negatively affect the achievement of the children. And the approaches used to effect change must be those that culturally disadvantaged parents will respond to.

Involving the Parents

Although more research is needed in the area of the relation between parent attitudes and pupil achievement, experience tends to support the hypothesis that disadvantaged pupils do better when their parents have a positive attitude toward school and when they are involved in school activities.

Some disadvantaged parents look upon the school with suspicion and pessimism. This may be due to their own unpleasant experiences as pupils, or to similar unpleasant experiences in their dealings with their children's school. Other disadvantaged parents feel that too much formal education—too much book learning—is bad for children. (Perhaps they feel threatened by the educational gap that results from a difference of educational level between themselves and their children.) The view that too much book learning is bad is prevalent among disadvantaged Appalachians.

Because literacy is a new phenomenon in many disadvantaged families, parents have a poor understanding of its significance in a modern society. This lack of understanding may be due, in part, to the few positive examples of educated persons in the parents' environment.

Most disadvantaged parents don't really have a basic understanding of the learning process. Too often, they view learning as some kind of magical process that occurs at school between the hours of 9:00 A.M. and 3:00 P.M. and fail to understand the supporting role which they must play twenty-four hours a day to help their children learn. (Even if they do understand it, many are unable to play this supporting role.)

Disadvantaged parents seldom make plans for their children's future—the exigencies of daily living preclude such planning. Thus the importance of education is not projected into the future, but is viewed in terms of the present. Education is not thought of as a continuum, but as a daily activity that children of certain ages must do. The failure to project the importance of education into the future is one of the things that prevents disadvantaged parents from developing attitudes and practices that support and sustain their children's efforts to achieve.

Finally, some disadvantaged parents who think of society as a battleground include the school in the enemy camp. These parents wage a kind of battle with the school, and their attitudes necessarily have a negative effect on their children. Fortunately, even some of those parents who have this negative viewpoint look upon the school as a source of hope. With most disadvantaged parents the school already has a head start.

When to Begin. The ideal time to involve disadvantaged parents in school activities and interest them in the school program is at the kindergarten level. This is an ideal time for two reason: First, if the parents can be influenced when their children start school, the tendency for disadvantaged pupils to fall farther and farther behind their middle-class peers may be arrested or diminished. Secondly, disadvantaged parents, like all other parents, are enthusiastic about their children beginning school. The school can capitalize on this enthusiasm by getting the parents involved at this point. If a good relationship with parents can be established right at the beginning of the child's school career, perhaps this relationship can be sustained.

Some school districts have conducted programs for involving parents of entering kindergarten children. These programs are a sort of Headstart Program for parents. Some districts operate an orientation program to explain the cooperative action of school and parents in educating children. In these programs parents are also taught the importance of answering their children's questions, talking to their children, pointing out things in their children's environment to stimulate interest and questions, taking their children on trips, and so forth. (Of course, the suggestions which are given must be possible for the parents to carry out.)

In addition to making parents aware of the supplementary role that they play in their children's education, these programs inform the parents about those areas that are their sole responsibility. (The importance of attending school regularly, showing interest in their children's progress, visiting school and participating in school activities, and providing an encouraging study atmosphere.) School districts that conduct this kind of orientation program are more likely to influence the attitudes of parents than school districts that wait until registration day to meet disadvantaged parents. The cold, formal registration process is not a good beginning for establishing parent-school cooperation.

School-Community Coordinator. A good relationship should be established with the parents of older children, too. These parents may not have had good relations with the school before. Many school districts have started programs to sustain or initiate good relations and to change attitudes of the parents in those areas that directly influence achievement. One of these types of programs involves a teacher or social worker whose job is to act as a liaison between the school and the home. This job is sometimes given the title of "school-community coordinator" or "school-parent coordinator."

The coordinator visits the homes, handles any problems that arise between the school and parents, explains to the parents how they can participate in the school program, and recruits parents for volunteer services. Coordinators also visit community organizations such as churches and clubs to talk with parents about the school program and ways parents can support the program. Some coordinators even conduct parent-education classes to help parents develop positive attitudes and practices that help their children. These classes are often held in the homes of parents, rotating among the parents enrolled in the class. Many of these programs are successful, and their success is probably due to the personal contact parents have with the school through the coordinator.

Often, the job of the coordinator is defined as it evolves. For example, in one Los Angeles high school the school community coordinator visited the home of a disadvantaged parent to find out why the parent could not attend a teacher-conference at school. When the parent told the coordinator that she needed a babysitter, the coordinator served as babysitter while the parent went to school.

Another time this coordinator held a conference in a neighborhood laundromat while a parent did the family washing. The coordinator even pitched in and helped to wash the clothes! While actions of this particular coordinator may seem unrelated to pupil achievement, the warm, friendly relationship that developed put her in a position to influence those parents for the benefit of their children. This coordinator lets the parents know through her actions that *the school is really interested in their children;* the parents can be expected to equal this interest.

Another type of program involving parents is one that teaches skills or gives help in particular areas where it is needed. Most schools, particularly high schools, have facilities to conduct parent-education classes in such areas as reading, home economics, automobile repair, industrial arts, and so on. Many disadvantaged parents are interested in or need help in these areas. Becoming involved in learning makes disadvantaged parents understand the learning problems of their children.

The PTA. Some districts have tried conducting classes in connection with PTA meetings. This seems like a good way to draw disadvantaged parents into PTA activities because it combines the meetings with something concrete and immediately useful. One aspect of this type of program should be to influence parental attitudes on education. Maybe the parents and their children could attend these classes together. In addition, these classes should be held on Saturday. This is usually the most convenient time for disadvantaged parents to participate.

While the PTA has been the traditional way of involving parents in the school, it has not been very successful with most disadvantaged parents. In many schools with disadvantaged pupils, more teachers than parents attend PTA meetings. In addition, the parents who attend the meetings are those who need to be influenced least. If the PTA is to be effective, it must draw in many more disadvantaged parents than it normally does.

There are a number of reasons why the PTA has not been effective with disadvantaged parents. First of all, the structure of the PTA, with its formalized leadership, its committee system, and its parliamentary procedures, is in conflict with the structure natural to disadvantaged parents. For example, within groups of disadvantaged parents, leadership usually emerges during the process of getting a job done. The ritualistic method of nominating and electing officers is contrary to the normal pattern for establishing leadership. In the parent groups, committee work is often replaced by a consensus for a small group to perform a particular job. Finally, parliamentary procedure can be a complicated process for conducting meetings made up of middle-class parents — it is totally inappropriate for conducting meetings for disadvantaged parents. Their meetings are usually conducted under the direction of a strong leader who has emerged from the group.

The PTA normally operates as if the parents and the school share the same educational attitudes and goals. This cannot be assumed when working with disadvantaged parents. The PTA must make room for different viewpoints and make provision for examining them. Too often the structure and orientation of the PTA shuts off the dissenting opinions that might point out where the PTA is missing the mark of effectiveness.

Another reason that the PTA has failed with disadvantaged parents is that it is often controlled by school people — teachers, administrators, and parents who attempt to push a particular point of view without considering different points of view or different ways of solving problems based on different cultural patterns. The only point of view that really needs to be pressed is that the role of the PTA is to benefit children. Eventually, disadvantaged parents will seek help on how to fill the role, and when they do, the school people can influence attitudes.

Finally, the PTA has often been unsuccessful with disadvantaged parents because meetings are held at inconvenient times. Unlike middle-class parents, disadvantaged parents normally travel long distance to jobs by uncomfortable means of transportation and they work harder physically than middle-class parents. They are unwilling — physically and emotionally — to attend a meeting after a hard day of working. A solution would be to hold the meetings on Saturday or Sunday. It would be interesting to see if this would increase attendance (assuming, of course, that other changes were made also).

The Banneker District Program. It is apparent that the PTA has usually failed with disadvantaged parents for the same reasons that the curriculum has failed with disadvantaged pupils: It has not changed to fit the experiences, behavior patterns, and characteristics of disadvantaged parents. One program that has been particularly successful in involving parents in school activities and changing parent attitudes on education is the Banneker District Program, a comprehensive effort to improve the achievement of culturally disadvantaged black children by involving parents and *mobilizing the entire community.* Teachers visited the families of their pupils, and merchants in the district were encouraged to report truancy cases to the school. The importance of education to disadvantaged pupils was outlined to community organizations, along with the role these organizations could play in helping pupils achieve.

Other means of bringing disadvantaged parents into the school are assembly programs, open-house programs, exhibits, and extracurricular activities. All of these afford personal contact and communication between teachers and parents.

Communicating With Parents

The most common means the school uses for communicating with parents are notes and bulletins. Many disadvantaged parents are, like their children, linguistically handicapped. They are poor readers. Thus they have difficulty understanding written communications from the school. A better way to communicate with these parents would be through personal contact, either by visiting their homes or by telephoning them. Personal contact is consistent with their cultural patterns of communication.

On the other hand, personal contact or telephone calls are inefficient. The schools simply can't make a personal contact every time communicating with parents is necessary. Phoning is time consuming and difficult because many disadvantaged parents do not have telephones; and home visits must be made after school hours. Apparently, because of the volume of routine communications needed, communication by notes and bulletins is unavoidable. It is essential, then, that notes and bulletins be written in clear, simple language, and that they contain only a few items. For nonroutine communications on important matters such as behavior problems or a pupil's achievement, personal contact should be used.

The difficulty of communicating with parents by notes and bulletins points out a particular area in which disadvantaged parents are often confused: communicating pupil achievement. Achievement usually is communicated by report card. As the language of the report card is not the language of the disadvantaged parents, they do not understand clearly what the school is trying to tell them about their children.

Almost all school districts use a district-wide form for reporting pupil achievement to disadvantaged parents and middle-class parents alike. Instead of using the same report card for all parents, the district should design one that can easily be understood by disadvantaged parents. A better method of reporting pupil achievement is a conference between the parent and the teacher. In addition, a conference at report-card time is an ideal way to meet with parents and obtain their cooperation.

Parents' Visits to School

Many disadvantaged parents visit school only when problems arise. This is unfortunate, because then school visits become associated with problems. During these visits disadvantaged parents are fearful, suspicious, and defensive. Not much progress can be made with people who feel this way. Thus it is important for the parents and the school to establish a cooperative working relationship so that when problems do arise, fear and suspicion don't handicap their efforts to solve the problems.

Relaxed Atmosphere. The physical environment of the school is a source of discomfort to many disadvantaged parents. Parents usually report to the main office when they visit. There they are confronted with a counter, files, switchboard, office sounds, and clerks—the same cold, official atmosphere of authority that may be associated with unpleasant experiences (welfare office, unemployment-compensation office, police station, finance office, and rent-collection office). Through a kind of stimulus generalization, some disadvantaged parents *expect* an unpleasant experience when they visit school. Schools located in disadvantaged communities should have a room that does not reflect officialdom where parents are received and conferences held. The conference should be conducted as informally as possible.

When conferring with a parent on problems, always try to say something positive about the child. It is especially important to conclude the conference on a positive note—that is, don't end the conference on the subject of any difficulty the problem might have caused. Instead, conclude with a positive statement about the pupil and the benefit the conference should have on his achievement.

Stereotyping. Another cause of difficulty when disadvantaged parents visit school is a double-barreled one: the stereotype many teachers have of the parents and the stereotype the parents have of the teachers. Some teachers think of disadvantaged parents as stupid, worthless human beings; they act so superior that the parents' feelings of inferiority are increased. Some specific ways that teachers communicate a negative stereotype are through rudeness, curtness, use of a vocabulary too difficult for the parents, and lack of interest in what the parents have to say. On the other hand, some disadvantaged parents think of teachers as haughty, snobbish people who are too good to talk to them, whether or not this may be true.

Both teachers and parents inadvertently reinforce the stereotype each has of the other. The teacher may do this by failing to communicate on a level that lets the parents know they are talking to another equal human being. Disadvantaged parents may reinforce the stereotype by not being able to communicate in standard English (their efforts to use standard English amplify their linguistic deprivation and make them appear stupid), or by failing to understand the topic being discussed.

Other subtle ways in which teachers and parents reinforce each other's stereotypes are through differences of clothes and grooming, socioeconomic class, attitude on education, and power base (the teacher is supported by the legal power of the state; the disadvantaged parent is dominated by the power of the state).

These stereotypes are unfortunate because they prevent communication. They disappear (as stereotypes often do) when teachers and parents work together *cooperatively* in the common interest of educating children. This is why it is so important for schools to initiate programs in which cooperative bonds between teachers and parents can be established.

Clear, Informal Communications. The language the teacher uses when conferring with disadvantaged parents is especially important. It's obvious that communication is impossible if the language level is above the parents' comprehension. The teacher should speak in simple, clear, informal English, without condescending in his choice of language.

Disadvantaged parents, on their part, are likely to try to use standard English, and the effort is likely to handicap their communication. It is important to be patient and to avoid making corrections either explicitly or through implication. If the conference is relaxed and informal, their ability to communicate will increase as the conference progresses. (Disadvantaged parents who speak a foreign language present a greater difficulty. Conferences with these parents require an interpreter, and this third party may prevent informality.)

Conflict between school and parents is often created by parents failing to make requested visits. The parents may be unable to keep their appointments because of lack of carfare, babysitter, or decent clothing, out of fear of dealing with authority figures, or the inability to come during school hours. The failure to honor requests to visit reinforces the stereotype that teachers may have of disadvantaged parents, or implies that disadvantaged parents are not interested in their children. Unfortunately some aren't—but many are.

Visiting the Home

Because of the difficulty many disadvantaged parents experience in coming to school, some educators recommend that teachers visit disadvantaged parents in their homes whenever a conference is necessary. Parents must always be notified before visiting. When requesting permission to visit the home, always give the parents the choice of conferring at the home or the school. This will give them the opportunity to prepare for the visit and another chance to visit the school, if they would prefer. Disadvantaged parents may be ashamed of their living conditions, and when they realize that the teacher intends to see them, they will often choose to see the teacher at school.

In the home the teacher should observe the following common sense rules: Do not appear shocked over the living conditions; make home visits last no longer than necessary; and accept any extension of hospitality, no matter how meager— refusal indicates superiority rather than politeness and reinforces the stereotype disadvantaged parents may have of teachers. (The neglect of disadvantaged parents to offer hospitality probably means that they are unable to or that they do not know middle-class courtesy patterns.) Female teachers should take care not to overdress when visiting the homes of disadvantaged pupils. Above all, the teacher should let the parents know that the visit was made for the benefit of the child.

Programs for Culturally Disadvantaged Pupils

While the *ratio* of culturally disadvantaged children in American schools probably has remained about the same over the years, the *number* of culturally disadvantaged pupils has increased. Educating these pupils is now one of the major problems of American education.

There are a number of reasons for the increased awareness of this problem. First of all, the growing population of culturally disadvantaged children magnifies their problem beyond the point that it can be ignored, dismissed, or hidden. Before World War II, the culturally disadvantaged population was dispersed throughout the general population or isolated in pockets of poverty. Further, the Great Depression of the 1930s covered most of the country with a cloud of poverty and hardship, and, in the economic fog, the culturally disadvantaged could not be distinguished from the temporarily poor.

When sunshine returned for the general population, however, the culturally disadvantaged remained under the cloud. One area where they did make hay, even though the sun shone only for others, was in population growth—their birthrate has been higher than the birthrate of the general population during recent years. Thus the number of culturally disadvantaged children in our schools has increased significantly. The growing concentration of the culturally disadvantaged in big cities and the resulting social and economic problems is another factor responsible for increasing awareness in this area.

Finally, as the curriculum of the American school changed to fit the general population (increasingly middle class in nature) and the increasingly complex needs of a complex society, it became more and more unsuitable for culturally disadvantaged pupils. They fell further and further behind in achievement, and their nonachievement drew the attention of educators. To meet the problem, educators began to devise new programs to help culturally disadvantaged pupils achieve.

Basic Types of Programs

There are basically two types of programs: compensatory programs and programs that utilize content, materials, and methods based on the pupil's cultural background. Both types of programs are usually called compensatory education, and both have the same purpose — to improve the achievement of culturally disadvantaged children. There is a distinction between the two, however.

Compensatory programs attempt to make up for the shortcomings and deficiencies in the pupil's background that prevent him from achieving. In other words, compensatory education attempts to give the culturally disadvantaged child those necessary experiences for achievement that a middle-class child normally derives from his cultural background. (The lack of these experiences penalizes the culturally disadvantaged because the school curriculum is based on them.) Programs like Headstart and enrichment programs (field trips and after-school and Saturday programs) are examples of compensatory education.

The second type of program uses the child's cultural background as a take-off point for instruction. These programs include content that especially interests disadvantaged pupils. For example, these programs may include a study of social problems relevant to disadvantaged pupils — disadvantaged black children may study the black man's role in American history. They also include materials appropriate to the pupils' backgrounds. Examples are the new elementary readers that include story characters in a mid-city setting and the high-interest books written in language approximating that of disadvantaged children.

Finally, these programs use methods and techniques that are adapted to the cultural background and learning style of the pupils. Many of these programs have small classes and staggered schedules; some include extensive counseling. Other techniques include stressing physical involvement in learning, permitting pupils to use their native language (foreign or non-standard dialect) without fear of criticism, and appropriate motivational procedures.

In actuality, no sharp distinction can be made between compensatory programs and programs based on the cultural background of disadvantaged children. Each necessarily has some of the other in it: compensatory programs must employ content, materials, and methods that are effective with disadvantaged children, and programs based on the backgrounds of disadvantaged children must compensate for their lack of experiences. The differentiation depends on the emphasis of the program.

Program Goals

Programs designed for culturally disadvantaged children, whether they are compensatory or based on the pupil's background, should differ from programs for middle-class children only in *structure* and *approach,* but not in goals. Programs for both groups must be designed to help pupils attain the general objectives of education. Each group has some specific objectives formulated on the basis of its particular situation, but the *overall general objectives of education are the same for both groups.*

This point is emphasized because some educators think that special objectives of education must be developed for disadvantaged pupils. James B. Conant implies this kind of recommendation in his book *Slums and Suburbs.* The confusion about objectives may be caused by the inability of disadvantaged pupils to attain standard objectives through regular programs. That is, educators note that disadvantaged children have difficulty attaining objectives through the regular curriculum, and instead of changing just the curriculum, they change both the curriculum and objectives. Furthermore, the order of change seems to be curriculum first, then objectives, and this results in the content and materials setting objectives.

Educational objectives imply behavioral changes in particular areas. For example, a general objective of American education is to understand and appreciate the democratic form of government (different school districts state this objective in different ways, but the essential meaning is universal). The behavioral change contained in this objective is to "understand and appreciate"; the area this behavior applies to is "democratic form of government." A basic task of educators is to organize appropriate sequential activities that will give pupils the experiences required for attaining the objective. These activities often are contained in a framework of subjects and units. The particular activities likely to produce the desired behavioral changes in the area stated in the objective constitute the curriculum.

Culturally disadvantaged children have difficulty attaining the objectives of education because the subjects, units, and activities are not appropriate for them, being based on the interests, experiences, and nature of middle-class children. Thus new curricula are needed for culturally disadvantaged children. Specifically, new programs of education must be designed that will permit them to attain educational objectives.

A worthwhile exercise for teachers would be to examine the programs for disadvantaged pupils in their schools and then look at the objectives of the total school program. During this exercise the teacher should ask himself: "Do these programs *really* lead to these objectives?" If the answer is negative, then new programs are needed that elevate students rather than dilute or lower goals.

This doesn't mean that programs for disadvantaged pupils should not contain specific objectives that are dictated by the conditions or the reality of deprivation. The attainment of these objectives is necessary before the higher, more general, and universal objectives of education can be achieved. For example, disadvantaged children must learn how to survive in their environment, how to improve themselves, and how to escape the clutches of all the destructive forces of a slum environment. But these objectives are *intermediate* objectives, not the final goal. If they become educational ends, they will keep the children outside of the dominant culture.

The need for establishing new programs for culturally disadvantaged pupils presents new challenges and new burdens to America's schools. To initiate the kinds of programs that are effective with disadvantaged children we need more teachers and more teacher-training programs, new materials, new equipment, and new buildings. All of these require more money, and a lack of money is a general characteristic of most school districts.

Elementary and Secondary Education Act of 1965

Fortunately, additional funds have been allotted to districts for the purpose of initiating programs for culturally disadvantaged pupils. The most significant new funds have come from the federal government with the passage of the Elementary and Secondary Education Act in 1965. President Johnson took the leadership in securing this most significant education bill in our country's history. Although it covers other aspects of education, the education of culturally disadvantaged pupils is its main emphasis.

The urgency of the need for the funds provided by the act is reflected in the short time it took from its introduction in Congress to its enactment. Committee hearings were held, congressional debates were held, final passage was accomplished, and the President's signature was affixed in less than four months.

The Elementary and Secondary Education Act authorized more than $1,300,000,000 in federal funds for educational purposes. Many existing programs for educating culturally disadvantaged pupils would not be possible without these funds. The largest allocation of funds ($1,060,000,000) was contained in Title I, intended to strengthen elementary and secondary education for impoverished youth. Other sections provide funds for additional textbooks, library books, and instructional materials (Title II); supplementary educational centers to provide specialized services (Title III); research (Title IV); and support of state departments of education.

In other acts the federal government has authorized funds to finance educational programs for culturally disadvantaged youth. Some of these programs are Headstart, the Job Corps, and the Neighborhood Youth Corps. However, although the funds have been decreased in recent years, the Elementary and Secondary Education Act remains the most important and extensive effort of the federal government to help with educating the culturally disadvantaged.

Programs in Operation

A list of the kinds of programs that have been designed for culturally disadvantaged pupils can be found in "A Schoolman's Guide to Federal Aid," *School Management* (June 1965), pages 94–164, by Buckman Osborne. The programs have been grouped under specific categories. The first category, "Educational Personnel," pertains directly to teachers of disadvantaged pupils rather than to the pupils—thus these programs are neither strictly compensatory programs nor programs based on the pupil's background.

Most of the programs in the list reflect only *structure*, not *approach*, though this often can be inferred from the structure. The approach to be taken is dictated by the nature of disadvantaged pupils (general characteristics, learning style, specific needs, and interests). Programs for culturally disadvantaged pupils often include more than one component. For example, a program may include special reading classes, field trips, and counseling services; or it may combine school-home co-ordinators, counseling services, and health services.

Student Achievement Centers Program. One example of a program that combines components to form a concerted, co-ordinated effort is the Student Achievement Centers Program conducted by the Los Angeles City Schools for disadvantaged students in junior and senior high schools. This program also combines the two basic program types: that is, compensatory education plus content materials and methods appropriate for disadvantaged pupils.

The core of the Student Achievement Centers Program is reading. Students are selected to enter a center on the basis of their reading scores. Poor readers (four or more years retardation) are programed into the basic reading classes with a maximum enrollment of twelve; students whose reading scores are less than four years below their reading-level expectancy are programed into reading-improvement classes with a maximum enrollment of fifteen.

In addition, all students are enrolled in social studies, math, and science classes that place equal emphasis on reading and content for these courses. Basic reading skills (phonetic and structural word attack, vocabulary building, comprehension skills, and so on) taught in the reading classes are reinforced in the social studies, math, and science classes. Maximum enrollment in these classes is twenty-five pupils.

The teachers in the Student Achievement Centers Program have received intensive in-service training in the teaching of reading. Teachers of social studies, math, and science classes are given specialized training in reinforcing basic reading skills. Every teacher attends a six-week workshop in methods of teaching reading to the culturally disadvantaged. In the workshops, teachers are taught effective methods of reading instruction, diagnostic techniques, use of special equipment and materials, and grouping techniques. In this way the students are assured of a massive teaching effort to help them improve their reading skills.

Each classroom in the Student Achievement Centers Program is equipped with a variety of equipment to aid instruction: tape recorders, overhead projectors, tachistoscopes, reading pacers, and so on. In addition, each classroom has a wide variety of textbooks, reading kits, and other reading aids, offering the greatest available variety of material. Each classroom also has small sets of supplementary books that appeal to many interest areas. Finally, the content of the social studies, math, and science classes has been changed to fit the particular interests and needs of disadvantaged students.

Teachers in the Student Achievement Centers Program are given clerical help to assist them in nonteaching duties. This extra help increases the time they can work directly with their students. Counseling is another component of the Student Achievement Centers Program. Attached to each center are counselors who work with students to help them solve emotional and social problems that are detrimental to learning. Each center has a school-home coordinator who works closely with parents on such problems.

Another component of this program is compensatory in nature. This is the extended-day and Saturday enrichment classes. In these classes, students can take courses in any area that interests them: music, art, industrial arts, dancing, computer math, and literature appreciation. Finally, each Student Achievement center is allotted many hours on Saturdays for scheduled field trips to cultural centers, industries, concerts, and exhibits. Thus, in addition to its reading-centered curriculum, the Student Achievement Centers Program of the Los Angeles City Schools utilizes many approaches to help pupils overcome the handicap of a disadvantaged background.

Banneker Schools Project. A program for culturally disadvantaged pupils that has received national acclaim for its remarkable success is the Banneker Schools Project in St. Louis, Missouri. The program was founded and is directed by Dr. Samuel Shepard, a black educator who refused to accept failure as a necessary product of deprivation. The Banneker School District is located in one of the poorest sections of St. Louis. The area has the highest crime rate in the city, the greatest poverty, the most ramshackle housing. It's a real slum and it is populated by blacks.

One of the first things Dr. Shepard did was to involve the parents of the school children. Every parent in the district was visited by a teacher. During these home visits, parents were urged to support the schools in their efforts to educate pupils. The importance of education as a means for a better life was pointed out, and parents were encouraged to take a pledge of cooperation. This pledge required parents (1) to send their children to school every day on time; (2) to provide the space and atmosphere in the home for their children to do homework; (3) to keep behind their children to do the homework (parents were kept informed of homework assignments); and (4) to constantly remind their children of the importance of education. This pledge was tacked up in the kitchen, or some other prominent place in the home, where it always could be seen.

In the beginning, Dr. Shepard spoke night after night throughout the district, hammering away on the disadvantaged position of blacks in American society and the role of education in changing this position. He persuaded parents and children to develop self-pride and conviction that achievement was possible — in other words, he worked on developing a positive self-concept for the entire population. He invited other speakers — especially successful blacks who had made it out of the slums — to speak on the same topic. Little by little, the parents were won over. Then they were organized in the schools' PTA's in order to sustain their enthusiasm.

Teachers in the Banneker District were given intensive in-service training on ways to teach their pupils. Pupil motivation was particularly stressed in the in-service training. Teachers were urged to stop looking at the IQ of the pupils and to make the pupils stretch to meet the content. The pupils were informed of their exact achievement levels in reference to grade norms in each subject matter. (The reality of nonachievement was faced!) And the pupils were urged by teachers and parents to get busy and close the gap.

Once the program got rolling, it was propelled by the new force of motivation. Pupils were given many enrichment programs to fill in their experiential gaps. Dr. Sam Shepard put all his eggs in a basket labeled motivation and hatched achievement. The significance of his efforts is that teachers, parents, pupils were motivated, and this triad of motivation made nonachievement virtually impossible.

The success of the program is remarkable. In the 1957–58 school year, 47 percent of the Banneker District pupils were below average; today, little more than 10 percent are below average. In the 1957–58 school year, only 10 percent of the Banneker District pupils were in the top group of achievement; today, more than 20 percent are in the top group. Attendance climbed above 90 percent.

The pupils who accomplished this remarkable record are from almost the same environment that produced pupils who scored abysmally low on national tests prior to the program. Only one thing changed in the environment — attitude. Perhaps this is the important ingredient in any program for culturally disadvantaged pupils.

The Student Achievement Centers program in Los Angeles, California, and the Banneker District program in St. Louis, Missouri, are examples of programs that combine compensatory education and education based on the pupil's cultural background. The programs differ, however, in their emphasis of *structure* or *approach*. The Los Angeles program emphasized structure, while the St. Louis program emphasized approach.

The emphasis on approach seems the most effective because its results are necessary for achievement regardless of structure. In fact, if culturally disadvantaged children can be taught to *believe* that they can achieve, to develop pride in themselves, and to recognize the importance of achievement, they can probably achieve within the structure of the regular curriculum. The greatest gains, however, are probably realized in programs that alter both structure and approach to fit the backgrounds, needs, and learning style of the pupils.

[For summaries of additional programs, see: *Compensatory Education for the Disadvantaged,* by Edmund W. Gordon and Doxey A. Wilkerson (Princeton, N.J.: College Entrance Examination Board, 1966.)]

Some Considerations in Establishing Programs

Some of the considerations in organizing programs for culturally disadvantaged pupils have already been discussed, for example, the overall school objectives for other pupils. The structure and approach of programs for disadvantaged pupils must be appropriate to their backgrounds, needs, and learning style in terms of content, materials, and methods. The distinction between programs for slow learners and programs for culturally disadvantaged children must be clear.

There are several other considerations. Often, school districts look to other districts for examples of programs. Many of these programs look good on paper, and many are good in practice. Some of the programs that look good on paper, however, have not been evaluated to determine their effectiveness. Therefore, before duplicating or adapting a program of another district, the program should be examined to determine if it has been adequately evaluated.

Secondly, educators must be careful not to design programs or adopt approaches that make disadvantaged children adjust to deprivation or become satisfied with the culture of deprivation. An effective program must make disadvantaged pupils dissatisfied with existing conditions. Satisfaction with deprivation erodes aspirations that are necessary to escape deprivation. One of the outstanding features of the Banneker District program is that *it did not permit the pupils to accept their roles in social tragedy.*

On the other hand, programs must not be so far above the child's level of existence that they fail to touch him. The cultural programs of many districts, in which disadvantaged children are taken to hear symphony concerts or operas, are examples of out-of-touch programs. Still, educators must be careful not to give disadvantaged pupils the same old stuff. The past experiences of failure cry for change. Change, however, must always be based on understanding.

Finally, educators must be careful not to place too much importance on gimmicks—whether they are scheduling devices, new kinds of teaching machines, or elaborate audio-visual machines and aids. *The most important component in any program is the classroom teacher.* All the gimmicks in the world cannot raise achievement by themselves.

Classroom Management

So far, the main focus of this book has been outside the classroom. These outside factors are significant, because they directly affect classroom learning. Thus teachers must understand these factors to be effective. The teaching-learning situation, however, is a classroom with one teacher working with a group of culturally disadvantaged pupils.

The first job of the classroom teacher is to determine the achievement-level of the pupils in his class. No effective instruction can be carried on until this diagnostic job is completed; the teacher must find out what the pupils know to be able to build on that. Part of the diagnosis can be made by informal methods. For example, having each pupil read orally to the teacher gives a rough estimate of reading ability; a simple composition or paragraph can reveal spelling and writing deficiencies; a short discussion can reveal language deficiencies.

Formal methods of diagnosing pupil needs should also be used; there are special tests designed for this purpose. Although the composite score really gives little direction for instruction, the real value of these tests is that they catalog the pupil's deficiencies. In addition, teachers should review the school records of each pupil (cumulative and health records) to determine pupil needs. Past teachers and other school personnel can also be questioned about pupils—this often is the most effective diagnostic procedure. Finally, a comprehensive understanding of culturally disadvantaged pupils (their way of life, their general characteristics, their learning style) is a kind of diagnosis that gives direction to teaching.

Classroom Environment

The classroom environment must be pleasant, stimulating, orderly, and beautiful if it is to be conducive to learning. The classroom may be the only pleasant aspect of the disadvantaged child's physical environment. Since these children often attend the older schools in the district, beautification is difficult. Still, teachers can make an effort to hang attractive pictures, construct eye-catching bulletin boards, and bring in a few plants. In place of the usual institutional shades, brightly colored curtains for the windows can make a big improvement and give the classroom a simple warmth disadvantaged homes often lack.

In the elementary classroom, especially in primary grades, the teacher should label many of the items. Labels should be printed in large letters on tag board or some other stiff, durable paper. These labels help the children become familiar with writing and they increase sight vocabulary. A good exercise for elementary pupils is to have the labels removed at the end of the day as they are spelled out, teaching discrimination between letters. The following morning, they can be replaced as the appropriate objects are named, requiring the pupil to read the word.

A classroom library is another important component of the disadvantaged classroom. The classroom library doesn't have to be elaborate — just a bookcase or table tucked in a corner. Pupils should be permitted to visit the library corner in their spare time. It can be stocked with regular books obtained from the central school library; in addition, teachers can include their old magazines, which otherwise are often discarded. Old magazines can be extremely valuable, especially for older pupils, as no others may be available. A newspaper can be included for the same reason — it doesn't matter if it is a day or two old.

Motivation

Motivation can be defined as "the incentives that initiate and sustain activities leading to particular goals." The task of the classroom teacher is to create conditions that produce incentives. In other words, the classroom teacher must make the student *want to learn*. Pupils may want to learn something in order to satisfy a particular need. Pupils may even be motivated to learn in order to please someone else. The important point is, learning is goal-directed, and pupils must want to reach the goals.

The goals of learning must be presented in terms culturally disadvantaged children understand. Furthermore, the activities to reach these goals must be appropriate for them. An activity to reach a goal often is satisfying in itself, and it gives reinforcement to continue on. In order to motivate his pupils, the teacher must understand them. This will make possible the selection of goals that will produce incentives. Sometimes, pupils themselves can offer goals; then the teacher can organize activities to reach them. When goals are prescribed, as are the overall education objectives, the teacher must select the content and material that arouse the pupils' interest.

Motivation, then, is *creating conditions that cause pupils to want to engage in particular activites for reaching goals.* This is what learning is all about.

Younger children, including younger disadvantaged children, seem to be motivated by their immaturity to learn. In other words, their *lack* of knowledge seems to propel them to acquire more learning. As they grow older, however, they lose this natural incentive. They become apathetic and negative toward learning—they can't be motivated. Their resistance may be explained partly by their consistent past failures. Some children may have experienced failure so often that they come to refuse to participate in learning activites that might produce further failure. Even if the goals are attractive to these pupils, the incentive that must be generated to reach these goals is smothered by expectations of failure. Sometimes the teacher contributes to these expectations of failure by letting his pupils know that he feels they are incapable of learning.

Part of the problem of motivating culturally disadvantaged pupils is to convince them that they can learn. This can be done by creating a success cycle. Some activities can be structured so that the pupils experience success. *Success is necessary to sustain motivation.*

Incentives toward successful achievement may be either extrinsic (lying outside the pupil) or intrinsic (lying inside the pupil). Examples of extrinsic motivation are vocational goals, prestige and status goals, striving for good grades, and learning to please the teacher. Examples of intrinsic motivation are pride in achievement, strengthening of self-confidence and self-concept, and learning to satisfy individual interests.

Most psychologists believe that intrinsic motivation is better because it is more potent and durable and yields greater learning. Intrinsic motivation, however, is more difficult to achieve with culturally disadvantaged children. It would seem, therefore, that if disadvantaged pupils can be motivated to achieve by wanting to please the teacher, identifying with the teacher, or by getting a reward (grades, praise, stars), then the teacher should capitalize on these. After all, the problem is to get the pupils learning. Once they become accustomed to experiencing success through learning, intrinsic motivation can develop.

Classroom Procedures

Lessons planned for culturally disadvantaged children must have built-in flexibility. That is, if the pupils show particular interest in an activity or topic, the teacher should continue with it and get as much mileage out of it as possible. Conversely, if they show little interest, the activity should be changed.

Other factors that affect attention span are radical changes in the weather, departure from regular school routine, and events outside the classroom that excite pupils. All pupils are affected by these factors, but culturally disadvantaged pupils seem to be affected to a greater degree. Lesson plans must take such factors into account.

Culturally disadvantaged pupils feel secure and perform best when an overall routine of lessons is maintained. The teacher should establish a routine early in the semester and let his pupils know that lessons will have a familiar pattern. The teacher can change topics, materials, and activities, but radical or frequent departures from an established routine cause troubles.

Culturally disadvantaged pupils must be given clear, simple directions when assignments are made. Write directions on the chalkboard in easy-to-follow steps, and repeat them until most pupils understand. Pupils who don't understand directions after they have been repeated should receive individual attention after the rest of the class gets started.

Always allow for plenty of time when planning lessons. Slowness is one of the characteristics of disadvantaged children. Close supervision during working periods will discourage them from wasting time. In addition, disadvantaged pupils require constant encouragement to finish an assignment. Positive encouragement will work much more effectively than berating their slowness.

Most lesson assignments should be planned for completion in one period. If assignments are carried over to the following day, much time is wasted in repeating the directions and getting the pupils started again. Also, the high absence rate of disadvantaged children prevents many of them from finishing carried-over assignments.

An unsuitable method often used in classrooms is similar to the recitation method of teaching used back in the days of colonial colleges: the pupils read a textbook, try to memorize information in the textbook, and then try to reproduce the information orally or in writing. This method of teaching is not very effective with any children, and it is particularly ineffective with culturally disadvantaged children.

For this method to be successful, the pupils must be highly motivated by the information in the text, and most textbooks are not very interesting to culturally disadvantaged pupils. Secondly, pupils must read, interpret, and understand information without the help of a mediator. Thirdly, disadvantaged pupils are usually limited in their verbal ability, and the recitation method depends entirely on verbal facility. Finally, the most severe shortcoming of this method is abstractness; it is contrary to the concrete approach required by the learning style of disadvantaged children. Unfortunately, the recitation method is often used with disadvantaged pupils by teachers who are marking time or by teachers unwilling to make the extra effort required.

The lecture method is also ineffective. This method also uses a verbal approach. It requires the pupils to listen to words; it requires speed of interpretation; and it requires focused attention on abstractions. These requirements are contrary to the learning style of disadvantaged children.

The committee method of teaching so popular with teacher-training instructors is another method that is usually ineffective —especially if the class is a heterogeneous group. Working harmoniously with others on an intellectual task is simply not a part of the disadvantaged pupil's background. Committee work requires a high level of cooperation and a democratic spirit. Disadvantaged pupils, on the other hand, are inclined to form groups that are totalitarian in structure. The strong rule the weak. Physical prowess, rather than intellectual leadership, indicates what is to be done and who is to do the "telling." Committee action is likely to be influenced by threat of a punch in the mouth after school, or even by a punch delivered during committee deliberations.

Because disadvantaged pupils lack the intellectual and social skills for effective committee operation, their committees often end up at one or the other extreme: either they are an inactive, uninterested collection of pupils or a brawling, disruptive mob. Of course, after proper preparation, disadvantaged pupils *can* learn to work in committees. This is difficult to achieve, however, because the committee method of teaching bucks the background of cultural deprivation.

Discipline

Discipline is one of the major concerns of the classroom teacher. Many teachers become so occupied with discipline that it becomes an end in itself. Some investigators have estimated that as much as 50 to 80 percent of classroom time is devoted to discipline or methods of controlling and coercing pupils. This is far too much time to devote to any one aspect of teaching, even a fundamental aspect like discipline. The teacher must always remember that discipline is related to all other activities as means to one end — and that end is achievement.

The term *discipline* has many meanings, all of which apply to the classroom situation. One definition is that it is "the imposition of external standards and controls on individual conduct." Standards and controls are necessary in order for children to become socialized; otherwise, they would grow up unprepared to live with others. External standards and controls are also necessary so that children can grow to them — in other words, so that they learn what adult behavior is. Finally, children are emotionally more secure when they are aware of controls. Ideally, external controls gradually are eased as children grow older and develop self-discipline.

The problem with culturally disadvantaged pupils in this regard is that many basic standards and controls are often lacking in their homes, or their standards and controls are different from those of the middle-class culture. When they get to school and meet with middle-class standards and controls, they rebel. But many of these are necessary for learning to take place, and on these the classroom teacher must take an arbitrary stand. This does not mean that discipline must be enforced with an iron hand; it does mean that standards and controls are set, and the reasons for them are related to learning. Frank Riessman stated in an address delivered at the seventeenth annual California Advisory Council on Educational Research, November 12, 1965:

> Everything the teacher says and does in the classroom should be related to learning. He should repeat over and over and over again: "I am here to teach and you are here to learn." This should be expressed in the teacher's every action and should be related to every rule and value. Thus, all rules related to punctuality, aggression, etc., should be strictly oriented toward their usefulness in relation to learning. We can't conduct a class if children fight, come late, walk around, etc.

Riessman's statement implies that pupils must understand the importance of education. The statement is a good general guide for classroom discipline.

Discipline can also mean the amount of order in a classroom. The importance of physical order has been pointed out; it is also important that pupils understand the importance of orderly deportment. Here again, its importance to learning should be made clear.

One of the primary requirements for good discipline is a good instructional program. Pupils are likely to behave themselves if the instructional program interests them and gives them valuable learning experiences. Perhaps the reason for greater discipline problems with disadvantaged pupils lies in an instructional program that is not very meaningful.

Some specific suggestions on discipline for teachers of culturally disadvantaged pupils are listed below.

1. Disadvantaged pupils seem to respond better in a classroom atmosphere that is highly structured—more of a traditional approach than a permissive approach should be used to control them. However, methods must not be unreasonable or overly strict.
2. Never use sarcasm to correct behavior. It sometimes gets immediate results, but it ruins chances for future rapport.
3. Don't use negative criticism. Disadvantaged pupils need constant positive encouragement.
4. Never make damaging remarks or use punishments that may hurt self-concept; teachers should heal self-concept rather than inflict further wounds.
5. Don't make a "big deal" out of little, unimportant incidents. For example, if one pupil swears at another during a moment of anger, don't give him a lecture on the evils of profanity. And don't make a moral case out of fighting. Swearing and fighting are patterns derived from a disadvantaged background, and preaching won't break these patterns. Instead of pontificating, as teachers often do, it's better to tell the pupils to "shut up" or bust up the fight. Then get them moving on their main task—learning.
6. Don't ask individuals to rat on each other. This is contrary to their value system and it even may be dangerous to the informer.
7. Don't punish the entire class for the actions of one individual. The innocent decide that they will get punished anyway, so in the future they, too, disobey.
8. Never back a disadvantaged pupil into a corner. There's only one way he knows to get out of a corner, and that is to fight—either verbally or physically. Many teachers who have been assaulted brought it on themselves by pressing an issue beyond the pupil's retaliation threshold.
9. Avoid physical force. Physical force is the usual way these pupils are controlled at home, and often it is the only way to get them to respond. Physical force, however, should be used in only the most extreme cases—when the district allows it—and *never* with high school students.
10. Be consistent in disciplinary procedures.

11. Make a few rules and stictly enforce them. Avoid making rules that become so numerous and complicated that they and their enforcement block the main task of teaching.

Discipline really results from understanding applied with common sense. Teachers must remember that effective disciplinary procedures will depend on their compatibility with the operant value system of disadvantaged pupils. Thus an understanding of these pupils is essential to good disciplinary procedures.

Human Relations

A part of good discipline is good human relations — the two can't be separated. Discipline implies control and order, but control and order must exist within a framework where each individual is respected and renders respect. To put it simply, human relations is mutual respect and the sustaining of that mutual respect in a social situation.

Human relations is important in any classroom, especially in a classroom of culturally disadvantaged children. These children often feel that they have been rejected by society, and they feel that they lack the respect of people in the dominant culture. Their continuing deprivation reinforces their feelings. In addition, many disadvantaged pupils are members of minority groups, and their membership has given them experiences with racial prejudice.

It is important for the teacher of culturally disadvantaged pupils to first of all establish that *each pupil is an individual to be respected.* If the pupils are members of a minority group, the teacher must also establish his lack of racial prejudice.

Some of the ways in which teachers can communicate respect to pupils have been mentioned previously. For example, taking time out to talk individually to pupils, showing a genuine interest in them and their problems, refraining from making disparaging remarks about them, and treating them as human beings are simple ways to transmit a feeling of respect. Making a sincere effort to teach pupils is perhaps the most effective means of transmitting respect.

Proving the lack of racial prejudice probably depends more on what the teacher does *not* say or do than what he does. For example, telling a group of black pupils: "Some of my best friends are Negroes"; or telling a group of Mexican-American pupils: "Mexican-American babies are so cute, I just *love* them!" will be certain to arouse suspicion. The adage about protesting too loudly in order to hide something has been reinforced in the area of racial prejudice many times for minority pupils.

Instead, teachers should let their actions show that they are not prejudiced. Actions *do* speak louder than words in this case, and minority pupils are much more practiced at detecting prejudice than teachers are in trying to explain a lack of it or in hiding it. The best way to prove the lack of racial prejudice is to be one's self—to use common sense and follow suggestions for good human relations.

This, of course, assumes a lack of prejudice. *If a teacher is prejudiced, then he shouldn't teach minority pupils.* Contact with minority pupils is likely to reinforce the prejudiced teacher's attitudes rather than change them, because the prejudiced person usually sees only what he is looking for.

Teachers of minority pupils should also learn the names and labels that minority group members find offensive. The common offensive labels are well known; however, there are others that a teacher might use inadvertently. Black pupils object to being referred to as "you people" or "your kind," and Appalachian pupils object to the term *hillbilly*; even the label *Puerto Rican* can be offensive to some Puerto Rican pupils (some prefer *Hispano*). Culturally disadvantaged pupils even object to the term *culturally disadvantaged*. In general, minority groups object to all labels that have a connotation of group deprivation.

While a teacher may not be aware of all the group labels that offend minority pupils, he is aware of individual personal names. The pupil's personal name, rather than any nickname, should be used whether the disadvantaged pupil is black, Mexican-American, Appalachian, Puerto Rican, or American Indian. Often, persons of the dominant culture use a nickname to indicate warmth and friendliness. However, many disadvantaged pupils interpret the use of a nickname as an attempt to downgrade them. Maybe their names are all they have as an identity label that holds dignity.

If a pupil's name is James, call him James, not Jim; if his name is William, don't call him Bill. A personal name is the primary identification label of an individual, and to change it or dilute it to a nickname is to dilute that person's dignity. Of course, nicknames can be used after the teacher knows a pupil and establishes a warm relationship with him. Never use a nickname during the initial stages of an acquaintance; make sure the pupil's permission is granted, either explicitly or by implication, before using it.

Another gesture that persons of the dominant culture often make to communicate positive feelings for another person, particularly a young person, is to touch the person while talking (usually, the gesture is laying a friendly hand on the younger person's shoulder). Many culturally disadvantaged pupils don't interpret this as a positive gesture, especially during a talk over some difficulty. Instead, they may interpret such contact during a stress period as aggression, and they usually meet aggression with aggression.

The teacher should also avoid communicating a "better than thou" attitude. Contrasting the pupils' behavior with the teacher's in terms that make their way inferior is not an effective way to change behavior. Some teachers constantly remind disadvantaged pupils that they are inferior because they don't act like the teacher or other people of the dominant culture. Instead, the teacher should merely point out the *advantages* of adopting a particular pattern. For example, instead of "knocking" nonstandard language, the teacher should accept the pupil's language and recognize that that language system works in particular situations. The advantages of standard English in specific situations should be pointed out—the time or situation when a particular pattern or way of doing something is most effective should be made clear. This is clearly preferable to telling pupils that their language is inferior and the teacher's language is better.

Summary of Main Points

1. The differences between groups of culturally disadvantaged pupils, and between culturally disadvantaged pupils and other pupils, are educationally significant.

2. Research plays a primary role in answering the question "How can culturally disadvantaged pupils be educated?"

3. Classroom teachers must become increasingly involved in research on educating culturally disadvantaged pupils and must keep abreast of this research.

4. Culturally disadvantaged pupils in schools with small disadvantaged populations are sometimes mistakenly classified as ordinary slow learners.

5. Pupils who are nonachievers because of cultural deprivation are a special type of slow learner.

6. Teachers must increase their understanding of their disadvantaged pupils through increased contact with the disadvantaged community.

7. The school should concentrate on influencing disadvantaged parents in those areas that directly affect the classroom achievement of their children.

8. Parents of culturally disadvantaged pupils also are culturally disadvantaged. The description of the pupils fits the parents as well.

9. Most programs for culturally disadvantaged pupils are of two types: compensatory education and education programs that use the pupil's background as a take-off point for learning.

10. Programs for culturally disadvantaged pupils must aim for the overall objectives of the curriculum, but change in structure and approach.

11. Programs for culturally disadvantaged pupils must not adjust them to their deprivation.

12. The classroom must provide a positive environment.

13. Lesson plans for teaching culturally disadvantaged pupils must have a built-in flexibility.

14. Effective disciplinary procedures depend on their compatibility with the operant value system of culturally disadvantaged pupils.

Questions for Discussion

1. What are some of the ways teachers can contribute to the research effort?

2. Examine the questions posed for research, and discuss possible answers to the questions. Discuss possible ways these questions can be answered through research.

3. Discuss the differences between slow learners who do not achieve because of limited innate mental capacity and slow learners who do not achieve because of cultural deprivation. What are the similarities?

4. What adjustments are needed in curriculum, methods, and materials for the latter group? How will these adjustments differ from the adjustments needed for ordinary slow learners?

5. Suggest additional ways that teachers can find out about culturally disadvantaged pupils.

6. Are culturally disadvantaged pupils' chances for achievement increased if their parents are involved in school activities? What are some ways to involve the parents?

7. Discuss ways the PTA can be made more attractive to disadvantaged parents.

8. What kind of report card could best communicate pupil progress to disadvantaged parents?

9. Discuss ways ESEA Title I funds can be used in your school or district to educate culturally disadvantaged pupils.

10. Examine a few programs for culturally disadvantaged pupils in your school or district to determine if the emphasis is on compensatory education or content, methods, and materials appropriate to the pupil's background.

11. Examine a few programs for culturally disadvantaged pupils in your school or district and determine if these programs are likely to help culturally disadvantaged pupils attain the overall educational objectives of the district.

12. Discuss the importance of diagnosis before instruction. What other ways can be used for diagnosis?

Bibliography

Ausubel, David P. "A New Look at Classroom Discipline," *Phi Delta Kappan,* Vol. XLIII (October 1961).

Baltimore City Public Schools. Early School Admission Project. *Promising Practices from the Projects for the Culturally Deprived.* Chicago: Research Council of the Great Cities School Improvement Program, April 1964.

Beck, John M., and Saxe, Richard W. *Teaching the Culturally Disadvantaged Pupil.* Springfield, Ill.: Charles C. Thomas, 1966.

Berry, Brewton. *Race and Ethnic Relations.* Boston: Houghton Mifflin, 1958.

Bloom, Benjamin S., et al. *Compensatory Education for Cultural Deprivation.* New York: Holt, Rinehart & Winston, 1965.

Bloom, Benjamin, ed. *Research Problems of Education and Cultural Deprivation.* Chicago: Research Conference on Education and Cultural Deprivation, 1965.

Clark, Kenneth B. *Dark Ghetto.* New York: Harper & Row, 1965.

Cody, William S., Jr. "Control and Resistance in a Slum School," *The Elementary School Journal,* 67:1–7 (October 1966).

Conant, James B. *Slums and Suburbs.* New York: McGraw, 1961.

Crosby, Muriel E. *An Adventure in Human Relations.* Chicago: Follett, 1965.

Cunningham, Ruth, et al. *Understanding Group Behavior of Boys and Girls.* New York: Teachers College Press, 1951.

Daugherty, Louise G. "Working with Disadvantaged Parents," *National Education Association Journal.* 52:18–20 (December 1963).

Dean, John P., and Rosen, Alex. *A Manual of Intergroup Relations.* Chicago: Univ. of Chicago Press, 1955.

Friggens, Paul. "Sam Shepard's Faith," *The PTA Magazine,* 58:18–20 (March 1964).

Goodman, Paul. *Compulsory Mis-Education.* New York: Random House, 1962.

Gordon, Edmund W., and Wilkerson, Doxey A. *Compensatory Education for the Disadvantaged.* New York: College Entrance Examination Board, 1966.

Gottlieb, D. "Teaching and Students: The Views of Negro and White Teachers, *Sociology Education,* 37:345–53.

Howe, Harold. "Growth and Growing Pains," *Saturday Review,* 68:20 (December 17, 1966).

Hunt, J. McV. "Experience and the Development of Motivation: Some Reinterpretations," *Child Development,* 31:489–504 (1960).

CHAPTER 6

IMPROVING LANGUAGE SKILLS: SPEECH

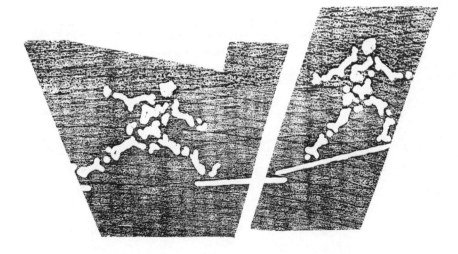

6

What Is Language?

Teaching Standard English to Blacks and Appalachians

The Language Problem of Mexican-Americans

This chapter is concerned with one more area in which disadvantaged pupils are handicapped. Most culturally disadvantaged groups speak nonstandard varieties of English. This language handicap is especially crucial because of the restrictions it imposes on academic achievement, vocational opportunity, and social advancement.

Language — specifically, standard English — is one of the keys to unlock the shackles of deprivation. That is, if culturally disadvantaged pupils acquire the ability to speak standard English, their chances for success are increased. Of course, acquiring the ability to speak standard English does not ensure success for disadvantaged pupils — they also have to acquire other middle-class patterns; but the ability to speak standard English is one of the essentials for success.

The role of the school in helping culturally disadvantaged pupils learn standard English is obvious. First of all, language is one area in which the school can affect behavioral changes. Secondly, behavioral changes in the area of language are essential for academic success. Thus teaching culturally disadvantaged pupils standard English is really one of the most important tasks of the school.

What is standard English? It is not the language of Dick and Jane. It is not the language of the pedantic English textbooks used at higher levels of education. And it certainly isn't the stuffy English of dowagers in any city's "four hundred." Instead, standard English is that English ". . . used to carry on the important affairs of our country," as Charles Fries, the noted linguist, has stated. In other words, standard English is that language system that is acceptable and understood by the vast majority of the people in our society, even those who may speak a nonstandard variety of English. It is the "universal dialect" of our society. It is the English spoken by most government officials, TV announcers, and educated people. More importantly, it is the language of the classroom.

What Is Language?

Language can be defined as "systematic noises people make with their vocal chords, and which carry meaning." The most important word in this definition is *systematic*. The speech sounds people make are not disorganized or random noises that serve only to stimulate other people's hearing—like the roar of traffic or the rustle of leaves. Instead, these noises stimulate other people's intellects and emotions as well, causing them to understand the ideas and feelings of the person making the noises. In other words, these noises *communicate*. A group of people making the same or nearly the same systematic noises are speaking the same language, and they can communicate with each other. Communication is adversely affected to the degree that certain noises differ from the system of the group; and this, in a nutshell, is the language problem of culturally disadvantaged pupils.

In addition, when these noises are symbolically represented in the form of writing, communication occurs through the process of reading. The problem of understanding this written communication is compounded for culturally disadvantaged pupils because they are required to derive meaning from symbols that stand for a variety of the language not quite the same in sound, grammar, and vocabulary as their own.

Even though the varieties of English spoken by the culturally disadvantaged are nonstandard, they are systematic. When culturally disadvantaged pupils try to learn standard English, their language system interferes with the standard system and handicaps learning. These interferences can be dialect interferences, as in the case of many black and Appalachian pupils, or native language interferences, as in the case of Mexican-Americans or Puerto Ricans. The interference is caused by the person imposing the sound and grammatical system of his own language on the language to be learned.

Many teachers are reluctant to recognize or admit that nonstandard English has its own rules of grammar. Instead, they choose to consider nonstandard English as *incorrect* English. A few teachers even look on nonstandard English as an inherent evil that reflects the quality of the speaker. In other words, "bad language, bad people." This is absurd because the particular language system a person uses has nothing to do with the worth and dignity of that person. Language is learned—it is not inherent, or genetically determined. Further, the language one learns is accidental. The fact that some people in our society do actually equate nonstandard English with negative personality qualities is one more reason for the necessity of the culturally disadvantaged student being taught standard English.

In summary, the English of the culturally disadvantaged is sometimes thought of as an inferior brand of standard English, or as being at one end of a linguistic continuum that stretches from incorrect to correct. Throughout this chapter, the English systems of culturally disadvantaged pupils are viewed as related to *but distinct from* standard English.

Should this view be unacceptable, perhaps the following experiment will be helpful. Select from a pupil's speech one pronunciation or grammatical item that deviates from standard English and try to incorporate this item into your speech. For example, try to incorporate the sound many Mexican-American pupils say for the sound represented in English spelling by the letters *ch*; or the particular conjugation of the verb *to be* that is used by many black pupils.

This experiment will illustrate the systematic nature of nonstandard English and the concept of interference of one language system with another. It will demonstrate the nature of the difficulty which speakers of a nonstandard variety of English have in learning standard English.

Interference

The school's attitude toward the language of its culturally disadvantaged pupils makes a great deal of difference in how language instruction is conducted. If the school holds with the concept of inferior language (this is more traditional and common), then language instruction takes the form of correcting pupils every time their English differs from standard English. For example, telling a pupil that he can't say *them boys* for *those boys* or *mouf* for *mouth* doesn't do a bit of good if in his language system *them* is a plural marker before nouns, and the final sound in *mouth* is /f/. (He may not even be able to hear the final sound in *mouth*.)

The proof that the traditional point of view causes ineffective language instruction for most culturally disadvantaged pupils is that many leave school after twelve years still speaking the nonstandard variety they spoke when they entered. (In fact, they often speak the nonstandard variety even better on leaving than they did when they entered, for when they were younger they were still learning the language of their group, and sometimes made mistakes.) In those instances where disadvantaged pupils did acquire standard English by the time they left school, the reasons for their success may be due as much to other factors as to school instruction.

If the school takes a different attitude—that the language of culturally disadvantaged pupils systematically interferes with their learning standard English—then instruction is based on the conflicts between the language of the subculture and standard English. For example, pupils who say "them boys" are shown the contrast between the way their language system uses plural markers before nouns and the way standard English uses plural markers. They are shown that *them boys* is equivalent to *those boys*. This contrast is followed by oral drill to establish the standard English pattern.

If pupils say *mouf* for *mouth* they are first taught to discriminate between the ending sound of *mouth* and the ending sound of *mouf*. Next, they are given extensive oral drills for reproducing the ending sound of *mouth*.

The instructional approach of the second point of view bases language instruction on the language of the pupils and the interferences, or conflicts, caused by their language. Unfortunately, not many language programs are conducted with this attitude. This kind of language instruction is consistent with the best practices for teaching a second language. Indeed, standard English can be treated almost like a foreign language in programs for culturally disadvantaged pupils.

Children begin to learn language long before they enter school. A child born into middle-class culture learns the language of middle-class culture; a child born into a disadvantaged subculture or a non-native culture learns the language of his culture. The child's first language teachers are his parents. If the parents speak a nonstandard variety of English, the child necessarily learns this as his language.

The culture into which the child was born continues to reinforce its particular language system in many ways. The most obvious reinforcement comes from exclusively hearing the language of one particular culture. When there is little contact with persons outside the culture, the child has little opportunity for learning any other language. This lack of opportunity for experiencing the language system of middle-class culture is severely penalizing.

In addition, children who grow up in a disadvantaged culture will have experiences that influence their language development in a way that does not fit the middle-class curriculum. At the same time, they lack many of the experiences that positively influence language. These are the experiences necessary for the concept development on which the middle-class curriculum is based.

Qualitative Differences

In addition to the difference in sound, grammar, and vocabulary between standard and nonstandard English, there is also a *qualitative* difference. Qualitative difference does not mean that one language system is inherently better than the other. What it does mean is that one language system (standard English) functions better in the dominant culture and, specifically, in the curriculum of the school. Some researchers have pointed out that the qualitative difference between standard and nonstandard English is most pronounced in vocabulary. Culturally disadvantaged pupils usually lack words that show fine distinctions within categories; they lack synonyms. Furthermore, they often use a great many cant or slang words that are not common outside their own cultural group. Thus many of the words they use among themselves are not very useful with others or in the classroom.

However, the qualitative difference between the vocabulary of standard and nonstandard English is much more significant than a lack of words or different and fewer words within conceptual areas. Vocabulary is an outgrowth of experience; the qualitative difference in vocabulary is a reflection of a qualitative difference in experience. Stated another way, *experiences are the building blocks of concepts, and words are the symbols of concepts.* If children lack experiences, their conceptual development and vocabulary will be restricted; or if they have different experiences, their conceptual development and vocabulary will not be the same as that of others. In short, vocabulary reflects culture. If the culture is disadvantaged, then the vocabulary it generates also will be disadvantaged.

(It is interesting to note that whatever is important or common in a culture will be expressed. Thus disadvantaged children have as many or even more words for certain ideas as middle-class children. For example, disadvantaged children have many words related to aggression. Within every disadvantaged group there is a large vocabulary on fighting and the kinds of blows delivered during fighting and in anger.)

The Handicap of Nonstandard English

Nonstandard language plays a significant deterrent role in learning to read. Of course, the culturally disadvantaged student's language system is not the only thing that handicaps him in learning to read. His impoverished experiential background, his inefficient learning style, his different value system, the inappropriateness of textbook content to his interests and background, and the general orientation and structure of the curriculum are other factors. Nonstandard language, however, is probably the most significant.

When a culturally disadvantaged pupil attempts to learn to read, his language system interferes with the language of the reading text. This is essentially the same difficulty encountered in teaching disadvantaged pupils to speak standard English and to understand the structure of standard English. The conflict in reading occurs between the vocabulary, sound, and grammar of standard and nonstandard English.

Many of the words in textbooks are not a part of the vocabulary of culturally disadvantaged children, and it is difficult for them to read these words. Teaching children to read words they already have in their listening vocabulary is simpler than teaching them to read words they have never heard before. Thus increasing the vocabulary of culturally disadvantaged children — specifically, giving them a variety of experiences that develop conceptual growth and vocabulary — should be stressed more than formal reading instruction.

This suggests that reading instruction for disadvantaged pupils should be delayed until after they have finished the primary grades. The emphasis in the primary grades could then be placed exclusively on language instruction. This appears to be a sound proposal from two viewpoints. First of all, there is no logical or practical reason why a first, second, or third grader must know how to read. A child *can't* read anything very well until he adequately understands the language of the reading material. Secondly, culturally disadvantaged pupils start school far behind average pupils and most of them never catch up, particularly in reading.

In fact, what usually happens is that the achievement gap between them and middle-class pupils grows wider as grade level increases. Delaying reading instruction until after the primary grades increases this gap at the beginning of the school career, but gives a much better chance of closing the gap in later grades — something that few culturally disadvantaged pupils accomplish, in spite of all the remedial reading-improvement programs designed for this purpose.

The sound system of nonstandard English also handicaps the culturally disadvantaged pupil in learning to read. For example, a child may not be able to hear certain sounds in some words because his particular language system does not contain these sounds in the manner in which they occur in standard English. He must contend with these, as well as with those sounds that are inaccurately represented by the English alphabet. For example, some black pupils say *rat*, the teacher says *rite*, and the textbook represents the teacher's standard pronunciation with *right*. In this case the pupils are dealing with one word represented three different ways.

Many disadvantaged pupils speak a variety of English that omits the sounds represented by consonants at the ends of words. This causes difficulty in reading by increasing the number of homonyms. For instance, *past,* when pronounced *pas* by a culturally disadvantaged pupil, would seem identical with *pass*. Also, the inflectional signals for meaning are missed by the disadvantaged reader. For example, the pupils who speak a dialect may read the sentence "We walked to school" as "We *walk* to school." The failure to hear and read preterit endings changes the tense of the sentence and gives an unintended meaning to the sentence.

Nonstandard speakers impose the grammar of their language system on reading. That is, they often translate reading into their particular system, and meaning may be confused in the translation. Many pupils who speak a dialect of English may read the sentence "We have taken a walk" as "We taken a walk." At first glance, it seems as if only the word *have* is omitted — not too serious an error. However, if these pupils use the past participle form of *take (taken)* for the past tense form *(took)* then the sentence takes the meaning of "We took a walk."

Of course, interference from nonstandard English also occurs when disadvantaged pupils attempt to express their ideas in writing. Their sound and grammar system is reflected in their writing and it causes difficulty for those who read it.

The importance of understanding the language systems of culturally disadvantaged pupils cannot be stressed too much. This understanding increases the teacher's effectiveness in reading and language instruction by helping him to distinguish between mistakes and interference. For instance, reading errors caused by nonstandard interference are difficult to detect unless a teacher knows the language system of his pupils. A teacher who is unfamiliar with his pupils' language system may confuse simple reading mistakes with pronunciation and grammatical interferences. Understanding the pupil's language system also helps a teacher to develop better communication.

The negative effect of nonstandard language on academic achievement, especially in reading, also affects vocational opportunity. Without education, chances for vocational and economic advancement are limited. Also, nonstandard language imposes a limit on the kinds of jobs disadvantaged pupils may obtain after they leave school. People who speak a nonstandard variety of English find it difficult to get jobs requiring verbal contact with the general public, especially if the contact requires extensive use of the telephone. The telephone amplifies the difficulty of understanding a nonstandard variety of English.

If vocational opportunities are restricted, then chances for social advancement are restricted, because low-paying jobs can't support a middle-class way of life. In addition, many individuals in the dominant culture have a negative reaction to nonstandard speech. People who speak a nonstandard variety of English may be rejected by members of the dominant culture on the basis of language alone. This means that even if a culturally disadvantaged individual satisfies all the prerequisites for entering and being accepted into the dominant culture, he still may be rejected on the basis of his nonstandard language.

The Language Program

While teaching culturally disadvantaged pupils standard English is necessary for academic, vocational, and social success, we have seen that the difficulties in so doing are enormous. The interference of their language system with the system of standard English is a *structural* interference. Another kind of interference contributes to the problem because culturally disadvantaged pupils may not recognize the need or have the desire to learn standard English. This is a *functional* interference.

Many of these pupils cannot realize any advantage in learning standard English. From their point of view, they are right. Standard English is a language system that is not functional in their cultural environment. Learning standard English sets them off from their primary group and identifies them with a group that has rejected them. In her book *Improving Patterns of Language Usage*, Ruth I. Golden reports that black high school pupils won't speak standard English because they fear that their friends and family wouldn't understand them and that their friends and family would consider them "uppity."

In spite of these *structural* and *functional* interferences, speakers of nonstandard English must be taught standard English. There is little the school can do to eliminate functional interference. To overcome functional interference will require basic changes in the attitude of society toward culturally disadvantaged people. Society must stop rejecting them. Also, the culturally disadvantaged population must be given greater opportunity to participate in the dominant culture—or, at least, to *know that the opportunity exists if they are prepared to meet it.* In this way they will accept the necessity for learning standard English. Greater participation will also increase meaningful contact with standard English speakers, and this kind of contact will reinforce classroom language instruction.

Fortunately, the schools can deal effectively with structural interference. All that is required is a change in attitude toward nonstandard language. Essentially, the school must quit trying to teach disadvantaged pupils standard English while ignoring the influences of their language on the learning process.

The language program for culturally disadvantaged pupils does not vary in sequence from the language program for middle-class pupils; it should, however, vary in the time spent on certain steps in the sequence and in the instructional approach. The increase in time should be both horizontal (more time within a grade level) and vertical (more grade levels for some steps). Briefly, the sequence of the language program is: understanding spoken English; speaking one's own language; and reading, writing, and speaking standard English.

In the primary grades, the emphasis in language should be on encouraging children to use their own language system, even if that language system is nonstandard. For culturally disadvantaged primary pupils, this means that the language program should include many activities that elicit verbal responses. Some appropriate activities are working with puppets, playing the roles of familiar people, and taking field trips (any excursions outside the classroom). The purpose of these activities is to get the pupils to *talk*.

Another purpose of these activities for primary children is to get them to *think with their own language and formulate concepts in their own language*. After they have gained concepts using their own language system, they can use them as a foundation for further learning in later grades. (When formal language instruction is introduced too early, before the children have learned to use their own language system, standard English confuses the children and prevents the formation of necessary concepts for further learning.)

In the middle grades, the emphasis in language should be on helping the child discriminate between the sound systems of his own language and those of standard English. The language program in the middle grades should include many listening activities that require the child to hear final consonant clusters, beginning and medial sounds, and inflectional endings. Furthermore, these listening exercises should be designed to focus attention on the points of interference between the child's language system and standard English.

For example, if the child substitutes a /d/ sound for the sound at the beginning of words like *that, the,* and *this,* he should be given listening exercises that require him to distinguish between the beginning sound of *Dan, dish, doze,* and the beginning sounds of *than, this* and *those*. (The tape recorder is useful for this kind of activity.) The emphasis in the middle grades should be on listening, because the pupil must *hear* the sounds of standard English before he can *speak* them.

In the upper grades of elementary school and in the secondary school, the language emphasis should be on helping pupils speak standard English. The focus on sound discrimination between their language and standard English should continue; in addition, the grammatical interferences between the two language systems should be dealt with.

For example, many black children do not use the ending sound on verbs in the third person singular, present tense ("he *go* to the store" — "She *talk* too much"). They must be shown the difference between the way they use verbs in the third person singular present tense and the way standard English uses these verbs. After they can tell this difference, they should be given practice and drill in using the standard English verb patterns. Many of the methods for teaching English as a second language can be used at the upper elementary and secondary levels.

The emphasis, then, in the language program for culturally disadvantaged pupils in the upper grades, should focus on the sound and grammar interferences between their language and standard English. (Functional interferences also should be dealt with in the upper grades, particularly in the secondary grades; pupils should be made aware of the advantages of learning standard English.)

The emphasis in language instruction at each grade level (primary, middle, and upper) is the same for all culturally disadvantaged pupils. The approach in teaching standard English, however, will vary according to their particular linguistic backgrounds. Many culturally disadvantaged Mexican-American and Puerto Rican pupils have difficulty learning standard English because of native language interferences. Thus the approach their language program takes should be similar to that of teaching English as a second language. They might also be given a remedial program to help them overcome native-language interferences.

Many culturally disadvantaged black and Appalachian pupils speak a nonstandard dialect of English. Because they rely on this language system to communicate with others in their primary environment, they do not often give it up. Standard English should be taught to them as an alternate dialect to be used in appropriate situations. In the past, the school has given the same language program to *all* pupils. This is one reason why so many pupils leave school still speaking the nonstandard variety of English they spoke when they entered.

Teaching Standard English to Blacks and Appalachians

What is Dialect?

Most culturally disadvantaged pupils speak some form of non-standard English. From one cultural group to another, however, the nature of the language handicap varies greatly. The specific language problem of black and Appalachian pupils is that they speak a nonstandard dialect.

A *dialect* is "a variety of language that differs in sound, grammar, and vocabulary from that variety of the language that is considered standard." There are a number of dialects in the United States—for example, New England, Southeastern, and Midlands. These are geographical dialects, varieties of English spoken by most people in a particular area of the country. There are also social dialects. Social dialects are varieties of English spoken by a particular ethnic class or social class within the population. Although these are useful terms, no clean distinction can be made between a geographical dialect and a social dialect. (Obviously, the variety of language spoken by persons belonging to a particular social class is influenced by the variety of language considered standard for a particular geographic area.)

The differences between American dialects are not great. In some countries the dialects of the national language are so different in sound, grammar, and vocabulary that communication between speakers of various dialects is extremely difficult. Italian and Chinese both have dialects so different from each other that they would seem to be different languages. Fortunately, this is not the case in the United States. Speakers of various American dialects can understand each other. Culturally disadvantaged blacks and Appalachians can communicate with speakers of standard English, although communication is difficult and their dialects often cause negative reactions in listeners.

Standard English is a kind of universal dialect that can be understood by all speakers of English, whatever their dialect. Pupils who speak a nonstandard dialect understand English much better than their own speech indicates—that is, their understanding of standard English is not as limited as their ability to speak it. Culturally disadvantaged pupils receive practice in listening to standard English from school, radio, television, and movies, as well as from personal contact with speakers of standard English.

It is interesting to note that speakers of nonstandard dialects can understand standard English much better than speakers of standard English can understand nonstandard dialects. The old stereotype of the head-scratching, foot-shuffling black probably sprang from the frustration he experienced in trying to make the Caucasian listener understand him.

The Development of Dialect

The black dialect and the Appalachian dialect developed out of the same factors: the early settlement history of the group, the population migrations, and physical and social barriers that isolated the groups. Black people spoke many languages when they first came to this country; slaves were taken from many different African cultures. The foreign languages they spoke undoubtedly interfered with their efforts to learn English, and slavery did not offer the best learning conditions. The social isolation built into slavery reinforced the nonstandard language patterns that inevitably develop when speakers of another language try to learn English. Furthermore, the slaves probably did not have good language models — there is no evidence that the overseers spoke standard English.

Since most blacks lived in the South until the time of Civil War, the dialect they developed resembled the dialect spoken by the dominant culture in the South. When they migrated to the North they brought their southern dialect with them. Continued social segregation has caused them to retain their dialect, so that blacks in northern ghettos speak a dialect more like the standard dialect in the South than the standard dialect in the North.

This pattern of social isolation causing the development of the dialect and perpetuating it applies also to continued segregation of the Appalachian group. Mountains and rural spaciousness have acted as physical barriers to cut off Appalachians from the dominant culture and reinforce their acquired dialect. When a member of this group leaves that geographic area and migrates to a northern city, he tends to lose his dialect more quickly than does a black because he does not experience such stringent social isolation.

Is There a Black Dialect?

The dialects spoken by many black and Appalachian pupils are not the same, although many of the same nonstandard items are found in the language systems of both groups. Some people question whether blacks speak a distinct dialect, or whether the dialect they speak is just a general lower-class dialect spoken by all lower-class people in the South. There is quite a lively controversy on this question among linguists. Many black people also oppose the view that blacks speak a distinct dialect. This opposition on the part of blacks, especially those who are active in the civil rights movement, is not surprising: *If blacks speak a distinct dialect, this is one more mark of difference that can retard assimilation.*

Some reject the idea of a black dialect because they equate anything identifiably "black" as something negative. Their reaction, too, is understandable, because things "black" have caused their alienation from the dominant culture. On the other hand, the more militant blacks hold that there is a black dialect, and they take pride in its existence. Their point of view results from the newly found identity that has grown out of the civil rights struggle. These people, understandably, tend to accentuate black traits.

The case for a black dialect is supported by research conducted at the Center for Applied Linguistics in Washington. This research indicates that the variety of English spoken by many blacks does differ from other varieties of American English. William Stewart, the originator of the Urban Language Study (a study concerning the speech of black children in Washington, D.C.), has definitely concluded that there is a black dialect. Furthermore, research suggests that the dialect is relatively uniform among culturally disadvantaged blacks throughout the United States, and that it differs from comparable nonstandard dialects spoken by other (e.g. white) groups.[1]

Research on the speech of black people in Harlem conducted at Columbia University by William Labov reached similar conclusions: ". . . many features of pronunciation, grammar and lexicon are closely associated with Negro speakers—so closely as to identify the great majority of Negro people in Northern cities by their speech alone."[2] Research conducted by other investigators has reached similar conclusions. The fact remains that many of the nonstandard features found in the speech of disadvantaged blacks are also found in the speech of lower-class whites in the South. Even if there is *not* a variety of English spoken exclusively by blacks, the great majority of culturally disadvantaged blacks do speak a nonstandard variety of English, and this nonstandard dialect has been labeled by linguists the "nonstandard Negro dialect."

---

1. William Stewart, "Observations on the Problems of Defining Negro Dialect," (mimeographed paper published by the Center of Applied Linguistics, Washington, D.C., April 1966).

2. William Labov, "Some Sources of Reading Problems for Negro Speakers of Nonstandard English," (paper read at the NCTE Spring Institute on New Directions in Elementary English, Chicago, March 1966).

Characteristics of the Black Dialect

Features of the nonstandard black dialect that deviate from standard English and systematically interfere with the efforts of black pupils in learning standard English or reading standard English have been isolated. Many of these features are found in the speech of Appalachian pupils and other speakers of nonstandard dialects, and not *all* of the features are found in the speech of every black pupil. Here are some of the most frequently encountered sound and grammatical features.

Simplification of final consonant clusters. The last consonant sound is often omitted in words ending in consonant clusters. For example, *hold — hol; rift — rif; past — pas; disk — dis.* Leaving off the final consonant creates a great many more homonyms in the speech of black pupils than there are in the speech of standard English speakers.

In addition, leaving off final consonant sounds causes black pupils to form plurals of some words in a nonstandard way; for example, *desks — desses; tests — tesses.* (Note how the plural formation follows the system of formulating plurals of words in standard English: for words ending in the same sound as the nonstandard *tes (test)* or *des (desk),* add another syllable *(es)* for plurals.)

R-lessness. The final sound represented in writing by the letter *r* is often dropped. Words like *door, store, floor,* and *four* are pronounced as if they were the words *dough, stow, flow,* and *foe.* This also creates many homonyms in black speech. The *r-* sound is sometimes omitted when it occurs in the medial position. *L-lessness.* The final sound represented in writing by the letter *l* is often dropped. Words like *tool* and *pail* are pronounced like the words *too* and *pay.* This sound is sometimes omitted when it occurs in the medial position.

Substitution of the sound represented in writing by the letter d for the sound represented in writing by the letters th at the beginnings of words. Words like *this, that, those, the* are pronounced as if they are spelled *dis, dat, dose, da* (this substitution occurs with the voiced sound — vocal chords vibrating — represented in writing by the letters *th*).

Substitution of the terminal sound represented in writing by the letter f for the sound represented in writing by the letters th. Words like *with, mouth, path* are pronounced as if they are spelled *wif, mouf, paf.* (The plurals of these words are *moufs* and *pafs.*) When the *th* sound occurs in the medial position, the sound represented in writing by the letter *v* is sometimes substituted *(mother — mover; brother — brover).*

Differences in individual words. For example, the words *credit, ask, children,* and *whip* are pronounced as if they were spelled *credick, ax, chilerun,* and *whup.* There are many other words that are pronounced differently from their standard English pronunciation.

Substitution of they *for* their. The word *they* is often used in place of the word *their.* For example, the sentence "They left *their* books in the locker" becomes "They left *they* books in the locker."

Substitution of them *for* those. The word *them* is often used in place of the word *those.* For example, the sentence "Give me *those* books" becomes "Give me *them* books." The word *them* is often used as a plural marker. *"Them books* in the locker." (The verb *are* is omitted.)

Addition of a plural sound (represented by the letter s *in writ-standard plurals) to irregular plurals.* The plurals of *child, man, woman,* and *foot* become *childrens, mens, womens,* and *feets.* Words that form irregular plurals like *wife, knife, wolf,* and *loaf* are pronounced in their plural forms as *wifes, knifes, wolfs,* and *loafs.*

Double negative. Sentences like "I don't have a pencil" or "None of the boys have pencils" become "I *don't* have *no* pencil" and *"Don't* none of them boys have *no* pencils."

Double subjects. Sentences like "My brother is a baby" and "That car lost its brakes" are "My brother *he* a baby" and "That car *it* lost its brakes."

Omission of the agreement sound for third person singular present tense verbs. This omission is one of the most frequent features of the Negro dialect. Sentences like "He walks the dog everyday" and "My father goes to work on the bus" are "He walk the dog everyday" and "My father go to work on the bus."

Addition of the sound represented in writing by the letter s *to third person plural present tense verbs when the subject is* they. Sentences like "They walk the dog every day" and "They look nice in their new clothes" become "They *walks* the dog every day" and "They *looks* nice in they new clothes." (Sometimes, the sound represented in writing by the letter *s* is added to first person singular and plural present tense verbs: "I walks" and "We walks.")

Dropping inflectional endings. This feature is especially marked for the preterit form represented by the letters *-ed* in writing. *Walked* becomes *walk.*

Reversal of the past-tense and past-participle forms of some irregular verbs. The past-participle forms of irregular verbs are used for the simple past tense. For example, the sentences "My father took a bus to work this morning" and "He went to the store" become "My father *taken* a bus to work this morning" and "He *gone* to the store."

The past-tense form instead of the past-participle form of some irregular verbs is used in the present perfect tense. For example, "My father has taken a bus" and "He has gone to the store" become "My father *have took* a bus" and "He *have went* to the store."

Other irregular verbs that are reversed in this manner are: *write, see, do, run.* (Some irregular verbs have the preterit ending sound represented in writing by the letter *-ed* added to their base forms in the past and present perfect tenses: *throwed* and *have throwed* instead of *threw* and *have thrown; knowed* and *have knowed* instead of *knew* and *have known.*)

The word done *sometimes substituted for* have *in present perfect tense.* Sentences like "I have walked to school" and "I done gone to school." Often, the substitution of *done* for *have* makes a statement emphatic.

Nonstandard use of the verb to be. The differences in the use of the forms of *to be* are so great in the Negro dialect that it is impossible to cover them all with one heading. This verb, *to be,* is the one most deviant feature from standard English in the speech of many Negroes. Some of the most outstanding deviations are:

- *Present and present progressive tense.* The standard form of *to be* is omitted in sentences like "He is going" and "Mary is running" ("He going" and "Mary running"). It is also omitted in sentences like "He is busy" and "He is here" ("He busy" and "He here").
  The sentence "He busy" means "He is busy *at this moment*"; the sentence "He here" means "He is here *at this moment.*" To show that someone is *regularly* "busy" or "here" at a particular time the dialect has the following form: "He *be* busy" and "He *be* here." To show that someone is *continually* "busy" or "here" (that is, all the time) the dialect has this form: "He *bes* busy" and "He *bes* here."
- *Past tense.* The form *was* is used in first, second, and third persons, singular and plural past tense (we *was,* you *was,* they *was*).
- *Present perfect tense.* The word *have* omitted in sentences like "I have been here" and "The meals have been cooked". ("I *been* here" and "The meals *been* cooked.")

■ *Future perfect tense.* The form *be done* is substituted for *will have* in sentences like "We will have gone" and "I will have been to school." ("We *be done* gone" and "I be *done been* to school.")

These are some of the outstanding features in the speech of many culturally disadvantaged black pupils. Again, it must be pointed out that many of these features are found in the speech of Appalachians and other speakers of nonstandard English. But all of these features are frequently found in the speech of culturally disadvantaged blacks. A knowledge of the sound and grammatical system of nonstandard black dialect enables the teacher to direct the language and reading instruction at the interferences that the dialect causes.

Slang. In addition to these sound and grammatical features in the speech of many culturally disadvantaged black pupils, slang is one other significant aspect of dialect. Black people have many slang words unique to the black subculture. Like the slang of other groups, this slang vocabulary keeps changing — new words are constantly added, while old ones are discarded. There is, however, a core of slang words that lasts and resists the normal tendency of slang to be dropped by a group. (One of the influences for dropping slang words from the black dialect seems to be the acquisition of these words by the dominant culture. As soon as the dominant culture begins to use a slang word, blacks discard it. The same thing seems to happen in nonlanguage areas — many of the popular dances originating in the black subculture, such as the Watusi and the Swim, were discarded by blacks when members of the dominant culture learned them.)

Many black pupils often do not realize that many of the words they use are considered slang by the dominant culture. Older black pupils, however, come to learn by experience that many of these words are nonfunctional in the dominant culture. Since blacks often lack standard English synonyms and use, instead, slang words for synonyms, they are handicapped in their ability to communicate outside their subculture.

The slang vocabulary of blacks is enormous by comparison with the slang of the dominant culture, and it is extremely colorful besides. Furthermore, the slang vocabulary reflects the black way of life and the things that are important or common in their subculture.

This phenomenon is consistent with vocabulary growth for any cultural group. For example, the Eskimos have a great many words for snow because it's so much a part of their environment and so important to their survival. Blacks have a great many words for whites because black-white relationships are so critical in their lives. Some of these words are: *ofays* (pig latin for foe), *fays, grays, Mr. Charlie, Miss Ann, the man, whitey,* and *pearls.*

Each one of these words has a special meaning. For instance, *Miss Ann* is an affectatious white woman with a marked attitude of superiority, and *pearls* are attractive young white girls (attractive young black girls are *sapphires*). *Fays* is a term referring to all Caucasians in a neutral way, but *whitey* is a derogatory term. The slang is metaphorically rich: *rib* (a girl friend); *tore up, wasted* (drunk); and *hog* (a Cadillac automobile—it is large, it does wallow smoothly down the road, and it does eat up a lot of money). This vast slang vocabulary could be put to work to benefit its users through their teachers' ingenuity—in teaching poetic devices, for example.

Instructional Methods

The essence of an effective instructional approach for children speaking a nonstandard dialect is that (1) language instruction should focus on the interference points and drills should be designed to deal with these; (2) standard English should be taught as an alternate dialect to be used in appropriate situations. (In the primary and lower elementary grades, the language program should emphasize sound discrimination and give pupils encouragement in speaking in their own language.) The general approach is the same for both black and Appalachian pupils.

The first step in the kind of teaching approach suggested here is for teachers to *accept the child's language.* After all, language is a very personal thing—it's a point of identity, and rejecting the way a child speaks is rejecting the child. Degrading the child's language degrades him and all those who speak his language—parents, relatives, friends, and neighbors. Finally, how can the child be expected to accept another language system if his own is not accepted?

The second step in this kind of approach is to determine which items in the pupil's speech require the focus of instruction. Conduct a diagnosis to determine what nonstandard items need attention in the speech of the particular pupils you teach. Identify the most deviant and frequent nonstandard features. You don't need to be a trained linguist in order to do this. All that is required is an attentive ear. The tape recorder is a valuable aid; record the pupil's speech and play it back to check for nonstandard items.

Another diagnostic method uses the pupil's writing—nonstandard features of speech often occur here, also. Another simple diagnostic procedure is to listen to oral reading, which also will reflect the features of nonstandard speech. Most important, however, is listening to the pupils' speech *analytically* instead of *critically*.

After identifying the nonstandard items that need attention, *only the most frequent and deviant ones,* you can begin teaching an alternate means of expression. It is important to begin to develop certain concepts of language. These concepts are so basic to successful learning that they must be introduced early and continually extended and reinforced throughout the language program. These concepts are:

1. *There are various language systems in our society.* If possible, have the pupils listen to recordings of various dialects to note the differences between them. The pupils should recognize that a Tennessee Mountain dialect is appropriate in the Tennessee Mountains, or that the nonstandard black dialect is appropriate for black speakers.
2. *Dialects develop for specific reasons.* Social and geographical factors should be emphasized.
3. *People can speak more than one variety of English.* This concept can be illustrated by pointing to examples in movies or TV or by showing what is commonly referred to as "levels of speech" that exist within one dialect. Teenage slang also can be used to illustrate this concept.
4. *Appropriateness is determined by ability to communicate.* The language system that communicates ideas and feelings effectively and the language system that is comfortable for both the speaker and the listener is appropriate.
5. *Standard English is the variety of English that is understood by most people, regardless of the particular varieties of English they speak.* Thus standard English is a kind of universal dialect in our society. Also, pupils should understand that standard English is used to transact most of the important business in our society.
6. *Standard English is appropriate in particular situations.*
7. *Standard English should be learned as an alternate dialect to be used in appropriate situations.*
8. *There are social, vocational, and academic benefits in learning standard English.*

Each lesson should deal with only *one* interference at a time, although standard items that have been taught can and must be reinforced in all subsequent lessons. This can be done by including the standard items in drills. For example, if the item being worked on is the nonstandard present progressive tense of the verb *to be* (He *going* to the store) pupils can be given drills that repeat the standard pattern of the verb and contain sounds worked on in a previous lesson (He is going to *the* store *with* his *brother* to buy *that tooth* brush).

Sounds can be reinforced in lessons on grammatical items, and grammatical items can be reinforced in lessons on sound items. The steps in a lesson should be:

1. Select one sound or grammatical item to teach.
2. Get the pupils to *hear* the sound or *recognize* the grammatical structure.
3. Get the pupils to *hear* or *recognize* the difference between the standard item and the equivalent nonstandard item.
4. Get the pupils to *discriminate* between the standard and nonstandard items. (Have the pupils select the word that ends with an *r* sound from a list of words: *door, stow, for, foe, floor, go,* and so on; or have the pupils select from a list the words that begin with the sound represented in writing by the letters *th: the, that, than, Dan, this, dish, doze, those.*)
5. Get the pupils to *use* the standard item in their speech. This is best accomplished in role-playing situations. Role playing is effective because it presents a situation in which the pupils are less self-conscious and teaches the pupils the kinds of situations in which standard English is appropriate.

These are the basic steps in a language lesson. The kinds of drills to include in the lessons are illustrated in the sample lessons on the following pages. Of course these sample lessons do not contain every kind of drill that can be used. They do, however, illustrate the basic approach and some of the types of drills that can be included in language lessons. The drills can be put on tape so that they can be repeated. (Spaces in the tape must be provided to give time for pupils' responses.)

Many of these techniques have been borrowed from those used in teaching English as a second language. Any good book on this subject will offer many other suggestions for constructing effective drills.

Sample Lesson 1   Noun Plurals

Objectives:
   To understand the plural ending for regular nouns.
   To develop standard pronunciation of regular noun plurals.

Procedures:
1. [*Instruct pupils to read the sentences that follow and pay particular attention to the underlined words.*]

Give this ball to that player.
Give these balls to those players.
A dog is chasing the cat.
Two dogs are chasing four cats.
A bus is parked outside the school.
Ten buses are parked outside the school.

2. Listen to the pairs of sentences as I say them. Pay close attention to the underlined words in each sentence, particularly to the ending sounds of the underlined words:

[*Read the sentences in Number* **1.**]

Did you hear the sounds that were added to the underlined words in the second sentence of each pair? I'll read the second sentence in each pair again . . . . These sounds were added to the underlined words because the words are plurals—that is, the words refer to two or more things. Look at the pairs of sentences again. Notice that there are other words in the sentences that make the underlined words take the ending plural sounds. For example, *this* ball, *these* balls; *that* player, *those* players; *a* dog, *two* dogs; *a* bus, *ten* buses. Now practice saying the ending plural sounds.

List I

pot — pots	street — streets
night — nights	cuff — cuffs
book — books	week — weeks
bank — banks	fight — fights
cup — cups	puff — puffs

Look at the first pair of words in List I. The words are: *pot—pots.* I'll say the words again. This time, listen carefully to the ending sound for each word: *pot—pots.* Now, say each word after me: *pot—pots.* The first word, *pot,* is singular. The second word, *pots,* is plural and the plural sound has been added to the word. The plural ending sound for all words in the list is like the plural ending sound of *pots.* I will say each pair of words in List I. You say the pair of words after me. Be sure to pronounce the ending sounds of each word. Here is the first pair. Repeat the pair after me . . . .

[*Work through List I.*]

Now look at the first pair of words in List II. We'll do the same kind of drill with these words. Again, listen carefully to the ending *s* sounds of the words in each pair. Say each pair after me:

List II

dog — dogs	friend — friends
car — cars	wave — waves
rib — ribs	chair — chairs
ring — rings	bag — bags

song — songs	pin — pins
paper — papers	sin — sins

[Words in List I end with the sound *s*; words in List II end with the sound *z*.]

3. Listen to these words as I say them. There are three words in each group. Two of the words are the same. So when I read, you will hear one of the words twice. Tell me the word I say twice. For example, if I say: *dogs—dog—dogs* you point out *dogs*, because that is the word I said twice. The ending sound of the word will tell you the word to point out. Listen carefully to the ending sound of each word. Here is another example: *cup—cup—cups*. Which word did I say twice? Now let's begin the drill:

book	books	book
bag	bags	bags
songs	songs	song
weeks	week	weeks
street	street	streets
rib	ribs	ribs
cuffs	cuffs	cuff
girls	girls	girl
pin	pins	pin
chairs	chair	chairs

4. Look at the first pair of words in List III. Listen while I say the first pair of words: *bus—buses*. I'll say the pair again: *bus—buses*. All of the words in the list have the same plural ending that *buses* has. The plural ending of words in this list rhymes with the word *fizz*. Listen again: *bus—buses*. This time you say it after me: *bus—buses*. Now let's say the words in List III. Again, listen to each pair of words and pay particular attention to the ending sounds. Then repeat each pair after me.

List III

bus — buses	bunch — bunches
glass — glasses	church — churches
place — places	wish — wishes
box — boxes	hedge — hedges

5. Listen to the following sentences. Pay close attention to the plural ending sounds of words in each sentence. After I say a sentence, you say it. Let's say one example.

Pack all the <u>pots</u> and <u>pans</u> in <u>boxes</u>.

Now, say each sentence after me. Remember to say the plural ending sounds clearly. Here is the first sentence:

<u>Pots</u> shouldn't call <u>kettles</u> black.

<u>Kettles</u> seldom like the <u>jokes</u> of pots.

Jokes told by pots often lead to fights with kettles.
Girls and boys should be friends.
Instead of being friends, their quarrels make them act like wild dogs.
Buses in bunches pass by stores and churches.
Glasses are cylinders, and boxes are squares.
Judges in courts sit on high benches.

Now we are going to do a harder drill. The nouns in the following sentences are singular. You repeat the sentences and make the nouns plural. Be careful—you may also have to change other words to make them agree with the noun plurals. For example, if I say:

The cup is over there.

You answer:

The cups are over there.

In the first sentence, *cup* is singular. To make the second sentence plural, *cup* was changed to *cups*. Also the word *is* in the first sentence was changed to *are*, because the verb *are* is used with plurals. Listen to the example again: The cup is over there.
The cups are over there.

Here is another example. Repeat the sentence, changing the singular noun to plural and changing any other word in the sentence that needs to agree. After you say the sentence, I'll say it correctly. Then you say it the same way. Let's try it. Here is the example:

The bus does not stop here (Pupils repeat in plural.)
The buses do not stop here (Pupils repeat this after the teacher to reinforce their correct response.)

Now we're ready to do the drill. Change all singular nouns to plurals:

I don't like to wash the dish.
I don't like to wash the dishes.
The car is parked.
The cars are parked.
The joke was not funny.
The jokes were not funny.
My friend has the book.
My friends have the books.
The boy and girl ate all the cake.
The boys and girls ate all the cakes.

6. [*Nouns ending in* st *and* sk *are special problem words. Many pupils do not pronounce the final* t *and* s *sounds in the singular forms of these nouns. Thus the plural forms of the words are pronounced like the plurals of words in List III—boxes, churches, buses, etc. Have the pupils look at word List IV.*]

List IV

wrist	wrists
test	tests
desk	desks
chest	chests
mask	masks
fist	fists
tusk	tusks

Look at the words in List IV. These are special problem words because their ending sounds are often left off. I will say the singular form of each word. Listen carefully to the ending sound for each word.

[*Pronounce singular forms.*]

This time, you say the singular form of the words after me. I'll say a word, then you say it. Be sure to pronounce the ending sound. Here is the first word:

[*Pupils pronounce singular forms after the teacher.*]

Now, let's see if you can really hear the ending sounds of other words like those you just said. I'll say a pair of words. You repeat the words. Then, if both words end with the same sound, you say "same." If each word ends with a different sound, you say "different." Let's try one example: Say the following pair of words after me, and then tell me whether their ending sounds are the same or different. Here is the pair:

guess — guest

Now let's do some more. Each time, tell me if the ending sounds are the same or different.

vest — west	chest — mass
task — west	pass — pest

7. Look at the plural forms of the words in List IV. The plural ending of these words is pronounced the same as the plural ending sound in *hats, pots, jokes,* and *cakes.* The plural ending sound for these words does not add a syllable. I will say the singular and plural forms of the words. Listen carefully to the ending sounds.

8. Repeat the following sentences after me. Be careful. Some of the words ending with noun plural sounds are tricky.

Babies chew their fists.
There are scratches on all the desks.
The tomatoes were eaten by garden pests.
The tests are in the boxes on the desks.
Ants are pests that a housewife detests.
Cats who are pests molest birds in their nests.

Sample Lesson 2   Third Person Singular Present Tense

Objectives:
  To pronounce the third person singular present tense agreement sound at the end of these verbs.
  To develop standard usage of the third person singular present tense.

Procedures:
1. [*Instruct the pupils to look over these words to see how many they recognize.*]

I	II
work	works
make	makes
walk	walks
take	takes
put	puts
meet	meets
live	lives
laugh	laughs
run	runs
play	plays
call	calls
go	goes
use	uses
catch	catches
dance	dances

Look at the list of words in the Column I. I will say the word and you say each word after me.

Now look at the words in Column II. An ending sound has been added to each word. These ending sounds are the same as the sounds you learned for the noun plural in the previous lesson. For example, the first word in List II, *works,* has an ending sound like *pots;* the last word in the list, *dances,* has an ending sound like *boxes.*

Even though these words have ending sounds like noun plurals, they are not nouns because they cannot be used as subjects of sentences. These words are verbs. They change their ending sounds when they are used with certain subjects.

Let's practice saying the words in Column II with the words in Column I. I'll say a pair of words and you repeat the words after me. For example: *work—works;* you say the pair after me. . . .
        [*Work through Columns I and II by pairs.*]
Now I'll use some of the words from Columns I and II in pairs of sentences. You repeat each pair after me. For example, I'll say

I <u>work</u> after school. He <u>works</u> on the weekend.

Then you say the sentences. Be sure to say the ending sounds.

They walk to school everyday.

He walks to school sometimes.

We live on the first floor.

She lives on the second floor.

I never take a nap.

My little brother takes a nap everyday.

I make money.

He makes money, too.

Older children seldom catch colds.

A baby catches cold easily.

2. [*Instruct the pupils to tell the difference between the underlined words in each pair of sentences above. Lead the pupils to recognize that the ending sound is added to the underlined words in the second sentence of each pair.*]

3. I will say four sentences, and you repeat each sentence after me. Sometimes the verbs will take an ending sound and sometimes they will not. Listen for the ending sounds.

I like to dance, but Tom dances poorly.

When we dance, he steps all over my feet.

He thinks he dances well.

Tom needs to take lessons.

In sentences like the ones we just had, the ending sound is put on the verbs when the subject is *he, she, it* or *a person's name*. In the ones we just said, the ending sound was put on for: *Tom dances, he steps, he thinks, he dances,* and *Tom needs.* These subjects are *third person.* The words we use for things are third person also. Whenever a subject is third person and the verb is present tense, the verb needs an ending sound.

Repeat these sentences after me. Notice the ending sound for verbs that are third person singular present tense:

My little brother watches "Batman" all the time.

He thinks that program is the greatest.

He tries to imitate Batman.

He wears an old kitchen curtain for a cape and puts a grocery bag over his head.

He waits for me to come home from school, and then he jumps out from behind the door.

I always act as if he scares me, and when I do, that scares him.

Then he cries. I always end up laughing while "Batman" cries.

Now, pay attention. This drill will be a little different. First, I will make a statement. Then, I'll ask you a question. You answer the question. For example, if I say, "*I work* every day. What does *he* do?" You answer, "He *works* every day." Here is another example:

"I like to dance. What does *Mary like* to do?" You answer, "*Mary likes* to dance."

I ask questions in class everyday. (What does he do?)
I sit in the front of the room. (Where does the teacher sit?)
Willie Mays likes to play baseball. (What does Jimmy like to do?)
I know the answer to the next question. (What do you know?)
I pass in all my subjects. (What do you do?)
Tom lives three blocks from school. (Where does Mary live?)
I need to stop talking. (What does your friend need to do?)

General Suggestions

1. Avoid making value judgments about the pupil's language. Don't refer to the language as "substandard," "incorrect," or "bad."

2. Constantly refer to the practical and vocational benefits of standard English.

3. Point out the differences between the pupil's language system and standard English. Pupils must *hear* the differences before they can learn the standard English item.

4. Teach standard English *as it is spoken*.

5. Concentrate on gross deviations, rather than fine grammatical points.

6. Record the pupils' speech often, and have them evaluate each other on those standard items taught up to the time of the recording.

7. Whenever oral reading is done, have the entire class (instead of just one pupil) read the material. This gives oral practice to everyone.

8. Arrange the furniture in the classroom so that pupils can talk to each other, instead of talking to the front of the room.

9. Understand the pupil's cultural background. Since language reflects culture, understanding the total cultural background will help the teacher to understand the nonstandard language.

10. Do not attempt to speak the dialect of the subculture—especially if you are not of the same ethnic background.

The Language Problem of Mexican-American Pupils [1]

Many Mexican-American pupils speak a nonstandard variety of English. The causes of their nonstandard English are not the same as for culturally disadvantaged blacks and Appalachians.

1. With acknowledgements to Phil Hernandez, Assistant Professor of Education, San Fernando Valley State College.

Many Mexican-Americans speak Spanish as their first language, and this causes interference when they try to learn English. Those who don't speak Spanish as their first language have Spanish interferences because they have grown up in a cultural environment where English is influenced by Spanish — and this is the variety of English they have learned. The specific language problem of many Mexican-Americans is that they impose the sound and grammar system of Spanish on English. This does not constitute a dialect in the sense in which we have been using the term.

Nonstandard language, however, handicaps Mexican-Americans in the same ways that nonstandard English handicaps blacks and Appalachians. It is important for teachers to understand that the interferences are from Spanish; thus an understanding of Spanish — or, at least an understanding of the interference phenomenon — will help teachers to understand this nonstandard language system.

Teaching Mexican-American pupils is loaded with sociological and psychological implications. First of all, these pupils are products of a *different* culture — that is, a way of life that differs both in *degree* and *kind*. Few English teachers are trained to teach English as a second language, and this is how English should be taught to those pupils who speak Spanish. Few teachers speak Spanish, and this can handicap them in working with interferences caused by Spanish.

A lack of understanding of the Mexican-American culture increases the difficulty; teachers are unable to plan language-arts programs consistent with the cultural background of the pupils. There is also a lack of effective materials for this group. On top of all this is the problem of limitations caused by the pupils' deprivation.

In general, Mexican-American pupils can be classified in four linguistic levels:

1. Pupils who speak more English than Spanish — English is their first language (many speak *only* English).
2. Pupils who speak more Spanish than English — Spanish is their first language.
3. Pupils who speak English half the time and Spanish half the time — some of these pupils speak a kind of hodgepodge "Spanglish" that Mexicans call *pocho*.
4. Pupils who speak only Spanish.

The English of all four groups is influenced by Spanish. Their language behavior tends to make English fit Spanish sound and grammar.

The teacher can most easily understand and teach pupils who are most assimilated into the dominant culture; thus the teacher will experience less frustration and more satisfaction with this group. Yet, these pupils generally do not learn standard English and often have a disinterested attitude toward all school work. The reason these pupils don't learn standard English is twofold: first, the English program is not slanted to deal with the particular interferences from Spanish; secondly, their attitude toward learning English (or any subject) is a negative one.

The inappropriateness of the English curriculum (and the total curriculum) and their negative attitude toward school are reflected in their declining achievement scores. The longer these pupils stay in school, the farther they fall behind — after the seventh grade, their achievement scores take an abrupt nosedive.

The explanation of their declining achievement as the grade level increases cannot be explained by examining only the schools. The explanation is contained in the frustration of straddling two cultures. Even though these pupils are more assimilated both culturally and linguistically, they still have one foot planted in the Mexican culture; this creates cultural and linguistic interferences. Still, this is the group that English teachers have the least problems with. The other three groups must be brought up to this transition level.

Teaching English to the second group of pupils (those who speak more Spanish than English) is as much a sociological and psychological problem as a linguistic problem. These pupils are reluctant to break the strong ties that bind them to their culture; their Spanish is one of the strands in the cultural rope.

In many cases, these pupils are the first generation of their families to be born in the United States. The first five or six years of their lives were spent in the tight family structure that is identifiably Mexican. Spanish most likely is their first language. Their primary experiences with English are limited to school contacts, and the English program in the schools often does not fit their particular problems.

The kind of English program they really need (English as a second language) is not given to them. Instead, the English curriculum (and the whole curriculum) is based on an assumption that all children enter school with certain experiences in their background and a particular vocabulary. With this handicap these children become nonachievers and, later, dropouts. They need a program that emphasizes language in the primary grades — the approach of this program should deal directly with interference items from their native Spanish. And the program should encourage them to use oral language.

The third group, the *pochos,* is the most difficult to understand and accept. Also, they are the most difficult to teach. There is a stronger pull in two directions on this group—the straddling of two cultures affects them more than other groups, as reflected in their hodgepodge language. They are neither Mexican nor members of the dominant culture. They reject much that is identified with Mexican culture; yet, they hold onto many Mexican cultural patterns. At the same time, the *pochos* try to adopt characteristics and patterns of the dominant culture that will make them more acceptable.

The last group, the Mexicans who speak only Spanish, belong in a classroom where English is taught as a second language. They need instruction only in English, because they will learn little in school until they do learn English.

The teacher should be aware of the nonstandard features of English spoken by Mexican-American pupils. The frequency and nature of the nonstandard items indicates the degree that their English is influenced by Spanish. Listed below are some common nonstandard pronunciation and grammatical features.

- *Difficulty with English sounds contained in these words:* miss—mees; brother—brouther; chair—share; very—bery; cap—cahp; rice—rize.
- *Accent on wrong syllables:* perfectly; office.
- *Final consonant clusters dropped:* The last consonant sound in a consonant cluster at the end of words is dropped.
- *Syllable added for preterit ending represented by the letters* ed *in writing:* jumped—jumpted; talked—talkted.
- *Use of double negative.*
- *Reversal of past-tense form of verbs and past-participle form of irregular verbs:* He should have gone—He should have went.
- *End agreement sound not pronounced for third person singular present tense verbs:* He runs all the time—He run all the time.
- *Double subject:* That man lives next door—That man *he* live next door.
- *Addition of the sound represented in writing by the letter s to irregular plurals:* men—mens; children—childrens.
- *Combining English and Spanish:* market—marketo; watch—watcho.

Mexican-American pupils should be given the kinds of exercises described earlier—specific interferences between their English and standard English in language lessons. In addition, the language program must encourage these pupils to *talk*—to stop being reluctant speakers.

Summary of Main Points

1. The ability to speak standard English is necessary for academic, social, and vocational advancement.

2. Nonstandard English systematically interferes with the learning of standard English.

3. Interference occurs because the nonstandard speaker imposes the sound and grammar system of his nonstandard language system on the sound and structure of standard English. This is structural interference.

4. Nonstandard English is reflected in reading and writing.

5. Standard English is the universal dialect—that variety of English understood by most people in our society, regardless of the particular dialects they speak.

6. Culturally disadvantaged pupils will not learn standard English by being told that their language system is incorrect, wrong, or bad. Instruction must be fitted to the specific interferences between their language and standard English.

7. The sequence of the language program should be: understanding spoken English; speaking one's own language; reading, writing, and speaking standard English.

8. Standard English should be taught as an alternate dialect to speakers of nonstandard dialects; standard English should be taught as a second language to pupils who speak a foreign language.

Questions for Discussion

1. What are some additional ways in which nonstandard English handicaps individuals socially and vocationally?

2. Give specific examples of how nonstandard English interferes with reading. (Use examples from a particular group of disadvantaged pupils.)

3. Discuss the following statement: Reading instruction should be delayed for culturally disadvantaged pupils.

4. List additional interferences from the nonstandard black dialect.

5. List interferences from the Appalachian dialect.

6. Select one nonstandard item from the speech of a particular group. Write drills that
   a. help the students hear the standard item (sound or grammar);
   b. discriminate between the standard and nonstandard items;
   c. reproduce the standard item; and
   d. use the standard item (role playing).

Bibliography

Ashley, Annabel, and Malnstrom, Jean. *Dialects USA*. Champaign, Ill.: National Council of Teachers of English, 1963.

Bumpass, Faye. *Teaching of English as a Foreign Language*. Washington: Educational Services, 1959.

Cobbs, Hawner. "Negro Colloquialism in the Black Belt," *Alabama Review,* 5:203–12 (1952).

Deutsch, Martin. "The Role of Social Class in Language Development and Cognition." Mimeograph from the Institute for Developmental Studies, New York.

Francis, W. Nelson. *The Structure of American English*. New York: Ronald Press, 1958.

Golden, Ruth I. *Improving Patterns of Language Usage*. Detroit: Wayne State Univ. Press, 1960.

Green, G. C. "Negro Dialect: The Last Barrier to Integration," *Journal of Negro Education,* 32:81–83 (Winter 1963).

Hall, Robert. *Linguistics and Your Language*. Garden City. N.Y.: Doubleday, 1960.

Johnson, Kenneth R. "Language Problems of Culturally Disadvantaged Negro Students," *California English Journal,* 2:28–33 (Spring 1966).

Labov, William, et al. *Preliminary Study of the Structure of English Used by Negro and Puerto Rican Speakers in New York City*. Cooperative Research Project No. 3091. New York: Columbia Univ. Press, 1966.

— — —. "Some Sources of Reading Problems for Negro Speakers of Nonstandard English." Paper read at the NCTE, Spring Institute of New Dimensions in Elementary English, Chicago, March 5, 1966.

Lin, San-Su C. "Experiment in Changing Dialect Patterns: The Claflin Project," *College English,* 24:644–47 (May 1963).

— — —. *Pattern Practice in Teaching of Standard English to Students with a Non-Standard Dialect*. New York: Columbia Univ. Press, 1963.

Loban, Walter. *The Language of Elementary School Children*. Champaign, Ill.: National Council of Teachers of English, 1963.

McDavid, Raven I. Jr. "The Dialects of American English," in Francis, W. Nelson. *The Structure of American English*. New York: Ronald Press, 1958.

McDavid, Raven I. Jr., and Glenn, Virginia. "The Relationship of the Speech of American Negroes to the Speech of Whites," *American Speech,* 26:3–17 (1961).

National Council of Teachers of English. *Language Programs for the Disadvantaged*. Champaign, Ill.: National Council of Teachers of English, 1965.

Prator, Clifford. *Manual of American English Pronunciation*. New York: Holt, Rinehart & Winston, 1960.

Shuy, Roger W., ed. *Social Dialects and Language Learning*. Champaign, Ill.: National Council of Teachers of English, 1964.

Stewart, William A., ed. *Non-Standard Speech and the Teaching of English*. Washington: Center for Applied Linguistics, 1964.

CHAPTER 7

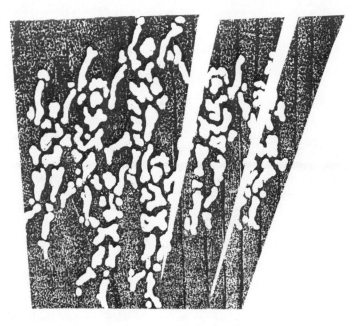

IMPROVING COMMUNICATIONS SKILLS

7

Teaching Reading

Teaching Writing

"How can culturally disadvantaged children be taught to read?" This question is frequently asked as if there were only one method of teaching reading. Actually, there is no one method to teach culturally disadvantaged children, or any children, to read. Children who are ready—who have all the prerequisites for reading—learn to read regardless of the method used to teach them. Culturally disadvantaged children generally lack the prerequisites to become good readers in the present school curriculum. No matter which method is used, many of them will fail to become good readers because they aren't ready—they aren't ready when they start school, they aren't ready after they start school, and most aren't ready any time during their school careers.

The achievement gap between disadvantaged children and their middle-class peers at the time of entering school increasingly widens as both groups progress. The failure of remedial programs to close the gap—or, at least, to keep the gap from widening—should indicate to educators that low reading achievement in culturally disadvantaged pupils is not solely the result of instructional methods. Yet educators keep devising remedial reading programs. This focus on remedial reading is probably the result of confusion between nonachievement due to cultural deprivation and nonachievement due to limited innate mental capacity. Slow learners and culturally disadvantaged learners are not the same, even though they both may be poor readers.

Although reading is a complicated, hard-to-define process, a definition is necessary to point out the reasons so many culturally disadvantaged children fail to read well. *Reading* might be defined as "obtaining meaning from printed language symbols." The ability to attach meaning to a symbol involves prior learning of oral language, which, in turn, stands for real objects. This ability grows out of the totality of language experiences of the child. All previous experience that increases a child's understanding of the world is involved in this complicated code of learning.[1]

Now, if the main points in this definition are related to the total description of culturally disadvantaged children, the rea-

---

1. Herman Warsh, "Teaching Culturally Deprived Children to Read" (unpublished paper, University of Southern California, 1965).

sons for poor achievement in reading are apparent. It is necessary only to contrast the definition of reading with a brief general description of culturally disadvantaged children to illustrate how the definition implies their failure. First of all, reading is a *symbolic* process, and culturally disadvantaged pupils generally *do not handle well the kinds of symbols that are necessary for learning reading in the middle-class curriculum.*

Many culturally disadvantaged pupils speak nonstandard varieties of English or different languages (English may be their second language). It is obvious that one should be able to *speak* the variety of English he will be taught to read—or, at least, to be able to *hear* the sounds of the variety of English he will be taught to read. Yet many culturally disadvantaged pupils can do neither. Part of their language handicap is due to the nonstandard varieties they speak, and part of it is due to the lack of concepts that generate a vocabulary for learning to read.

This points out a second factor which contributes to reading failure: culturally disadvantaged children have had neither the expected experiences that yield the concepts essential to learning to read, nor the expected experiences that teachers can build on to help pupils develop necessary concepts—and subsequent language skills—for learning to read. Their cultural background has not prepared them for reading: that is, the kind of preparation for learning to read that middle-class pupils receive almost automatically in their culture is not part of the culture of deprivation. Pupils from a deprived culture are programed for failure in reading. Because reading is so important for achievement in other subjects, disadvantaged pupils become multiple failures.

Finally, the learning style of culturally disadvantaged pupils, their lack of literacy as a tradition, the inappropriateness of most reading materials, and their anti-intellectualism are negative factors that contribute to poor achievement in reading. The reason remedial programs generally fail to close the reading-achievement gap (thus the *whole* achievement gap) is that the school does not base the reading program on the experiences of the disadvantaged child.

The school must realize that unless the curriculum is changed to fit the child, programs in reading must be conducted concurrently with remedial programs in language (remedial language programs based on the interferences of a particular linguistic group), programs for acquiring the experiences for building additional concepts (compensatory education), and programs for developing a mature learning style. Nevertheless, it is doubtful whether many of these pupils would learn to read well even if the schools were to take such steps; too many of the causes of deprivation—the causes of nonachievement in reading and all other subjects—are beyond the influence of the school.

Teaching Reading

The Reading Lesson

The reading lesson can be divided roughly into six parts: (1) motivation, (2) vocabulary, (3) guided silent reading, (4) discussion, (5) oral rereading, (6) skill development and follow-up (independent activities). In upper grades the reading lesson should be divided into two parts, as the entire lesson can't be covered in one period. Reading should be taught every day. In addition, reading skills should be reinforced and extended in other subjects. Reading and the other language arts are the keys to academic success, and they can't be overemphasized.

Motivation. This first part of the reading lesson is a crucial one for culturally disadvantaged pupils. The problem of motivating disadvantaged pupils is not segmented into individual attempts preceding each reading assignment; rather it is an overall problem. These pupils must be helped to develop positive attitudes that make them *want* to achieve. Admittedly, this is very difficult to accomplish. Culturally disadvantaged pupils must want to achieve, and their general propensity for achievement involves improving self-concept, generating a success cycle, seeing practical and immediate applications of school learning, and studying a curriculum suited to their needs and interests.

This general motivation for achievement is required before culturally disadvantaged pupils can be motivated for a particular reading lesson. Without it, motivation for any particular lesson in reading or any other subject becomes a disjointed, uncoordinated effort, rather than the continuing and reinforcing effort that is required for achievement.

Part of the motivation problem in reading is due to the inappropriateness of the reading materials. Many of the materials include characters unlike any people the disadvantaged pupil knows. To his way of thinking, the characters go through strange actions in unfamiliar settings and, to top it all off, they speak an almost incomprehensible language. The prospect of reading these materials doesn't generate much motivation in a culturally disadvantaged child. Fortunately, publishers are now making effort to produce reading materials with more appeal. Motivating disadvantaged pupils to read will be a little easier as these materials increase.

In the meantime, the teacher has to work with the materials

that are available. The problem becomes more difficult as age and grade level increase, and as the reading material increases in difficulty. Reading material seems to become increasingly inappropriate as the need to read becomes increasingly important. So—the question is, *how can the available materials be made attractive?*

In motivating culturally disadvantaged pupils to read particular materials, the teacher must relate the content to the pupils' interests, needs, and level of understanding. This requires a great deal of stretching some of the time, and a great understanding all of the time. Usually, the problem or conflict of a story is universal and cuts across cultural boundaries. The trick is to structure the discussion to fit the experiences of the pupils. Obviously, if the teacher does not understand his pupils, the trick cannot come off well.

The better the story, the easier it is to relate it to the pupils' experience—good literature has a universality that transcends cultural boundaries. Even though the reading level of good literature is usually more difficult, it is easier to motivate disadvantaged pupils to read good literature than it is to motivate them to read the kinds of stories usually found in reading textbooks. This is understandable: children with the monumental problems of deprivation cannot be aroused to read about storybook characters who grapple with such problems as finding food for a pet rabbit, trying to find a way to ask the new girl to have a soda, or any of the other relatively bland conflicts and crises that are common to these stories.

Vocabulary. Introducing new vocabulary is the second part of the reading lesson. The problem here is that culturally disadvantaged pupils have no familiarity with much of the story vocabulary, or else have only a casual lexical acquaintance with it. Reading texts list new words to be introduced in a story; however, the teacher must go over the story to pick out additional words which are not in the pupils' speaking or listening vocabularies. Even though the disadvantaged pupil is least able to handle new words, his language handicap requires him to handle *more* new words than his more fortunate middle-class peers for whom the books are written. This fact, alone, indicates a need for more appropriate textbooks.

Before reading, introduce all unfamiliar words *in sentences.* (Sentences containing the new words can be written on the chalkboard or reproduced on worksheets.) Underline the words and discuss the structural and phonetic clues. Also, ask the pupils to give a synonym from their speaking vocabulary for every new word. (Slang words should be accepted—they may be the only synonyms known.)

It is important that each pupil be able to hear the new words; that is, he should be able to hear all the phonetic elements. Part of the difficulty of building vocabulary is that the disadvantaged pupil studies a new word that is in neither his speaking nor listening vocabularies; nor can he hear the phonetic elements in the word. If the word is part of his speaking and listening vocabularies, he often gives it a nonstandard pronunciation that interferes with his ability to learn to read it.

Again, the kind of oral language instruction discussed in Chapter 6 is recommended. This instruction should *precede* formal reading instruction in the lower grades, and be concurrent with and coordinated with the reading program.

Guided Silent Reading. After new words have been introduced, the teacher helps the pupils get started reading. The teacher can do this by reading aloud the first few paragraphs of the story. Or he can have students read one or two paragraphs to answer specific questions or obtain specific information for a brief discussion.

After the pupils have begun the story they can continue on their own. This reading should be purposeful. That is, the pupils should read to find out specific information or answer specific questions, perhaps those raised during the motivation period.

Obviously, the pupils must realize the purpose for reading before they begin — otherwise, they won't know what to look for. Assigning questions only after the story has been read is not only inefficient, but it fails to focus the pupils' attention on the story. They can't interact with the story unless they have a purpose in mind. Finally, the purpose for reading should tie in with their experience and interests. In other words, the purpose should be *inherently* motivating.

Particular reading skills that can be reinforced during guided reading are comprehension, word recognition and vocabulary expansion, phonetic and structural analysis, and reference and organizational skills. During this guided reading period, the teacher should circulate around the classroom helping any pupils who have difficulty. Or, if the reading group is small enough, the teacher can be seated conveniently for giving help. The point is, the guided reading part of the reading lesson should be exactly that — guided. *The teacher should not leave his pupils on their own.*

Discussion. After guided reading is completed, the teacher conducts a discussion to determine if the purpose for reading has been satisfied. During this discussion period the story can be interpreted. This part of the reading lesson can be the most enjoyable and profitable, giving the class an opportunity to react in a number of ways. First of all, they have an opportunity to organize and express their ideas and extend their language skills. Secondly, reading and discussion of reading is one area of the curriculum that makes the pupil's experience an integral and functional part of the curriculum. Characters and theme become meaningful through the pupil's experience. Out of this meaning, the pupil can extract understanding of himself and others. (This, of course, depends on how effective the teacher has structured the motivation and guided reading.)

Oral Reading. A good time to reread parts of the story orally is during the discussion and interpretation part of the reading lesson. Pupils can read parts aloud to answer questions, prove a point, support a particular interpretation, or to further enjoyment. It is doubtful if orally rereading the entire story is helpful, especially at the upper grades. For one thing, it's a slow process. In addition, many culturally disadvantaged pupils read so poorly that it is difficult for others to follow. Finally, extended oral reading by poor readers probably reinforces the reading faults of other poor readers.

Thus oral reading should be limited to reading short passages for a particular reason. Other reasons for oral rereading are to convey meaning through the use of proper expression, to practice standard pronunciation, and to gain confidence in reading.

Skill Development and Follow-up. The last past of the reading lesson is the follow-up. This is the workbook section of the lesson. Generally, teachers use the workbooks that accompany the reading text. Most of these are very good. Other reading materials, such as reading kits, are also used. Sometimes workbooks and other reading materials don't include enough help on the specific skills needed by a particular group of readers. Thus classroom teachers often have to design their own follow-up activities. *The purpose of this part of the reading lesson is to reinforce and extend reading skills introduced or covered during previous parts of the lesson.*

The follow-up activities should be divided equally into two groups: activities that cover vocabulary skills (including word-attack and dictionary skills), and activities that cover comprehension skills (including interpretation, reference, and organization skills.)

Teaching Basic Reading Skills

The basal reader program is the most frequently used program for teaching reading in the elementary grades. Basal readers differ in their approach to teaching reading, and they also differ in emphasis. Most basal readers do a good job with middle-class pupils, but a very poor job with culturally disadvantaged pupils. The accompanying workbooks, too, do a poor job of developing and reinforcing basic reading skills. Teachers must make the best of these reading materials until publishers bring out readers that are specifically designed for the culturally disadvantaged. Meanwhile the teacher must devise his own ways of teaching skills.

The same thing applies for secondary teachers. The problem is even more acute at the secondary level. Here the readers are much more difficult and require a mastery of basic reading skills that culturally disadvantaged pupils lack because of the cumulative ineffectiveness of reading materials in the elementary school. Also, less time is spent on developing basic reading skills at the secondary level. This is ironic, because these basic skills are really necessary if pupils are going to read at the secondary level. Of course, a teacher can always give his pupils elementary reading materials — but the content of these materials are usually inappropriate for secondary students. Thus secondary teachers, too, need to devise their own ways of teaching basic reading skills.

Sight Vocabulary. Most culturally disadvantaged pupils need to increase their sight vocabulary. (Sight vocabulary, of course, is dependent on the pupil's speaking vocabulary — thus the importance of language and its interrelation with reading becomes evident.) The sight vocabulary of younger pupils can be increased by placing large, clearly printed labels on objects in the classroom. All pupils can be helped by listing familiar words that belong to particular categories. On Monday, words pertaining to a sport can be written on the chalkboard for the pupils to copy and work on during the week. The words should be suggested by the pupils — in this way, the teacher can be sure that the words will be familiar to them.

For example, the teacher can write the heading *baseball* on the chalkboard, then ask the class to suggest words that fall in that category. *Bat, ball, glove, base, player, walk, hit, foul, strike,* and *mound* may be suggested and included in the list. Then the teacher can conduct a short discussion on baseball, pointing to the words on the chalkboard as they come up in the discussion. Even if the pupils should already have most of the words in their sight vocabularies, such a discussion will provide reinforcement.

Making word families from one word in the sight vocabulary can be the activity for Tuesday. For example, the word *mound* can yield a big family of phonetically related words.

Once the pupils understand the base word, substituting initial consonants gives *bound, found, hound, pound, round, sound,* and *wound.* Other word families can be propagated by words in the baseball category. The consonant blend *str* in the parent word *strike* can be used to give birth to a large family of words beginning with this consonant blend. This exercise promotes recognition of a large number of unknown words.

On the third day, the same list of words can be used to write a composition—in this case, a composition about baseball. After the pupils write their compositions, they should be encouraged to read them. They read their own writing better than the writing of others, and this gives them an increased measure of success.

Sight vocabulary can also be increased by showing pupils a stimulating picture and having them describe it. Key words can be printed on the chalkboard and used similarly to the baseball words. As pupils describe the pictures, they can try out the standard English patterns they are working on in language.

Phonetic Word-Attack Skills. A sight vocabulary is a good starting place for teaching word-attack skills (phonetic and structural analysis). Phonetic word-attack skills can be taught in the manner described above or they can be taught during the vocabulary or follow-up parts of the reading lesson. When teaching phonetic word-attack skills to culturally disadvantaged pupils, *special attention must be given to those sounds not in the pupils' language system.* For example, if the pupils substitute a *d* sound for the sound represented by the letters *th* in writing, then this sound should be given special attention when phonetic word-attack skills are covered. Also, this sound should be given the kind of emphasis recommended during the language period. Pupils *must hear* a sound before they can learn to read words that contain that sound or to develop word-attack skills.

The phonetic elements to be emphasized in reading are:

- Sounds of initial consonants
- Sounds of final consonants
- Long and short vowel sounds
- Consonant blends *(br, cr, fr, gr, pr, tr, bl, cl, fl, gl, pl, sl, sp, sc, sk, st, str, spl, sn, sm)*
- Consonant digraphs *(ch, th, sh, wh, cr, wr)*
- Phonograms *(ain, an, and, ake, at, ar, ack, all, ark, ay, ell, eat, et, ot, oat, ight, ing, ill)*
- Diphthongs *(oi, oy, ow, ou)*

Structural Word-Attack Skills. Structural clues as an aid to reading should also be covered during the introduction of vocabulary or follow-up parts of the reading lesson. Teachers often assume that the most common prefixes and suffixes are a part of the disadvantaged pupil's speaking vocabulary, while this is not the case. Reading materials, too, often reflect this assumption. Actually, culturally disadvantaged pupils must be taught the meaning of the most common prefixes and suffixes. They often substitute a word that has the same meaning for a prefix or a suffix.

The common prefixes and suffixes should be taught inductively rather than deductively. Supply base words that are in the pupils' speaking vocabulary and ask the class to use the words in a sentence to express a meaning that could be communicated by a prefix or suffix attached to a key word. For example, ask the pupils to use *happy* in a sentence to show that someone is not happy. If the sentence offered is "He ain't happy," show that the word *ain't* can be replaced by the prefix *-un:* He is unhappy. Or ask the class to use the word *power* in a sentence to express the lack of it. To teach the suffix *-less,* show the pupils that "The people don't have no power" can be translated as "The people are powerless."

Many examples like these should be given to illustrate the function of prefixes and suffixes. Pupils can reach this generalization if they are shown many examples of words used in sentences contrasted with sentences containing these words with a prefix or suffix added. *Do not begin by giving the meanings of the prefixes and suffixes!*

Phonetic and structural word-attack skills should always be taught by example rather than by rule. Too often, rules are abstract, and disadvantaged pupils don't respond to abstract presentations. Also, teaching word-attack skills by presenting rules first is a deductive method of teaching and this is contrary to the learning style of disadvantaged pupils. Finally, in teaching the meaning of prefixes and suffixes, disadvantaged pupils should be permitted to contrast the meanings with their nonstandard ways of expressing the same meanings.

Inflectional endings must also be taught. Again, the disadvantaged pupil must hear an ending sound before he is required to read it. Many culturally disadvantaged pupils don't pronounce the preterit ending sound. The same is true for other inflectional endings. Also, the pupils must compare the way they express meaning with the way these meanings are expressed by inflection. For example, they must recognize that "them apples" equals "those apples" or "the apples" and that the terminal letter *s* in writing means more than one.

Another structural word-attack skill is that of dividing words into syllables. Pupils must know what a syllable is and be able to sound out syllables if they are to read. But teaching syllabication is difficult, especially to culturally disadvantaged pupils. Their nonstandard language systems often create different numbers of syllables than standard English has for some words, and the syllables of many words in their systems begin or end with sounds different from the beginning or ending sounds of syllables in standard English, even though they may be imperfectly represented by our graphic system. The imperfect graphic representation makes the problem of teaching reading—particularly phonics and syllabication—extremely difficult.

Linguists have not yet formulated a definition of a syllable that they all can accept; consequently, there are a number of definitions, any one of which is too difficult for disadvantaged pupils. The best method for these pupils may be definition by example. One way of teaching syllabication is to start with pupils' names.

Have the pupils say their names, noting how many times their mouths, tongues, or lips move. The number of movements to begin sounds indicates the number of syllables. Point out that if the mouth, tongue, or lips move at *the end* of a sound or at *the end* of a name—for consonant stops, for example—this does not make a syllable. (It ends, rather than begins, a sound.)

After a pupil can determine the number of syllables in a word through hearing it, he can be taught how to distinguish syllables through visual clues. This is closely connected to phonetic and structural elements in the word-attack skills. Most of the basal readers and other reading materials include many activities to teach syllabication, but more preparation must be given to culturally disadvantaged children before they can do the activities listed.

Context Clues as an Aid to Reading. Using context clues is another reading skill that culturally disadvantaged pupils particularly need. A simple way to help pupils understand what is meant by getting meaning from a context clue is to have them supply a *known* word that is missing from a sentence. For example, the class can be given the sentence "He opened the door, sat behind the wheel, and drove the _____ away." The pupils can see that the words *car* or *automobile* fit in the blank, and they can explain how they know the word fits. This will help them to realize that the other words in the sentence and the thought expressed by the sentence give clues to an unknown word.

Next, pupils can be given sentences containing an underlined unknown word. For example, "He opened the door, sat behind the wheel, and drove the *vehicle* away." Assuming that the pupils know all the other words in the sentence, they will know that *vehicle* is the word for something that can be driven and ridden in, even if they can't sound out the word with phonetic clues.

The reason culturally disadvantaged pupils have such trouble with context is either that they can't read enough words in sentences to give them the overall meaning of the sentence, or that the unknown word symbolizes a concept they don't know. Often, even though they can determine the meaning of a word in context, they lack the phonetic and structural word-attack skills needed to sound it out. This lack is often due to interferences from their nonstandard language systems.

Pupils can be shown that the *types* of expression help determine the meaning of a word. For example, some sentences give definitions: "The *filament* is the thin wire inside a light bulb that glows and gives off light." Even if the pupils don't know the word *filament,* the type of sentence (definition) gives them a context clue. Some sentences restate the meaning of a word: "The *chassis,* or bottom part of the frame of an automobile, is made of steel."

Another type of sentence that gives context clues is the sentence containing such typographical aids as quotation marks, italics, boldface type, or parentheses. These sometimes set off meaning clues for an unknown word in the sentence: "Fires are fed by *combustible materials* (paper, rags, woods, or gasoline)." Pupils can be shown that the words in parentheses stand for *combustible materials.*

Still another type of sentence that gives context clues is a sentence that compares or contrasts. Sometimes the meaning of an unknown word can be determined if a similar or opposite idea is included in the sentence or in another sentence close by. Often, signal words such as *while, other, but,* and so forth provide a clue to this type of sentence. For example: "Playing is always enjoyable, but work can be drudgery."

Culturally disadvantaged pupils must be given many drill exercises that include these types of sentences. Further, these pupils should be told why they are given drills. They should be aware that the drills deal with particular types of sentences that give clues for unknown words.

The Main Idea of a Paragraph. The ability to categorize is a prerequisite for understanding the main idea, and this skill should be emphasized in reading readiness and reading programs in the primary grades. When developing this skill, the teacher first presents concrete objects to categorize. The program in the primary grades generally does a good job of teaching pupils how to do this. The instructional movement in developing categorizing skill must be *from concrete objects to abstract ideas*. There is, however, a transition stage that is crucial in teaching this skill to culturally disadvantaged pupils.

One activity that can be used at this intermediate stage is to show a picture that portrays action or something else of high interest to disadvantaged pupils. Direct the pupils to look at the picture and think about a title for it. Before they title the picture they must list all the important details in it. List these details on the chalkboard as the pupils give them. (This will help increase speaking and sight vocabulary.)

When all the details are listed, the pupils discuss them to determine which are important for giving a title to the picture. Then the pupils title the picture. This title will generally express the main idea. A similar activity that is less concrete is to read a short story or poem that the pupils can understand. Have the class suggest details or important events that contribute to the title, discuss which are important, and then give a title.

Later, pupils can be given lists of words or sentences to be categorized. After they can do this, have them write newspaper headlines that express the overall idea of a news story. For example, the pupils read a short news story (or you read the story). Then have them write a headline for it. Compare this headline with the original one.

To help the children write the headline, have them list details under the headings *who, what, where, when, why,* and *how*. (These headings can also be used with pictures, stories, and poems.) These activities will help pupils understand what is meant by the main idea of a story or paragraph. When they can determine the main idea of a paragraph they read themselves, they can be shown that the main ideas of each paragraph make up the overall meaning of the story or selection read.

Following Directions. Culturally disadvantaged pupils must be taught to follow both written and oral directions. Teaching these pupils to follow written directions should be an integral part of the reading program. The following steps in reading directions should be taught:

1. Read the directions all the way through to get a general idea of what is to be done.
2. Read the directions a second time to understand all of the steps.

3. Try to get a mental picture of each step and the reason for each step.

The follow-up part of the reading lesson is a good time to develop the skill of reading directions. Pupils can be given simple directions to turn to a particular page, look at the picture, count the number of people in the picture, and write the number down. The directions given during the follow-up period can be made more difficult as the pupils' skill in reading directions increases.

The practice in following written directions might be correlated with phonetic and structural word-attack skills. For example, pupils can be given written directions to locate a particular word by phonetic or structural clues. Mature pupils can be given the directions on medicine bottles. This kind of activity gives the class practical help in reading directions, while emphasizing the importance of reading directions accurately. The need for accuracy can also be emphasized during a discussion on the effects of *not* following directions as they are written.

Closely related to the ability to read and follow directions is the ability to take tests. Culturally disadvantaged pupils are often doubly penalized in taking examinations by their limiting cultural backgrounds and their inability to follow directions. These pupils must be taught how to take tests, and this should be an integral part of the reading program, specifically that part which deals with following directions. The following points should be taught:

1. Be prepared.
2. Read all directions carefully and understand them before executing them. Ask questions if you do not understand.
3. Read all test items carefully.
4. Ask questions about unknown words.

If disadvantaged pupils can be taught how to take tests, their scores probably will increase in spite of their lacking the motivation of most middle-class pupils. Knowing how to take tests can offset some of the negative effects of inadequate motivation.

Inference. Culturally disadvantaged pupils tend to interpret written sentences literally, and this affects their reading comprehension. These pupils often fail to understand that metaphorical and exaggerated statements, for example, are used to convey a quality rather than to express fact. Give the class such sentences as: "She wore a dress that was a block long" or "He was a tiger on the prowl when tracking the criminal."

After they read the sentence, the pupils can discuss the quality that the sentence means to emphasize through metaphor or exaggeration. These pupils have difficulty understanding figurative speech expressed in standard English.

These pupils also have trouble with figurative language that depends on a different experiential background for understanding. This does not mean that they have difficulty with figurative speech as a poetic device — their rich understanding of slang shows that they do understand and use the poetic device of figurative speech, including metaphoric and exaggerated statements. The kind of figurative language they encounter in readers, however, does not fit their linguistic or conceptual backgrounds. This also makes it difficult for them to get meaning by inference, and they often have trouble determining the direction of a story, anticipating action, and understanding the motivation of characters. Thus the clues in a story that help the reader draw inferences must be pointed out.

Another handicap related to inability to understand figurative speech is failure to separate fact from opinion. During reading and discussion periods, distinguish between statements in the reader that are supported with facts and statements that are not supported with facts. In the follow-up period, pupils can be given sentences to label *fact* or *opinion:* "That is the ugliest picture in the world;" "The picture is hanging on the south wall;" "The baseball team won three games last year;" "The baseball team will win more games and the championship next year."

It is extremely important that culturally disadvantaged pupils be able to separate fact from opinion and understand the techniques of propaganda. Culturally disadvantaged people suffer from the negative opinions others have of them, and if they can recognize the cause of their suffering they will be in a better position to counteract it. Also, once they learn to distinguish opinion from fact, the pupils will no longer feel that the negative opinions expressed by others mirror reality.

Propaganda techniques, especially in advertising, are used to exploit the culturally disadvantaged. Pupils should be taught that propaganda gives only one point of view, that it is heavily opinionated and lacks supporting facts, and that it attempts to influence people in only one direction. A good exercise for mature pupils is to give them advertisements and have them list all the facts.

These suggestions on techniques that can be used for teaching reading concepts and skills do not fit into any particular method for teaching reading. Children will learn to read in spite of the method of instruction so long as they have the appropriate conceptual and linguistic background necessary for learning to read. Readiness is the determinant factor in teaching culturally disadvantaged pupils to read.

The lack of reading readiness in culturally disadvantaged pupils results from the causes of deprivation. It has been pointed out that the school cannot remove or affect many of these causes of deprivation; therefore, the school cannot properly prepare culturally disadvantaged pupils to read. The problem, then, is to teach them to read *in spite of* their lack of expected readiness. The problem of the school is *to use the backgrounds of these pupils as a foundation for teaching them to read.* In other words, cultural deprivation is their reading readiness.

If a reading program is to be based on the above rationale, new methods and new materials must be developed. These methods and materials must be consistent with the background and learning style of the pupils. The problem in teaching reading to culturally disadvantaged pupils really boils down to these two choices: either the school gives these pupils the kind of readiness for reading that middle-class children receive automatically, or the school uses new methods and materials that are suited to disadvantaged pupils and considers their experience of deprivation to be their readiness.

The school has traditionally made the former choice in designing programs for the disadvantaged (Headstart and other compensatory programs are products of this choice). The limitations of the school in making up for deprivation, however, seem to indicate that the latter choice might be more effective. Few programs are based on this choice, possibly because of the lack of research findings in this area.

In traditionally making the choice for compensatory programs, the school has taken on a monumental job. Also, this choice has been responsible for promoting the view of culturally disadvantaged pupils as *slow learners* rather than, perhaps, *different learners.* Consequently, many reading programs for culturally disadvantaged pupils are identical to reading programs for slow learners. The structure of these programs has resulted in identical reading materials for both groups of learners.

More and more reading materials are being published that seem more appropriate for disadvantaged pupils, especially books that have characters and settings with which culturally disadvantaged pupils can identify. Some of these reading materials are good — especially the trade books. The ones that are not good duplicate the ineffectiveness of traditional materials.

Some trade books that are especially appropriate for culturally disadvantaged pupils portray minority group characters in situations interesting to disadvantaged pupils — particularly pupils of the same ethnic identity as the characters. But not all books with minority characters are good. Many of the books being published with black characters illustrate a common flaw: many educators and publishers assume that if textbooks include black characters or stories about black people, black pupils will be motivated to read.

This is a reasonable assumption. However, many of the books and stories about black characters are poor because the characters are portrayed unrealistically. They are the same old white middle-class characters painted brown and sporting new names. They are unlike any real black people—or any real people at all, since the white characters that are hidden behind the brown faces are themselves unreal.

Many of these stories with black characters have the same worn-out plot: some "nice" black person is fighting for acceptance and finally makes it because of some special skill he has (if he is a boy, he can run or excel in some other athletic skill—girls are usually singers). This kind of story is mildly offensive to many blacks—and it should be—because this *is* often the only way they can be accepted. What black people want is *acceptance as individuals,* not acceptance because of a particular rare skill or quality that only a few can possess.

How silly many of these stories are! And how unrealistic! Most urban blacks living in ghettos don't even come into contact with Caucasians socially. In large cities, most disadvantaged blacks attend schools that are predominantly black. How strange it must be for these black pupils to read about one black person in an all-white school battling with his special skill for acceptance. Stories about blacks should be realistic and fresh. They should dramatize conflicts other than that of acceptance.

Also, stories about blacks should have some soul. (In black slang, *soul* means "that which can be exclusively identified with the black subculture.") In other words, the interest, actions, and responses of the character should be those of black people who are products of the black subculture, not brown white folks who are products of the dominant culture.

Of course, if stories are to reflect the cultural identity of black people, publishers and school districts will have to admit that our society is a segregated society, and that segregation has been a cause for the development of a unique black subculture. Publishers and school-district officials are reluctant to reflect this reality or their recognition of this reality in textbooks. Instead, black characters are usually portrayed as having only one insignificant difference: the color of their skin and the problems of being accepted because of their skin color.

Our past failure in teaching reading to blacks and other culturally disadvantaged pupils indicates that our methods and materials are inappropriate and ineffective. The first step to bring about improving the reading skills of disadvantaged pupils is being taken in changing reading materials. But if the stories in the new books are not realistic, if they are not be-lievable, if they are not *good* — the step will be without effect on reading achievement. And if the effort is not undertaken to find new methods based on a rational consistent with their cultural backgrounds, many of these pupils will probably con-tinue to do poorly in reading.

Teaching Writing

The Writing Program

The purpose of the writing program is to teach pupils how to (1) organize ideas, and (2) write them down so others can understand them. Writing programs for all pupils have this same purpose, and the skills to be taught in a writing program are the same for all pupils. The difference between the writing program for disadvantaged pupils and for other pupils is in the ideas to be organized (specifically, the experiences out of which ideas are formed), and in the specialized instruction disadvantaged pupils require in language (specifically, instruc-tion in standard English).

As stated in the foregoing paragraph, the purpose of the writing program implies a two-part definition of writing. First, writing is "the organization of ideas"; secondly, writing is "ideas that are symbolically communicated in language that other people can understand." Furthermore, the definition implies two roles in the communication process of writing: that of the organizer and recorder of ideas (the writer), and that of the receiver of the ideas (the reader).

Correcting Pupils' Writing. Teachers generally spend much more time teaching the second phase of writing — that is, writ-ing in language that other people can understand. The prover-bial red pencil derives its notoriety from the disproportionate amount of time teachers spend scratching corrections on pu-pils' papers to make the papers readable — in other words, translating the pupils' language into standard English.

These red marks are really warning signs that tell the teacher to spend *less time doing translations and more time on teaching language.* This problem is not unique to culturally disadvan-taged pupils — all pupils make the kinds of mistakes in writing that cause difficulty for the reader. But culturally disadvan-

taged pupils make these mistakes plus mistakes caused by interference from their nonstandard language system.

Now, this is not to suggest that teachers stop correcting the
writing of culturally disadvantaged pupils. What is suggested
is that more emphasis be placed on teaching language, and
that corrections be correlated with the language program.
Corrections should be *diagnostic* — they should point out those
items that require special emphasis in the language program.
Corrections should focus on the particular interference from
the pupils' nonstandard language system. (In a sentence like
"Them boy play in the street," a red line should not be drawn
through *them* and a red *s* should not be added to *boy* without
pointing out to the writer that the word *them* is not a plural
marker and that the way to show more than one in writing is
to add the letter *s*.) Finally, correlating the writing program
with the language program means that the corrections made
in pupils' writing should relate only to those items covered
in the language program.

There are two advantages in correcting only one item in
each written assignment: concentration on one item gives
more reinforcement for establishing the desired pattern; second, the pupils' papers will not be severly marked up. (It may
be that there is an inverse relation between the number of red
marks on a paper and the motivation of pupils to keep trying
to write: as red marks increase, motivation to try decreases.
Thus teachers should make fewer and more meaningful corrections.) In addition, written corrections should receive more
emphasis as the grade level increases. In both the lower and
upper grades, the main emphasis should be on *getting pupils
to put their ideas down in writing*. In the upper grades writing
standard English patterns should receive a secondary emphasis.

Organizing Ideas. Teaching pupils to write standard English
patterns is only one phase of the writing program. The other
phase, teaching pupils to organize their ideas for writing, is
the more difficult. One cause of difficulty is that many of these
pupils do not have many ideas to organize. They have not had
the rich experiences that generate ideas. With few ideas, they
have little to say and little to write about. Another difficulty
is that disadvantaged pupils are often assigned writing topics
that have no relation to their experiential background.

The need for providing rich experiences must be discussed
further. What is meant by the word *rich* as it relates to writing
is "an experience that excites and motivates pupils to think
about the experience and discuss the experience with the
teacher and other pupils." During the discussion of an experience that the pupils have shared, each individual contributes

an idea that triggers additional ideas in others. Thus a discussion that follows a shared experience generates more ideas than were generated by the experience alone. This is one reason why it is important to precede a writing assignment with a short, intense discussion. (However, the discussion should not be so long as to reveal *all* the ideas).

A more basic reason for providing rich experiences is that culturally disadvantaged pupils constantly need new experiences that generate thought, discussion, and ideas for writing. The interest-need spectrum of young children is narrow, and the school can provide experiences that cover this spectrum. Also, so much is new to young children that the novelty of an experience is interesting. At the upper grades, however, the school curriculum is not designed to cover the students' interest-need spectrum. Activities that are supposed to give experiences to these older children are ineffective because they don't fit the students' interests and needs.

All disadvantaged pupils, at all grade levels, have had out-of-school experiences. These, too, can be used as a resource of ideas to be organized for writing. The problem is that disadvantaged pupils' experiences fall in an intellectual vacuum; that is, there is no one to interpret and explain the experience meaningfully so that the pupil formulates ideas and relates the idea to others. It is important to give these pupils in-school experiences, regardless of grade level, that provide a professional mediator—the classroom teacher.

Another problem in using out-of-school experiences as a resource of ideas for writing is that the cirriculum is not geared to these ideas. In the previous paragraph it was suggested that the curriculum be changed so that activities to give idea-generating experiences fit the interests and needs of disadvantaged pupils. Here, the curriculum must change its expectations of the ideas disadvantaged pupils bring to school.

The problem of curriculum expectations not fitting the ideas (experiential background) of disadvantaged pupils is best illustrated by examining the kinds of topics some teachers and most textbooks give as writing assignments. Such topics as "Winter in the Woods," "A Visit to the Antique Shop," "My Favorite Pet," and the ubiquitous "My Summer Vacation Trip" are examples of topics that are obviously inappropriate for disadvantaged pupils.

In summary, the writing program consists of two parts: teaching pupils how to organize their ideas for writing, and teaching pupils how to express their ideas in writing so that other people understand them. The writing program for disadvantaged pupils must give them experiences that fit their needs and interests so that they can formulate ideas to write about; also, pupils must be given an opportunity to write about the ideas they already have. After they put their ideas into writing, the teacher's corrections should correlate with language instruction.

Teaching Basic Writing Skills

Most language textbooks do a poor job of organizing the writing program. Teachers of disadvantaged pupils can use these textbooks as aids in teaching writing, but textbooks can not take the place of the teacher. The teacher must do some good teaching of writing skills *before* his disadvantaged pupils will be ready to use textbooks. Most teachers who like to teach writing use textbooks very little in their teaching. Instead, they use their own materials and their own techniques. This is especially true of good teachers—not only do they use their own materials and techniques, but they adapt textbook materials to fit the learning style of their pupils.

The writing program begins in the primary grades, before pupils are able to write even one sentence by themselves. The experience chart is more than a readying aid; it is one of the best means that teachers have for teaching good organization in writing. The experience-chart technique can also be used in the upper grades, including high school. Formulating and writing a few sentences or an entire paragraph or composition through class participation is a good exercise for teaching writing skills, especially organizational skills.

When primary pupils graduate from experience charts to writing their own sentences, teachers should concentrate on *what* the pupils write, rather than *how* they write it. The teacher should not emphasize standard grammar, correct spelling and punctuation, or even neatness. Encouraging pupils to write down their own ideas in their own language in a logical sequence should come first. The teacher should help his pupils to develop pride in their ideas expressed in their own words. (It is doubtful if they can develop pride in their writing if their papers are returned to them with many red correction marks.)

Writing paragraphs. The concept of the paragraph should be introduced in the middle grades. Pupils must be taught that a paragraph is a group of sentences that develop one idea. This concept can be taught along with the reading skill of finding a main idea in a paragraph the pupils have read. Give pupils practice in writing a sentence that expresses the main idea of a paragraph. After they can do this, they can understand that a topic sentence functions in the same way—that is, it states the main idea in a paragraph, the idea that is supported or developed by the other sentences in a paragraph.

Pupils should be moved from writing a sentence that expresses the main idea of a paragraph to writing their own topic sentences soon after they understand the concept that paragraphs have a main idea. An inductive way of teaching how to write a topic sentence is to have pupils write three sentences about something specific. For example, have them write three sentences about what they saw on the way to school, their favorite television character, or the costume the character wears. When they have finished, ask individuals to read their sentences and have the class formulate one sentence to summarize each set of three. This sentence can be the topic sentence for a four-sentence paragraph.

Pupils should also be given an exercise that requires them to write three or four sentences supporting a topic sentence. This exercise, and the one described in the foregoing paragraph, should be repeated several times before pupils are given the assignment of writing a complete paragraph. (The teacher will have to write the topic sentence for some pupils long after others have learned to write it themselves.)

Pupils should be taught to plan their paragraphs before they write. A simple method of teaching this is to encourage the pupils to think about what they want to express — the main idea they want to develop. This is the topic sentence, and it should be written exactly as it will appear in the paragraph. This means that they should revise the topic sentence, if necessary, before writing the supporting sentences. After the topic sentence is written, four details that support the topic sentence should be written. These details do not have to be expressed in sentences. The outline for a paragraph is as follows:

Topic sentence
1.
2. Supporting details
3.
4.

An example of a paragraph outline about Batman's costume might be as follows:

Batman dresses funny.
1. mask
2. cape
3. long green underwear
4. big belt

When disadvantaged pupils first begin to plan their paragraphs, they need as much individual help as possible. One way to help all the pupils at once is to involve the whole class in planning a paragraph. Write the topic sentence and the supporting points on the chalkboard; then have the pupils write the paragraph from the outline. Cooperatively formulating a paragraph plan is a desirable intermediate step to formulating a plan individually.

It should be noted that the described method of planning and then writing a paragraph is a deductive method. If disadvantaged pupils have difficulty learning to plan a paragraph by this method, reverse the procedure and teach them to plan a paragraph inductively. This is easily accomplished by having them write the supporting points first, then the topic sentence.

Teaching disadvantaged pupils to write a good paragraph should be the primary writing objective of the intermediate grades of elementary school. Of course, if there are pupils who are ready and can be taught to write a three-paragraph composition, let them do it. However, writing a three-paragraph composition should be the primary purpose of the upper grades of elementary school and the early grades of junior high school. The same method can be used for planning a three-paragraph composition as was suggested for the paragraph. A title for the composition can be inductively formulated by expressing the main idea of the three topic sentences.

By the time pupils reach the end of junior high school, and certainly when they enter senior high school, they can be taught that the topic sentence of a paragraph suggests a particular method that can be used to develop the main idea of the paragraph. For example, the topic sentence "Batman wears funny clothes" suggests that *details* should be used to develop the idea expressed in the topic sentence. The topic sentence "I don't like Batman" suggests that *reasons* should be listed to develop the main idea. A topic sentence that suggests the listing of *examples* to develop the main idea is "Batman helps the police of Gotham City." Finally, the topic sentence "Batman and Mighty Man are something alike" suggests that *similarities* and *differences* be listed to develop the main idea. Other methods for developing a paragraph that can be taught are contrasts and comparisons, steps in a process, and cause and effect.

Each method should be taught individually. Again, it is recommended that *the entire class be involved.* That is, write topic sentences on the board and have pupils cooperatively develop the paragraph with the method being taught. After pupils learn the methods for developing paragraphs, the method should be listed in the paragraph outline.

Teaching pupils to write is difficult; teaching culturally disadvantaged pupils to write is extremely difficult. Of the three language-arts skills, speaking, reading, and writing, writing is the most difficult to teach. The three skills are listed in the order of advancement pupils must progress through before beginning a subsequent skill. In other words, pupils should not begin to learn how to read until they have acquired some speaking facility, and they should not begin to learn how to write until they have developed some ability to read. Culturally disadvantaged pupils are taught these three skills before they are ready, often by methods and materials that are not appropriate to their backgrounds.

The importance of culturally disadvantaged pupils learning the language arts cannot be overemphasized. *The language arts are the primary tools for academic success, and academic success can be the master tool culturally disadvantaged pupils use to fashion a better life.* The fundamental purpose of the schools in educating the culturally disadvantaged must be to help them acquire this master tool.

Summary of Main Points

1. There is no *one* method for teaching reading to culturally disadvantaged pupils.

2. The main cause of poor reading ability in culturally disadvantaged pupils is that their cultural backgrounds have not adequately prepared them for reading instruction in the middle-class curriculum.

3. *Reading* can be defined as "obtaining meaning from printed language symbols."

4. Pupils should be able to hear the *sound* of the language and *speak* the language before they are taught to read it.

5. Remedial reading programs generally give poor results because reading instruction is not coordinated with remedial instruction in language or with efforts to provide disadvantaged pupils with the experiences they need for learning how to read.

6. More research is needed to determine how a disadvantaged background can be utilized as the basis for an effective reading program.

7. The reading lesson can roughly be divided into six parts: (1) motivation, (2) vocabulary, (3) guided silent reading, (4) discussion, (5) oral rereading, and (6) follow-up.

8. Writing is the most difficult language-arts skill to teach culturally disadvantaged pupils.

9. The order for beginning instruction in the language arts is speaking, reading, and writing.

Questions for Discussion

1. Give other definitions of reading and relate them to the characteristics of culturally disadvantaged pupils in order to determine the implications for an effective reading program.

2. Select a familiar story for a particular grade level and discuss how it can be related to the experiential background of disadvantaged pupils.

3. Select one nonstandard pronunciation characteristic of disadvantaged pupils in a particular linguistic group and discuss how it interferes with teaching phonetic word-attack skills.

4. List common reading mistakes made by a particular group of disadvantaged pupils and relate the mistakes to either the experiential or linguistic backgrounds of the pupils.

5. What are other divisions that can be made in the reading lesson for disadvantaged pupils?

6. Compile a bibliography of appropriate books for disadvantaged pupils. What should the criteria be for selecting books?

7. Discuss ways that the background of disadvantaged pupils might be used positively to teach reading and writing skills.

8. What are some suitable topics that disadvantaged pupils can use in writing assignments?

9. Discuss the following: Should instruction in other subjects be delayed for disadvantaged pupils until they have acquired basic language-arts skills?

Bibliography

Artley, A. Sterl. *Your Child Learns to Read.* Chicago: Scott, Foresman, 1953.

Betts, Emmett A. *Foundations of Reading Instruction.* San Francisco: American Book, 1954.

Claremont College Reading Conference. *Yearbook, 1964.* Claremont, Calif.: Claremont College, 1964.

Conference on Reading, University of Chicago. *Proceedings* (1964 Conference), *Meeting Individual Differences in Reading.* Chicago: Univ. of Chicago Press, 1964.

Corbin, Richard. *Literacy, Literature, and the Disadvantaged.* Report of the Incoming President. Champaign, Ill.: National Council of Teachers of English, 1964 (pamphlet).

Fader, Daniel N., and Shaevitz, Morton H. *Hooked on Books.* New York: Berkley, 1966.

Fernold, Grace M. *Remedial Techniques in Basic School Subjects.* New York: McGraw-Hill, 1943.

Figurel, J. Allen, ed. *Vistas in Reading.* Proceedings of the Eleventh Annual Convention, International Reading Assn., 1966.

Harris, Albert J. *How to Increase Reading Ability* (4th ed.). New York: David McKay, 1961.

Hildreth, Gertrude. *Teaching Reading.* New York: Holt, Rinehart & Winston, 1958.

Kottmeyer, William. *Teacher's Guide for Remedial Reading.* St. Louis: Webster Publishing, 1959.

Loretan, Joseph O., and Umans, Shelly. *Teaching the Disadvantaged.* New York: Teachers College Press, 1966.

Miel, Alice, ed. *Individualizing Reading.* Practical Suggestions for Teaching, No. 14. New York: Bureau of Publications, Teachers College, Columbia, Univ., 1958.

National Council of Teachers of English. *Language Programs for the Disadvantaged.* Champaign, Ill.: National Council of Teachers of English, 1965.

Penty, Ruth C. *Reading Ability and High School Drop-outs.* New York: Teachers College, Columbia Univ. Press, 1956.

Smith, Nila Banton. *Reading Instruction for Today's Children.* Englewood Cliffs, N.J.: Prentice-Hall, 1963.

Spache, George D. *Reading in the Elementary School.* Boston: Allyn & Bacon, 1965.

Strang, Ruth. *Diagnostic Teaching of Reading.* New York: McGraw-Hill, 1961.

Umans, Shelly. *New Trends in Reading Instruction.* New York: Bureau of Publications, Teachers College, Columbia Univ., 1963.

Ware, Kay. "Ways to Develop Reading Skills and Interests of Culturally Different Youth in Large Cities," *Improving English Skills of Culturally Different Youth in Large Cities.* Bulletin No. 5, 1964, U.S.Office of Education. Washington: Government Printing Office, 1964, pp. 150–51.

Whipple, Gertrude. *Appraisal of the City Schools Reading Program.* Detroit: Detroit Public Schools, 1963.

Witty, Paul A., ed. "Reading and the Underprivileged," *Education,* Vol. 85, No. 8 (April 1965), pp. 450–506.